Open Verdict

A Hong Kong Story

Ken Bridgewater

PARTRIDGE
A Penguin Random House Company

To order additional copies of this book, contact
Toll Free 800 101 2657 (Singapore)
Toll Free 1 800 81 7340 (Malaysia)
orders.singapore@partridgepublishing.com

www.partridgepublishing.com/singapore

Endorsement

Having lived in Hong Kong since 1965, I followed the proceedings of the **MacLennan** case with as much amazement and fascination as anyone else. Although crafted as a novel, 'Open Verdict' is based on archival material studiously researched and dexterously presented as a page-turner of a real life detective story. Chapter by chapter, it unveils a mystery that has long languished unsolved, along with the fate of Amelia Earhart, the *Marie Céleste* and what really happened that fateful Friday November 22, 1963, in Dallas, Texas.

Peter Moss—author
The Singing Tree among other titles

About the Author

I came to Hong Kong in 1973 to take up the post of Physicist with the Hong Kong Government. I headed the team of Bio-medical engineers in Hospitals

During this time, my wife was hosting a talk show on Commercial Radio and I wrote **"Talk of Hong Kong"** based on her experiences. This was about the thrills and spills of radio talk back. It was published by Phoenix Books and became a best seller.

I completed my Government contract and went on to be C.E.O. of the Hong Kong Institution of Engineers. I became speech writer for Legislative Council members.

In 2000, I was commissioned by Random House, London, to be the writer for Dr. Mosaraf Ali. We published four books, **The Integrated Health Bible, The Ultimate Back Book, the Nutrition Bible** and **The Neck Connection.** Three were best sellers and one was an e-book. Dr. Ali is the internationally known personal physician for the British Royal Family.

I am currently engaged in writing the life story of a well known architect and Interior Designer.

Card or Series title page

Talk of Hong Kong published by Phoenix Books

The integrated Health Bible with Dr. Ali published by Random House

Dr. Ali's Ultimate Back Book published by Random House

The Nutrition Bible Published by Random House

The Neck Connection Published by Random House

Dedication

To Joe and Katie MacLennan

Preface

The book arose out of my wife hosting a radio talk show during one of the most devastating periods of Hong Kong history. No day went by without some event or threat alerting me to the pressures experienced by the media during a public outcry against Government or criminal activity on a massive scale.

Introduction

Open Verdict was written about a talk show that was deeply involved in the MacLennan affair. John MacLennan died with five bullet wounds in his chest and was found with a suicide note. The gun was wiped clean and no pen in the apartment wrote the note. An inquest formed after media pressure returned an open verdict. The MacLennan family employed a detective who lived with us during his investigations and we became aware of the true facts of the case hidden from the public. **Open Verdict** is written as a novel although largely factual and the true story has not been revealed until now.

Prologue

Around 1980 the underlying threat in Hong Kong was not Al Qaeda, but an ancient Chinese brotherhood known as the Triads, which surpassed Al Qaeda and even the Mafia in power, terror and crime. Traditionally they were patriots, who played pivotal roles in regime changes in China over the centuries However, in the 1950s they became immersed in corruption and extortion, for which Hong Kong's laissez faire structure provided an ideal home. Yet the Handover to China in 1997 passed peacefully, when many expected these agents of crime to play their traditional terrorist role in ending a dynasty.

Why did they leave Hong Kong untroubled during such an opportunity for disturbance? We know Beijing took no chances. Their close surveillance within China revealed terrorist activities timed to disrupt the Handover, which were ruthlessly put down. In Hong Kong itself their job was hampered by the British presence. So undercover deals were struck directly with the Hong Kong triads to keep them quiet. It worked. In the event the most violent part of the Handover was the fireworks, a rich volcanic display in Hong Kong's glittering harbour defying the permanent backdrop of gaudy neon lights and even the rain.

Instead these gangsters diverted their attention to New York, San Francisco, London, Sydney, Vancouver and other great cities. There are many explanations for this. Maybe it was their hunger for greater power. Perhaps they were scurrying from what they saw as a sinking ship. But one theory stems from the story of a Hong Kong Police Inspector, who was found dead in a locked flat with five gunshot wounds in the chest and from the subsequent public anxiety expressed on Aileen's radio talk-show.

For some people the line was never drawn under the subsequent Inquiry and for years relevant disclosures continued to appear. There are still those today who remember the case, not for its furore, not for its brush with triads or the homosexuality revealed, not even for the improbability of the declared suicide, but for the whitewash and the attempted justification.

Open Verdict is a true story; that is to say the bare truth has been moulded to comply with the rules of story telling. To improve the narrative flow, topics discussed at different times are compacted into the episodes to which they relate. Lengthy press conferences are edited down. Though almost all names are those of the actual people involved, the contributions of some of the minor characters are condensed into the parts played by 'supporting players'. Aileen and Kevin are based on real people.

Bearing this in mind I would like you to imagine you have just been called for jury service and your judgement is required on the content of this book. At the end you will have received the evidence, the great majority of which can be supported by existing documentation or recordings, and you will be given a summation. Where the jury convened for the actual hearing returned an 'open verdict', what will your verdict be?

Ken Bridgewater 2013

Chapter 1

Autopsy

When John MacLennan invaded the life of Aileen he was already dead. He was on a dissecting table with a pathologist cutting out his heart.

Aileen was about to host her daily talk show on Hong Kong Commercial Radio, called *Aileen's Phone-in*, as she waited for the red "On Air" light she scanned the news headlines. An almost unknown company, Carrian Investments Limited, had bought the prestigious Gammon House for HK$1 billion, a huge amount in the 1980s. She wondered how such a low profile company came by that sort of money. A policeman had been killed in a shooting incident. "No foul play was suspected". She sighed. She was familiar with that expression. A torso in a sack had recently been dredged from the harbor with no arms or head and "no foul play was suspected". "Oh, not another," she thought and no doubt that reaction was discernible to her listeners a few seconds later as she broadcast the information. Her honey-tongued drawl revealed a hint of her Irish background but concealed the venom she had at her disposal.

Her show was introduced by a signature tune, appropriately listed as "On the Go", after which it was her routine to open the lines to everyone. Usually they were queuing up.

"Hello, Aileen, I'm Augustine. I live in 700 square feet with my mother and father and seven brothers and sisters. The TV is always on.

1

The airport flight path is across our window and there is a factory next door. Where can I study for my exams?"

"That's tough. Where do you live?"

"Tsuen Wan." This was one of the noisiest, smokiest, dirtiest industrial areas in Hong Kong.

"I'm sure there are plenty of others with that problem. Here's an idea. How about talking to one of our listeners, a retired fishmonger called Bob Saunders. He's started a study group in Tsuen Wan for students like you. He has the use of an old go down with lots of desks and chairs donated from a school that has closed down. You can go there any time. The rule is—no talking. OK? My producer will give you his number." The phone light lit again.

"Hello, Aileen? I'm Frank from Sai Kung."

"I know Sai Kung. You're at the seaside where they have all those bubbling fish tanks so you can choose which one you want for supper."

"That's right. Well, round the corner in the square is a restaurant called Pebbles. I go there quite often. I like to sit at the tables outside in the square. Only every so often the police come and clear us away."

"Maybe no one's allowed to put them there."

"Probably, but its bloody silly because they're not in anybody's way, and anyway the Chinese restaurant across the corner in the square puts tables out too and they don't get cleared away, In fact the police often come and eat there in uniform."

"You don't say? That's odd. We'll take it up with the Police Public Relations Bureau, better known as PPRB. Tune in again tomorrow to see what they say." The phone light was still on.

"Aileen, this is Elsie. Elsie Elliott." Of course everyone knew her. She was the first to disclose the triad demands for protection money from the mini-buses and had established a reputation as an English Urban Councilor renowned for her crusades for justice and for her condemnation of police corruption. "I've been listening to your last caller. I suspect the police cleared away Pebbles' tables because they hadn't paid their protection dues. That's not what PPRB will say, of course. But that's not why I am ringing. This policeman who died in a shooting incident. How can they say 'no foul play is suspected'? I knew him. His name was John MacLennan. He was the victim of a scandal because he was investigating high ranking policemen. He would never have shot himself. He wasn't the type."

"Are you saying he was murdered?"

"I'm saying they shouldn't jump to conclusions."

At the autopsy John MacLennan's somewhat overweight naked body was being photographed in various positions to show entry and exit wounds. His heart weighed 380 grams and was healthy apart from a hole through it.

The first bullet had clipped the fifth rib, penetrated horizontally the right ventricle of the heart, the diaphragm, the liver, a main artery (the aorta) and lodged in the ninth thoracic vertebra.

The second bullet had penetrated horizontally the rib space, the heart sac, the diaphragm, the spleen; the diaphragm again, fractured the ninth rib at the back and lodged in the underlying muscle.

The third bullet was directed slightly downwards into the abdomen, through the stomach and the tenth rib space, before exiting.

The fourth shot, close to number three, was also directed downwards. It had penetrated the transverse colon and the mesentery of the small intestine and had also exited. The fifth shot was fired downwards into the lower left abdomen. It penetrated muscle of the abdominal wall before it too excited.

Because of a request made to him at the death scene the pathologist, Dr Wong, had the deceased's anus photographed to see if it showed possible homosexual activity. He took blood samples which subsequently showed a low alcohol content. The brain was healthy and the gullet empty.

Later that day, as the sun fell towards the mountains on Lantau Island, west of Hong Kong, a third of the way round the world on the Black Isle, near Inverness in North Scotland, it was early morning, dark and snowing hard in ear tingling silence. Katie MacLennan was bringing her chilled crofter's cottage back to life by lighting the oil lamps. Her eldest son Ron had already lit the log fire before he left for work on the farm. She boiled the kettle on the kerosene stove for her husband Joe's tea and turned on the radio. With no telephone this was their only contact with the outside world. This had been Joe's job till cataracts blurred his eyesight and now he was the one to be waited on. Over the air came the announcement "This is the BBC Scottish Region's nine o'clock news. First the headlines:

"President Carter has praised the united Nations General assembly's resolution calling for the withdrawal of Soviet troops from Afghanistan;

Elvis Presley's physician appears before the Tennessee medical examiners to answer charges related to drugs he prescribed for the singer;

Chaos occurred last night in Glasgow Central Railway Station, leaving hundreds stranded when deep snow caused points to malfunction:

A local boy, John MacLennan, who was a Police Inspector in Hong Kong, has died in a shooting incident. He was about to be arrested on eight charges of gross indecency."

That was all. The BBC had no more to tell. Katie staggered against the doorpost, dropping the tray. The china and the tea crashed on the floor.

Chapter 2

Disposal of body

Richard Lidster, the representative of the Royal Hong Kong Police in the Hong Kong London Office in Grafton Street, arrived at work after a freezing ride on British Railways Southern Region and a tiring trudge through London slush to find a telex waiting for him. It read: Inspector John MacLennan died 7 am local time from gunshot wounds. Contact parents at Togorm Farm Inverness Scotland and break news. Obtain their permission for autopsy and their wishes for funeral arrangements. Cremation recommended as airlines object to freighting bodies.

The name was familiar to Lidster. Two years earlier John MacLennan had been concerned in an internal scandal involving triads. Lidster, who had been part of the investigation, was therefore not entirely surprised MacLennan had come to a sticky end. He would, of course, have been well aware that the Royal Air Force had a special unit on standby for flying bodies back to England, so it wouldn't have been difficult for him to read into the message some urgency to get rid of this one before too many people saw it.

He soon discovered the parents had no phone. He did however manage to contact the neighbouring farmer, Angus Macdonald of Togorm Farm, who undertook to go round to the cottage and contact the parents. Macdonald sent a labourer out to bring the MacLennan's' elder son Ron home while he put on big gum boots and camel hair duffle coat with the hood up. Fifteen minutes later, he was knocking on their door.

"Can I come in, Katie. I have some verra bad news."

Katie was weeping. "Aye, come in Mr Macdonald. But you're a wee bit late. We heard it on the radio. We canna believe it."

He did his best to console them, knowing as little about it as they did. Then he got on to the difficult bit.

"I hardly like to mention it, but the Hong Kong Police have to know. With a sudden death they have to have an autopsy. And they need your permission. I'm sure it's only a formality, just to make certain everything's in order." Katie's voice was breaking up so Joe stepped in.

"I'm sure you know best, Mr Macdonald. Tell them to go ahead. We understand." Joe was surprisingly calm, as if he had had a premonition.

"And they'll want to know the funeral arrangements. Have you any special preference?"

Joe asked. "Dee you mean for here or Hong Kong?"

"Why Hong Kong, I suppose. When we get him back we can have our own funeral service here."

Katie had recovered a bit. "Can we talk it over when Ron comes?"

"Aye. Of course. Then I'll be leaving you. Will you be alright? I'm sure Ron will nay be long.—Oh . . ." He hadn't forgotten. He just hadn't known how to raise it. Now he knew he had to. "They'll need to know what you want done with poor Johnny. Maybe you could talk that over with Ron too." After that effort he couldn't get out fast enough. He knew he hadn't put over half of Mr Lidster's message, but that could wait.

Ron arrived soon. The family decided they needed help. Johnny after all had always been a keen churchgoer and had regularly said his prayers. The snow had eased so they dragged themselves round to the kirk, where the pastor advised them to ask for Psalm 23, The Lord is my Shepherd, and a Hymn, Eternal Father Strong to Save.

"Leave all the arrangements to me," he said. "We will have a regular burial service when they bring him back." As soon as the family left he ordered a six-foot grave to be marked out and the turf removed at Fodderty Cemetery. Cremations were unheard of in the Black Isle.

The MacLennan's called in on Angus Macdonald on the way home.

"Don't worry," he said. "I'll ring London right away."

Once he was through he handed the phone to Katie. "But Mr Lidster," she murmured, "we don't do cremations here. De y' ken, it's against our belief . . ."

"But we have already arranged to have a regular funeral and burial here . . ." She continued, scrimmaging through her bag for a hankie.

"Oh well, if you insist I suppose we will have to agree." She blew her nose noisily and wiped her eyes

So it was that Mr Lidster sent a telex at 11.35 that morning, giving funeral instructions and permission for an autopsy that had already been in progress for a whole day because of the time difference, adding "Next of kin wish deceased to be cremated and ashes sent to them in UK."

A week or so later Angus MacDonald received a telephone call from Aberdeen Airport, inquiring if he would ask a member of the MacLennan family to come and collect a casket of ashes. Angus was furious. "I'll do nothing of the sort. What dee ye think it is; the groceries?"

He collected the ashes himself and took them to Donald Cameron & Son, the undertakers. The invoice contained an item 'supply new brass plate'. This was because the casket had been sent with the wrong name on it.

In Hong Kong the Coroner, Mr Hanson, acted immediately on receipt of Lidster's telex. He signed an order for a cremation to be carried out five days later, even before he had the results of the autopsy. Indeed, he knew it was still in progress because he ordered tests for gunpowder to be carried out on the hands and on the sweater MacLennan had been wearing, together with fingerprint tests on an alleged suicide note. The following day he was replaced by a new Coroner, Mr David Leonard, and the tests were never conducted.

Exactly one week after John MacLennan's death a funeral service with full honours was held at the Union Church in Kennedy Road, Hong Kong Island. The coffin was covered with a Union Jack and many of the top brass of the police force attended the funeral (not normal with a suicide). Afterwards the coffin was taken to Cape Collinson and cremated.

Chapter 3

Opening studio

In the week following, Aileen had only sporadic calls from listeners about the death. Most expressed surprise that it was possible for anyone to shoot oneself more than once, but in the absence of any detailed information there was not much more that could be said. The newspapers had hardly picked up the case at all. Not so Elsie Elliott. She had been writing letters demanding an inquiry, which was turned down. After ten days of such rejections she asked Aileen if she could come into the studio. At that time Aileen still had no warning of the upheaval John MacLennan's death would cause in her life, so it was with expectation and not a little excitement that she dressed in a Dior design crisp linen suit, copied from a fashion magazine by a local tailor, casual but elegant. She believed that, even on radio, listeners can sense from your voice whether you look a million dollars or a slob. With a final glance in the mirror, which revealed a beauty emanating more from sheer vitality than from bone structure, she almost danced down the corridor of their flat into the dining room to find her husband Kevin tucking into bacon and eggs, with something of the detachment of a nuclear scientist, while devouring the newspaper at the same time. She gulped down a mango juice.

In the kitchen an elderly Chinese woman dressed in black and white pyjamas or *Baak Saam* was pouring coffee into a flask. She had been trained in an era when expatriates required their amahs not only to wear uniform but to speak in 'pigeon English'. She placed the flask in a string bag along with an apple. She came out and thrust it all into Aileen's hand.

"You plenty not eat, you get muchee thin."

"No chance on your cooking, Ah Sun."

Kevin looked up.

"Talking of cooking, I see some Chinese have been eating dog again and everyone's up in arms about it. How could they do that to man's best friend!"

"Don't ask me, Dear Boffin. Ring me up on the program and yell with indignation. Everybody else will."

"No fear, not me. But I hope you've got your bulletproof knickers on."

She kissed him—not so much a kiss as four seconds of passion full on the mouth—crumpling his newspaper like a morning sheet. Then she was on her way

Down in the car park the amahs were doing their *Tai Chi*, a ballet of slow motion karate chops, imaginary sword fights or simple balancing acts, while breathing deeply the soft morning air of a sunny January day.

Aileen gave them a cheery wave as she slipped into her red open-top Alpha Romeo Spider to drive to the radio station. From her Plantation Road flat, high on the Peak, she drove first on the subtropical south side of Hong Kong Island, with several sheer drops on the right, viewing far below the deep blue South China Sea spattered with little islands and stretching to the horizon. Then the narrow road twisted down under trees through a gap to the north side, revealing the mass of towering buildings before the azure harbour, in which a multitude of small craft buzzed about the rusting freighters, while a few remaining junks with their red batwing sails wove among the ferries. The wind ruffled her silk leopard scarf and her short wavy auburn hair as she made the steep descent. Once through the narrow city she curved into the car ferry terminal, reached a slender arm to pay the toll and collect the English newspapers and joined the queue of vehicles for the ferry.

This was her routine. Someone was sure to ring the show and refer to an obscure paragraph on page six, which would be a slip on her part if she had not read it. She noticed with distaste the policeman in his dark blue uniform collecting the protection money from the wrinkled hands of the street hawkers. By the time the ferry was ready she had scanned the

South China Morning Post, but the *Hong Kong Standard* and the tabloid *The Sun* had to wait till she had eased the car up the ramp and onto the sopping wooden car deck. She quickly whipped through the remaining newspapers and climbed out to stretch her shapely legs, her sleek white suit contrasting sharply with the mixture of office wear, tee-shirts, denims and sailors' uniforms of others on board.

Tourists came from all over the world to see that crossing and it still filled her with wonder. On one side were tall buildings, grinning like concrete teeth, topped with huge neon signs, edging their way halfway up the mountains and stretching their serried ranks for miles along the coast. On the other the flat triangle of Kowloon, crammed solid with lower buildings, limited for the safety of the continuous stream of aircraft making one of the most hazardous and awesome approaches in the world, and also backed by distant mountains. The entire crossing was accompanied by junks and chugging sampans, yachts and buzzing speedboats, weaving their way into the patchwork spectacle, displaying the living energy that is Hong Kong.

The drive through Mongkok, the most densely populated area on earth, with as many as a thousand residents crammed into areas the size of a football pitch, was bumper to bumper traffic. As she passed the minibus terminus she saw a heated argument with arms waving and plenty of tuneful Cantonese expletives flying about. She gathered they were debating how much of the takings the drivers had to pay to the triads, a really thorny problem that had been going on for years and which the police seemed powerless to control—to the point where suspicions were aroused that they might actually condone it. The incident reminded her of her forthcoming interview with Elsie Elliott and she spent the rest of the journey working out how to get the best out of that rare experience.

At last she arrived at the radio station in the foothills which gave their name to Kowloon. In Chinese Kowloon (*Gau Lung*) means nine dragons, which is said to be the number of peaks (actually only eight) separating the city from the rural New Territories—the area under a 99-year lease that expired after June 1997 and took the rest of Hong Kong with it back to the sovereignty of China. The ninth dragon was added to this range in honour of Zhao Bing, the eight-year-old last emperor of the Song Dynasty who sought refuge briefly in Kowloon while fleeing the invading Mongols.

Frena, Aileen's producer, an intense unsophisticated young Chinese in tee-shirt and jeans, was already busy. Totally bilingual, she had spent ten years in Australia as a journalist, winding up as researcher on a talk show with an aggressive, rude, highly successful Australian host. She had returned to her birthplace to continue her career. She looked up as Aileen spoke.

"Morning, Frena. I think we might get a call on that ferry collision." Safety in the turbulent harbour was always a worry.

"Marine Department have already rung to say they would like to comment."

"Fine Let's include yesterday's call from that student who took down some life belts and found they had gone rotten" Then as an afterthought she added "Perhaps we can get the Ferry Company to upgrade their reply of 'no comment' . . . oh and you'd better lay on a couple of experts on cooking and eating dog," and she bustled into the inner room.

The studio was quite small, with good air-conditioning, which coped adequately with the dozen or so cigarettes Aileen smoked during a program. A heavy soundproof door led from the corridor into the outer production side. The technician and the producer sat at a console, equipped with disk and tape players and vertical faders, facing a double glass window into the inner studio. Behind them was just enough room for a steel filing cabinet. An attempt to brighten up the dark wood and black sound absorbent panels with some gaudy posters was only marginally successful. Another heavy door led into the inner studio which was even duller because there the sound absorbent panels had to be left free to eliminate echo. Aileen sat at a desk facing the door, but slightly skewed towards the producer's window at her right. Her guests sat opposite her with individual microphones, so they were less conscious of the producer. The word dull could aptly be applied to the empty studio, but Aileen brought to it such exuberance that it was lifted to a virtual glitter throughout the talk-show. Her Shakespeare-loving parents must have had prescience of her magical spirit when they named her after his sylphlike raiser of tempests. In fact her mother had played in the BBC Shakespeare series, which is where she met Aerial's father, who was on the engineering staff. Aerial's education was somewhat disturbed by her father's periodic postings but she showed sufficient talent to finish up in a Drama School in the outer rooms of the Royal Albert Hall. At this point she met, fell in love with and married Kevin, another BBC engineer, who was later posted to Hong Kong. He subsequently transferred to the Hong Kong Government engineering department under the Director of Public Works, which entitled them to a married quarter high up on the hill behind the city. Aerial's background enabled her to apply for a job as an announcer in a local radio station, where she advanced to host the talk-show.

Chapter 4

Elsie in studio

Elsie arrived well ahead of the program. John MacLennan's funeral had been held two days before and now she was taking her place in the studio during the signature tune and sharpening her knives.

She was a frail, grey haired lady who looked as if she should be dressed in lavender and spending her time harmlessly knitting socks for her grandchildren. She had come to Hong Kong thirty years before as a missionary, living for a while in a tiny brick hut, beside a large Army tent, which served as her school. Later, as she saw injustice all around her, she made it her mission to expose these wrongdoings. She had done this with such success that she had become something of a thorn in the side of the authorities and a much loved figure in the eyes of the public at large. In particular she had caused such a nuisance over police corruption that all the hawkers greeted her as she passed and taxi drivers refused to charge her a fare, a kind gesture that she rejected on the grounds that they had to make a living. She now dwelt in ethnic exile in her Chinese school deep in smoky, industrial Kwun Tong. That school, however, had become almost a shrine. People with problems came from all over the territory to lay them before the one person they knew would listen sincerely and try to get them a fair deal. She had a nose well attuned to the smell of injustice and corruption. It was her unremitting appeals and nagging a decade before that had caused the disclosure of huge corruption

13

syndicates operating in Hong Kong and brought to justice top policemen and others who were making colossal fortunes out of graft. Indeed, many regarded her as the founder of the Independent Commission against Corruption or ICAC, which now held a unique place in Hong Kong and perhaps the world, though obviously the colonial administration took the credit for this.

The "On Air" light came on.

"Hello folks, you're with Aileen's Phone-In and as always you can call into the program, on 3-361181, with anything you feel strongly about today. Later in the show we'll be talking about pawn shops. They were invented by the Chinese 3,000 years ago and now are part of the Hong Kong way of life. But to begin our program we have Urban Councilor Elsie Elliott in the studio to talk about Inspector John MacLennan who died last week. Good Morning Elsie, welcome to the studio. I hear you have asked for an inquiry. Why is that?"

"Because I don't think we have been told the full facts. You see, I knew him. He came to me about a year ago when he was framed on a charge of gross indecency."

"Framed?"

Aileen wondered if accusations like that should be broadcast to the whole of Hong Kong. But Elsie was away. There was no stopping her now.

"Yes, the charge was brought with no witnesses. Yet the Acting Commissioner of Police, Roy Henry, considered it sufficient grounds for his dismissal. That's when John approached me. So I wrote to the Governor. I explained that he had been grilled for several hours by a magistrate, who came to the conclusion that not only was he innocent, but that because his job had involved investigation of triads and homosexuals there may have been a motive to get rid of him if some high-up policemen were involved.

"John MacLennan was reinstated in a matter of days but he was warned by his superiors that he wouldn't get any more promotion. From then on he was obviously a target."

"But Elsie, are you saying that this frame-up was within the police department? That the police themselves were falsifying evidence against their own?"

Aileen had mixed feelings. This was gripping stuff, but upstairs her boss would be glued to the monitor. Nick Demuth was a guard dog for the station image. Any threat to that and he would phone the lawyers. He'd be doing that now. Oblivious, Elsie sailed on:

"Oh yes. As far as I can see the outdated colonial laws on homosexuality, where consenting adults can get life imprisonment, are very convenient for that sort of thing. They have been dormant for a long time, but seem to have been resurrected recently. They encourage blackmail and intimidation."

"Elsie, you have been lobbying for a change in the law for years. Are you saying the authorities want it there?"

"Of course, you can see various cases involving triads and so on where boys give evidence in court and are subsequently discredited. They are often paid by the police to tell lies in court. Why don't they investigate who sent the boys to court?"

"Because they would be investigating the investigators, you mean?"

"Exactly, but they won't change the law because as it stands it is so useful to the police. After all, so many people have been complaining about it for years."

"And no homosexual dares to plead his own case."

"I know, but plenty of other people have pleaded who are not homosexual. It's so unfair. Also it doesn't apply to women."

"Perhaps they don't want gay rights demonstrations in Hong Kong like they get in Amsterdam and San Francisco."

It was about this time that Aileen glanced into the production studio and saw the boss, Nick Demuth, looking more harassed than usual behind his wrinkles and thinning grey hair. He had come down from on high and was glaring at her. Well, not so much glaring as glassy eyed. His index finger flashed from left to right across his throat. The message was clear.

"It may be the Chinese," Elsie was saying. "People say the Chinese wouldn't like it to be legalised. But in China they don't make it criminal either . . ."

Aileen shrugged her shoulders to Nick to show that nobody could stop Elsie, who energetically continued . . .

"One of the top Chinese, a legislative councilor, only the other day said there was no such thing as a Chinese homosexual . . ."

Nick was giving the cutting throat signal with increasing precision. Aileen pretended not to see him, reckoning you don't just cut off a celebrity like Elsie Elliott.

". . . and all the time a Chinese procurer was running the racket providing boys to give false evidence. I can name him." but don't. Please, please don't.

"Which is why I think it is so unfair trying to pin it on the expatriates all the time."

"Elsie, are you saying that John MacLennan was driven to suicide because of persecution?"

"Not necessarily."

"But you *are* calling for an inquiry."

"Yes. I do not doubt the persecution, I doubt the suicide. As soon as I heard he was dead I immediately thought—oh, no! Not suicide. He wouldn't do that. I knew him too well. And then I heard he had four or five shots in him."

Aileen forgot about Nick. "Four or five?"

"Yes, there are conflicting reports."

"But even four. Self-inflicted? That's very strange."

"Yes, even police friends of mine have been voicing their doubts. I understand people who knew him are scared to speak."

"But do you really think it might not have been suicide?"

"How can I know, Aileen, how can anyone know? But I'll tell you this. Murder by five shots is a triad signature. During the triad initiation ceremony they have to swear 36 oaths, mainly concerned with loyalty to the brotherhood, and more than half of them end with the promise: 'If I break this oath I will be killed by five thunderbolts.'"

A call came in. "I'm a soldier. I was in Northern Ireland and I've seen people shot. I can tell you they just go down. Shooting yourself four times! Bloody ridiculous!"

Then another—all confidential she was. "It's the police, you know. How do you think that body in the sack did the deed? Did they saw the head off first and then the hands? Or if they did the hands first, how did they hold the chopper to do the head?"

By this time Elsie caught the mood of the listeners. "Perhaps they held the chopper with their feet and fell on it."

"Then how did they climb into the sack and sew themselves up? No, that's silly," said the caller.

Aileen turned to Elsie. "Only two days ago I read out a news item about a triad gang threatening to sever a man's leg." (Little did she know that some years later one of her own successors would be chopped nine times with a butcher's knife as he entered the radio station for something he had broadcast). "You see, Elsie, we hear of these incredible cases, but how many are there we don't know about?

Another caller commented "I think there are a lot of police suicides that we do know about. I've seen some in the press. Is there any way we can find out the number?"

"I can ask PPRB. It's a reasonable request for Police Public Relations."

"Will they tell the truth?"

"Oh yes."

"Including the one in the sack?"

Elsie added, "It's not the ones in sacks I am worried about. It's the ones in ashes. Two days ago they cremated John MacLennan's body."

"Cremated the body! How can they have?"

"I don't know. There should have been an independent examination of the body—by someone not connected with the police. All I know is the coroner signed the cremation authorisation within 48 hours of the death and it was carried out the day before yesterday."

"But surely, Elsie, in cases of foul play or suspected suicide there must be some ruling against cremation of the body."

"You would think so, wouldn't you?"

"What? Even when they knew there had been a public call for an inquiry they still cremated the body within the week?"

"Yes."

Elsie, sensing a suitably dramatic ending, summed up with: "There's a lot more in this than meets the eye."

Aileen looked up. Nick had gone no doubt to place the entire legal profession on standby alert.

Within half an hour the police rang up and demanded a tape of the program.

"Very uptight, they seemed," said Frena.

"Well don't send it to them."

"But . . ."

"Send it to Elsie first. If she says it's O.K.—send it to them."

Aileen listened to it herself. She thought it was pretty stirring stuff but she couldn't see anything actually libellous in it. She didn't mention it to Nick. In fact she avoided him for a few days to let him get over it. Elsie couldn't see anything wrong with it either so it was duly dispatched.

When Aileen had time to think about it she had to admit the interview had left a lot of question marks. Was John MacLennan hounded? Can you shoot yourself more than once? No, it just wasn't good enough, so she joined Elsie in demanding an inquiry. Soon the rest of the media took it up, but Chinese New Year intervened, so it was two frustrating weeks more before the authorities announced there would be an inquest.

Before it started Chief Inspector Bailey turned up at the studio.

"Would you mind certifying that the tape which you sent to Police Headquarters was a true and unedited record of the discussion which took place between you and Mrs Elsie Elliott on Hong Kong Commercial Radio on Thursday 24th January 1980?" He spoke as if he was reading what he was about to write down.

"Sure," Aileen said, "come in."

He pulled out a form Poll 154—Royal Hong Kong Police STATEMENT/Report. He wrote out what he had just said and she signed that she had read it and certified it to be correct. It seemed pretty innocuous, but he was obviously up to something.

Three weeks later the inquest actually opened, but far from the iconic image of a blindfold Justice balancing even scales, this one started without a corpse and with a presumption of suicide.

Chapter 5

Chinese Lunar New Year was a very special festival in Hong Kong, a time of reunion and renewal of the spirit. Also known as the Spring Festival, it was traditionally the time to celebrate the end of winter, the renewal of life in the soil and the start of planting. It was also one of three occasions in the year for debt collection. Creditors pursued their debtors, sometimes with the help of strong arm methods of the triads for larger debts, right up to New Year's Day. On that day there was an amnesty, folks visiting relatives, the heat lifted from debtors who could breathe again and even the triads joining the festivities, which lasted between five and 15 days according to people's means and inclinations. Hong Kong was festooned with red and gold ornaments. Especially in the villages, doorposts were adorned with images of the Kitchen God. Chairman Mao Zedong proclaimed that this emblem be replaced with his portrait, though little notice was taken of this even in China and certainly not in Hong Kong.

For Aileen and Kevin Chinese New Year meant some hardship. For their amah, as for thousands of others, visiting did not just mean popping next door, but embarking on an exhausting journey across the border to China. Ah Sun was no exception. Towards Chinese New Year she changed. Normally her loyalty was boundless. If there was work to be done no power on earth would get her to bed. Even on her day off the morning cup of tea arrived before she left, and when she returned in the evening she had always spent time in the market buying goodies for Master such as mangoes or his favourite fish, which she called *gow yue*.

But now the fish was not for Master. She was thinking of the family in China. She came back with bags of it and hung it up to dry.

"That way muchee cheap. Three dollar two piecy."

You could smell it down in the street.

The day before she was due to go, Aileen crept up on her in her bedroom with a tape recorder and collected a treasure of an interview. Ah Sun told her how her family was so poor. She was the rich auntie who sent them money every month. They would all be there to meet her to see what she had brought from the golden city. Then they would all retire to their little wooden hut and eat suckling pig. Aileen asked her if she would stay for a week.

"No, Missy, I no sleep."

"Why not?"

"No room, no bed—and we not stop talking all the time."

So the next day off she went, her white jacket changed for a black one and a straw hat which was just a rim, the hole in the middle filled with a piece of black cloth covering her head, to complement the black veil all around the rim. In the fields these hats were worn with a towel in the middle and they were very cool. She looked extraordinarily fat.

"What on earth are you wearing, Ah Sun?"

"Six piecy jumper, Missy, then I no pay money."

All the amahs did this. The Customs must have known exactly what they were up to but for some reason they let them get away with it. Nowadays of course regulations are much easier.

Then out came a bamboo pole and two enormous nets full of packages. It was all Kevin could do to heave one of them into the lift for her, but once downstairs she slung one on each end of the pole, put the pole on one shoulder and off she waddled carrying at least her own weight. Aileen drove her to the station. What a sight! Hundreds of amahs, all dressed exactly alike, all with bamboo poles and huge packages for their families. In those days they had to disembark at the border and carry everything across the bridge at Lo Wu to board a Chinese train to Canton. It seemed unlikely she would survive.

She did. Three days later Aileen suddenly found her bustling about in the kitchen as if nothing had happened, looking as thin as ever, all the extra clothing left behind, along with her voice.

"Ah Sun, you got bad throat?"

"No Missy," she croaked, "I plenty blabbermouth."

It was a different sort of hardship for Superintendent Marc Pelly, appointed as investigating officer in the case of Inspector John MacLennan. He had been given advance warning that an inquest would be held three weeks after Chinese New Year so he hoped to be able to use the holiday time to fully acquaint himself with the facts. Unfortunately for him too many potential witnesses were on leave and others were on unusual shifts because of the festivities. If he was tall and lean before, he was almost wasting away by the time he had interviewed eighty witnesses. Some he could invite to his rather bare and boxlike office in the Homantin Police Station; others, such as the Commissioner of Police, he had in due deference to visit himself. First, however, he turned his attention inward, for John MacLennan had been on his staff and he had counselled him not long before he died.

Chapter 6

At about 5 pm on 14th January, the evening before the death, Marc Pelly had been in the kitchen of the Homantin Officers' Mess or common room, high up in the tall building that gave a spectacular view of the lights coming on in Kowloon and Hong Kong Island beyond. With jacket off and sleeves rolled up he sauntered out to the Mess bar, into the familiar surroundings of light coloured wooden tables and chairs, standard government issue, and a few rather worn leatherette sofas which had long suffered from Mess games and spilled drinks. What caught his attention was a lone figure standing by the window, looking worried.

"Hello, John," he said with his usual kindly twinkle in his eye. MacLennan was startled.

"Something wrong?" inquired Pelly.

"I dinna ken, Marc. The boss has asked me to be in his office tomorrow at the behest of the Special Investigation Unit." The stocky Scot's brow was furrowed and the usual affable grin had given way to a tight-lipped seriousness.

"Jack Trotman told you that?"

"He did. The SIU are supposed to be investigating queers. I don't know what that's got to do with me, unless it's about an incident that occurred about a year past in Yuen Long. There was a complaint against me; you probably heard about it."

"I heard rumours," Pelly admitted.

"Well, it was totally without foundation. I always thought it was triad-inspired. They couldn't prove anything so they dropped it. But obviously somebody was pushing pretty hard because at one time I was actually dismissed, but then I appealed and was reinstated. I assumed all that was in the past, but obviously it's not. You know, the SIU are Special alright. They are a rotten lot, Marc, They've got nothing better to do than go round hounding people. And with all the crime around too."

"Look, come and have a talk about it. I've got some food cooking in the kitchen."

"Aye, alright."

"You haven't got a drink. What'll you have?" "Thanks. A vodka and tonic." Marc Pelly did the duties of the absent barman, signed the chit and together they went into the kitchen.

"You know, I canna believe it, Marc. They say they are concerned with the procuring of boys and I am simply not into that. Yet once they get an idea in their heads, you canna shift it. It's persecution. Absolute persecution, and groundless too."

"But, John, they must have some reason."

"Well, I don't know what it is, but I have an idea. While I was in Special Branch, I became aware of the investigation of a lot of queer hawks. I saw the list of suspects and what looked like the whole of the top of the police force was on it and there were other implications too that I reckon could have blown the lid off Hong Kong."

"My God."

"They know I know, and I suppose they are afraid I'll blab or something."

"That's not very logical, John. You'd be much more likely to come out with it if you were under pressure yourself."

"Well, I don't know. Perhaps they think that because I was interested in the case I was queer myself. But if that's what they think they are barking up the wrong tree. The truth is, they've been taken off the real job of the police, busting crime, and now they don't know what to do with themselves. What do you think I should do, Marc?"

Pelly thought for a while and knowing the SIU's propensity for hounding and arresting people he cautiously offered: "If I were you I'd get a solicitor. You need to be careful from the start. Try Hampton, Winter and Glynn. Michael Winter himself is pretty good."

"I've already tried them because I knew they handled police cases. I had a chap called Llewellyn on the Yuen Long case, but I can't get hold of him. I couldn't even contact Mike Winter. Perhaps I should have another go."

John went into the bar, but in a couple of minutes he was back.

"I've got Stephen Llewellyn on the phone now. Would you have a word with him, Marc?"

"Sure, don't let this food burn, will you?"

Marc Pelly spoke to Stephen Llewellyn who explained that he couldn't come in the morning as he would be in court. "How serious is it?"

"I don't know. Where are you now?"

"South Kowloon Court. I'll be leaving soon."

"Why don't you come round to the Homantin Mess and we can talk about it?"

"Yes, alright. I'll be about an hour."

Marc went back to the kitchen. "He's coming round about six thirty."

"Oh, good . . . Er . . . Marc . . ."

"Yes?"

"What's the worst that can happen to me?"

"Don't be such a pessimist, John. Let Stephen Llewellyn handle it."

"Oh, I will. But I think it's as well to be prepared."

"Well, I really don't know. I mean the SIU don't deal in kids' stuff, if you'll forgive the expression. I suppose the worst than can happen is you might be required to put up bail."

"That's torn it."

"Why?"

"I haven't got a penny."

"Oh. Perhaps you were right to think about being prepared."

"How much would it be?"

"There again, it's hard to say, but I should think you ought to aim in the region of five grand. Can't you raise it from friends?"

"How on earth can I do that? None of my friends have got a penny either. I couldn't ask them anyway, it's dreadful. I mean, it's one thing if you've done something, but how on earth can you defend yourself against something you haven't even been involved in? Honestly, the SIU would be better employed on more serious crimes like robbery and burglary than investigating allegations that in most other countries is not a crime."

"Now, John, I know you feel incensed about it. Anyone would. But do stay calm. There's nothing worse at an interview of this nature than to get all uptight. Now, my advice to you is, see this lawyer, then get an early night and be fresh to face whatever they have to say in the morning." John gulped the rest of his vodka tonic. "And I shouldn't drink too much if I were you."

At 6.15 Stephen Llewellyn arrived. They went downstairs to Pelly's office where it was more private. Llewellyn explained to Pelly that he could not attend himself and asked if the interview could possibly be deferred.

"You'll have to ring the Head of the SIU, Superintendent Brooks."

Pelly called the number and handed the phone to Llewellyn.

But Brooks was adamant. The arrangements were firm and could not be changed. He then described at some length his displeasure that Inspector MacLennan should have been told the reason why he was required in Jack Trotman's office and particularly that the SIU was involved.

"He seemed right steamed up about it," Llewellyn said to Pelly. "But he won't change the time so I'll have to see if someone else can come." He rang his office and found Paul Stevens was available so it was fixed that he should attend. Then John MacLennan had a session with Llewellyn. Marc Pelly could see little else he could contribute so he went home about 6.30. He would never see John MacLennan alive again.

Chapter 7

It was during his investigation that Marc Pelly discovered what had happened next. Llewellyn left soon after 7.30 and at 7.50 John picked up his personal typewriter, his briefcase, some stationary and a bundle of case files, put through a call to Dc Leung, his detective constable, to tell him he had some important personal business to attend to, and left the station, presumably returning to his flat.

The remaining hours of John MacLennan's life seemed clouded in a certain mystery. At some time between 8 pm on the 14th and 5.30 am on the 15th he delivered a stack of completed case files to the office of his superior, Senior Inspector Charles Grant, but otherwise nobody could be found who knew his whereabouts. Despite some energetic detective work, Marc Pelly could only discover that WPC. Poon received a phone call in the report room between 1.30 am and 2 am on 15th January from a person who said he was Inspector MacLennan. The conversation was in English. MacLennan said he wanted a wake-up call at 5.30 am. He gave the telephone number. Miss Poon wrote the number in the duty officer's book and went for tea break between 5 and 6 am. The procedure was quite normal.

PC Lam made the wake-up call at 5.32 am to the number given. He said "Inspector MacLennan?" A voice said "Yes." "This phone is morning call to wake you up. I see you write down on the duty board." The person at the other end seemed to have some difficulty in understanding so the message was repeated. The response was "Thank you," in a voice that sounded very tired.

Station Sergeant Li Chi-man was on duty at 5.55 am on the 15th when a man came in wearing a dark-coloured winter jacket. "I am Detective Inspector MacLennan and I need a gun \because I am going out for a raid." He spoke very quickly.

"Excuse me, sir?"

"Raid. R-A-I-D—CID raid." He showed his warrant card.

"Yes sir. I recognise you. Please go downstairs and collect it."

Sergeant Li phoned down to the armoury.

"Armoury? Mr MacLennan is coming down to get a gun because he has a job to do. So when you see him give him a gun."

PC Lee Hok-lun gave evidence at the inquest that he was in attendance in the armoury and received a phone call at 5.56 am from Detective Sergeant Li to say that Inspector MacLennan was on his way down and should be given a gun. The man who came to collect the gun arrived at 6 am. He spoke in Cantonese. He said, "Good morning, I'm Inspector MacLennan." He showed his police warrant card.

PC Lee could not find a short barrelled CID gun so he gave him a normal one, number 4894, with six rounds of ammunition. The man signed the register in the wrong column and started to put 0500 instead of 0600 as the time. P.C. Lee asked him to correct these errors. The procedure was not normal and the change of shift stamp was subsequently entered in the wrong place. PC Lee also described the man as DDI (Divisional Detective Inspector) HMT (Ho Man Tin) CID which was not Inspector MacLennan's post. However, the gun was drawn and was next seen in John MacLennan's flat when he was found at 11.55 am in his locked bedroom with five bullet wounds in his chest. Sandra Hills, a physiotherapist who lived two floors above MacLennan was woken by several bangs over a period of minutes, perhaps five or ten, at "6—something" by her digital clock.

Pelly elicited the clearest account of the events leading up to MacLennan's death from Chief Inspector Michael Quinn, the deputy head of the SIU. The case went back to John MacLennan's joining the Hong Kong Police in 1973. He did not do well in Police Training School (PTS), but in subsequent postings was well thought of, regarded as honest, with high professional standards, jolly and extrovert. At the end of his first contract he expressed a preference for work in Special Branch on his return, so he was fully vetted, his character, personality and temperament being studied. This included being watched during a stopover in Bangkok where he was observed to indulge in the Thai sex scene with enthusiasm, but only with women. He returned in March 1977 and was posted to Special Branch where he gained incidental access to various highly confidential files, including one known as the Rumour File containing the names of important suspected homosexuals, including Assistant Commissioner of Police, Roy Henry. Naturally this file too was highly classified.

After a month MacLennan resigned from the force to join the London Metropolitan Police, saying that life in Hong Kong did not suit him. He was interviewed on 6th June 1977 to confirm his resignation and was struck off on 17th July. In December, however, he applied to rejoin the Hong Kong Police saying his reason for leaving Hong Kong was the health of his mother, who had now recovered. He was re-engaged and returned in March 1978. He was posted to the New Territories District, initially to Yuen Long, a small town in the North West not far from the Chinese border. It was here that a youth made a complaint against him of attempted gross indecency before promptly emigrating to Scotland. The file, however, was circulated for months with a pair of yellow briefs as one of the enclosures.

On the basis of this unsubstantiated complaint, and against the advice of several senior officers, MacLennan was dismissed by the Acting Commissioner of Police, Roy Henry. However, he bucked the system by appealing outside the service, to Elsie Elliott and thence to the Governor. There was no doubt in Quinn's mind that he was guilty as charged. He was therefore watched and during 1979 the SIU built up a case against him. By July they had eight charges of gross indecency buttoned up with as many male prostitutes prepared to give evidence against MacLennan in court. They put him on the immigration stop list, so he couldn't escape from Hong Kong, and he remained under surveillance. The Attorney General himself authorised the Inspector's arrest, which was set for 10.30 am on 15th January. In order to keep it strictly correct they decided the arrest should be made in the office of MacLennan's divisional commander, Senior Superintendent Jack Trotman. Much to the chagrin of the Special Investigation Unit, Trotman, in ordering MacLennan to attend the interview, disclosed that it was at the instigation of the SIU. When asked why he was concerned at this disclosure, Quinn replied that he didn't want MacLennan destroying evidence or trying to flee the Colony.

Chapter 8

At 9 am on 15th January there was an SIU briefing in Police Headquarters on Hong Kong Island with Quinn, two Inspectors, Loughrin and Tin, and Sgt Leung. Quinn instructed Leung to arrange an exhibits officer and a photographer. At 10 am the arrest party gathered, consisting of Quinn, Loughrin, Tin, Sgt Leung, Detective Constable Cheung (Exhibits Officer), DC Poon (Photographer) and two other DCs, a total of eight. They proceeded in two cars through the Cross Harbour Tunnel to Homantin Police Station. At 10.10 am solicitor Paul Stevens arrived at Trotman's office. He was sent to wait in MacLennan's office.

At 10.40 am the arrest party arrived. There was already concern that MacLennan had not appeared. Quinn and Tin went into Trotman's office and showed him the search warrant. They officially told him they had come to arrest Inspector John MacLennan. Trotman telephoned various places in the station where MacLennan might be, including the canteen and the mess. He then telephoned MacLennan's flat three times. He encountered an engaged tone twice and finally heard ringing with no reply. This seemed the time to suggest to Quinn that the arrest party go to MacLennan's flat. Quinn invited Trotman to accompany the party and also took the solicitor Paul Stevens and the Divisional Staff Relations Officer, Lee Siu-leung. The total was now eleven. They left in a Land Rover and two cars between 10.50 and 11.00 am.

They arrived at MacLennan's quarters between 11.12 and 11.15 am. They first contacted the manageress, Janet Gafoor, and proceeded to flat

410B on the 4th floor. The outer corridor stretched the length of the block and was open to the elements, with a drop over a waist-high wall to a concrete courtyard below. Finding the door locked they knocked and rang the bell but no one answered. Inspector Shaw from the next door flat came out and joined the throng, as did Inspector Muller from the flat downstairs. Quinn sent for Janet Gafoor, who arrived with the master key. This failed to open the door. She fetched an odd job man, making a total of 15 people gathered in the narrow corridor. After 25 minutes of advice and speculation, with much banging and hammering and splintering of wood around the door handle, during which Quinn sent Li Siu-leung for a crowbar, the door was broken down at 11.35 am. The door handle remained in place, allowing it to be photographed in situ from the inside. The flat was in darkness. The door had been secured with two locks, a bolt and a security chain. Quinn entered the flat over the shattered door and switched on the light.

Just inside the entrance there was a kitchen on the left and a bathroom on the right. The lounge was furnished with a standard Government Issue desk and two chairs, a settee, a bookcase, a coffee table and a nest of small tables. A jacket hung on the back of one of the chairs. Quinn was followed by Trotman, Stevens, Poon the photographer and Janet Gafoor. Quinn and Trotman looked round the flat. Quinn picked up from the desk and showed around a brown manila envelope, on the outside of which was a handwritten note. It said:

> *Please Please tell my family*
> *this was an accident and that*
> *I was a good Police Officer*
> *JM 06.10 h.*
> *15/1/80*

Paul Stevens was directly behind Quinn. Trotman looked at the windows, whose blinds were drawn, and checked the bathroom. The bedroom door was locked. Quinn examined the type of lock, later identified as a twisting bar type, and ordered the photographer to start taking photographs of the room, the broken front door and the bedroom door.

Quinn then ordered that the bedroom door be broken down and went next door to Shaw's flat to use the telephone. He and Trotman summoned Chief Inspector Kong, forensics, another photographer, ballistics, fingerprints, CID and an ambulance. By this time Li had brought the crowbar and he broke down the bedroom door quite quickly, by 11.55 am. The room was in darkness and the curtains drawn. Quinn entered and switched on the light followed by Trotman. There was a body on the far side of the bed which was identified as John MacLennan. He had apparently changed his shoes, because his bedroom slippers had come off and there was a police revolver, number 4894, at his feet. Quinn went over looking for signs of life, observed the gun and counted the wounds. The room was then left to the photographer.

It was a small flat, not designed for so many visitors. The lounge and the bedroom were 15 sq. metres each, hardly room to swing that proverbial cat. Indeed the bedroom contained a queen size bed, which had not been slept in, two tables, one supporting a red telephone, and a chest of drawers, leaving almost no room for significant movement. The only space that could be described as ample was a walk-in wardrobe by the door, itself a sixth of the size of the whole of the bedroom.

At 12.17 two doctors, Wong and Yip, arrived and confirmed MacLennan was dead. CI Kong arrived at 12.20 and took over the job of Evidence Officer. Ballistics officers Cimino and Nichol arrived at 12.27. Three officers from CID arrived at 12.30 and stayed 15 minutes before deciding CID was not involved. Marc Pelly arrived at 12.35 and in his report described the scene as "a state of chaos". In fact up till then some 25 people had visited the flat and up to 17 of them had spent some time in the bedroom—not counting the corpse.

At 1 pm Wan For—hing, another of the reinforcements ordered by Trotman, arrived and was told to search the body. This was no doubt because the rest of the clothing had not held MacLennan's warrant card. It was not on the body either, in fact it never turned up.

At 1.10 the fingerprint expert arrived and noticed that photographs were still being taken.

Trotman, Pelly, Kong, the three CID officers and others searched the flat for evidence of the presence of another person in the flat at the time of MacLennan's death, and declared they could find none. There was no sign of a struggle. They all reported the windows to be closed or secure and that there was no means of exit other than the door locked from the inside. In any case the bathroom window was too small and the other windows all faced a sheer drop from the fourth floor. The flat upstairs was empty but secure.

The remainder of Pelly's discoveries concerned allegations of improper inducement to gather evidence against MacLennan, which involved a letter written to the Coroner by a Crown Council, Howard Lindsey, referring to Elsie Elliott. Lindsey had also been arrested on charges of gross indecency after falling out with the Attorney General and had been confronted in court by the same male prostitutes as were later involved in the MacLennan case. Being an experienced lawyer, he had been able to tear their evidence to shreds, discrediting them all as liars, and he was acquitted. However, his contract was not renewed. He had written to accuse the Attorney—General of culpability in the MacLennan case because of his inaction in response to warnings before the death.

There had also been a headline in the *Sun* newspaper "'Suicide' cop was framed", suggesting that there was a cover-up, that 'high-ranking' policemen might be involved and stating that Elsie Elliott had therefore recommended an independent inquiry. Furthermore, the Police Public Relations Bureau held a transcript of radio interviews by Aileen with Elsie Elliott in which reference had been made to murder and frame-ups. Pelly therefore interviewed Elsie at some length. The implication was that the charges against MacLennan might have been improperly supported. Pelly formed the opinion, however, that Mrs Elliott's approach was emotional and prejudiced and had little to offer in the way of evidence to any inquiry.

In conclusion Pelly, who had introduced the word suicide several times in his report, entitled it "SUICIDE MR. John MacLennan" and concluded there was no evidence of anything other than suicide. He added that MacLennan seemed to have lived a double life, partly one of high values and principles and partly a twilight life both immoral and illegal, to conceal which he committed suicide.

He reckoned without the Inquest Jury.

Chapter 9

The inquest was held in the North Kowloon Magistracy, just below the Kowloon Hills on the outskirts of the city. Aileen approached it by driving along the foothills from Commercial Radio and turning south towards Mongkok. The main road from there took her past the magistracy, or rather, it would have done had she not noticed an empty car park just before she reached it. Such a rarity in Hong Kong. She swung her red two-seater confidently in past the notice that said 'authorised vehicles only' and parked it in a corner where it couldn't be in anyone's way.

The Magistracy was an old and not very impressive building. The court was on the fourth floor and the door led straight on to long benches for the public. Aileen saw Elsie already seated in the first row and sat next to her. In front was a barrier and immediately past that was a table at which sat a jury of three, backs to the public. Past them on the left was the witness box. There was a throne seat for the Coroner, back centre facing them, and balancing the jury on the right was a second table at which sat three lawyers, also facing forward. On the other side of the same table sat three court officials. As there was no clerk of the court present, the Coroner himself had to take down the entire proceedings in longhand.

The Coroner, Mr David Leonard, was tall and thin with little charisma. A permanent frown seemed to indicate the seriousness with which he regarded his task. Before the proceedings even started he asserted himself by ticking off the foreman of the jury, who was a

European, for speaking to a member of the public outside the court, urging him not to do so again. The foreman apologised, explaining that he had been asking the way to the toilet which he now knew, so it would not happen again.

The other two members of the jury were young Chinese women, one of whom rose and said: "Excuse please, I not wish be jury because case of men relations. I not think good for young Chinese girl also my English not good too."

The Coroner told her to sit down and get on with it. He then got stuck into legal matters and declared open the inquest on Inspector John Richard MacLennan. He explained that the purpose of an inquest was to ascertain who died, when and where, and what caused the death. He would not allow—he said—evidence that had no bearing on the case to be submitted.

Counsel for the police, Andrew Hodge, was tall and youthful with a bland charm that he put to good use as an encouragement to the witnesses. He opened the proceedings with the statement: "I submit that as to cause of death, the evidence will clearly state that this was a premeditated suicide.

Elsie turned to Aileen, eyes wide in amazement, "That's a fine way to begin a so-called open inquiry!"

"There remains," Counsel continued, "the matter of state of mind. We can either look for a bald reason why the young officer should take his life, or take a broader view, which is the preference of the Commissioner of Police, that we declare that all the circumstances affecting his state of mind are explained and all eighty witnesses who have made statements be called before the jury.

"I request that we investigate regarding the1978 dismissal of the deceased. What was his reaction to the dismissal, did he allege he was framed, by whom, was it true? Regarding the recent allegations, was he framed, was it part of a vendetta by police to get rid of a man they had failed to get rid of before? Did he believe this?

"Was he hounded to death by unscrupulous police officers or was he driven to suicide by his knowledge of guilt of homosexual activities?"

The Coroner remained silent but scribbled furiously.

Chapter 10

On the first day of the inquest they learnt a little about the past of the deceased. John MacLennan joined the Royal Hong Kong Police Force in October 1973 at the age of 23, and after a period at the Police Training School or PTS was posted to Kwun Tong police station, where he was quartered in a small single mess. The Mess had only ten quarters on two floors and John tended to be a loner. In any case, police shifts have the effect of throwing the officers together and away from the public. So, with such a small choice of friends, he kept himself very much to himself. He developed his interest in books and collected those he liked best. He kept up his regular letter-writing to Katie, his mother, and she to him, and he treasured those letters as the only tangible link with home.

For the most part he spent his time being a good police officer. He revelled in having men to command. He wanted to develop his new faculty, Cantonese, that he had been taught at Police Training School. He made a point of listening to his men and to the Chinese inspectors. He took a lot of time out to listen to his 'Major' that was the station sergeant or second-in-command. He would especially listen to his own detective constables and understand what they had to say. Soon he came to know the people he had chosen to work with and the place they shared.

The men liked his methods. If he thought they were wrong he would rebuke them. If he thought they were right he would say nothing until they had finished a job, then he would praise them. He didn't encourage them with carrots, such as offering a few beers for a job well done, a frequent practice with some other inspectors. He told them what to do, what he expected of them and they did it because they respected him. It was his experience in Scotland that enabled him to do this. He had been through it all himself and had empathy. He looked after them properly and honestly and they liked him for it and were very loyal to him.

It took a lot out of him and in the evenings he didn't want to do much more than get out of himself. Hong Kong was hot. Not the place for cross-country running or even walking in the hills as he loved to do in his native Scotland. His rare socialising was limited to a few beers with other lads. It soon began to show on his waistline.

In 1976 a new Inspector joined the station, Matthew Handley, who took up residence in the room opposite John. Matt was a slim, sporty fellow with a smooth mop of hair, moustache and a perpetual cigarette. They became very friendly and John got out more, discovered the great international cooking available in Hong Kong, and the night spots. Soon he was in with a crowd of police who led a similar life. They liked him. He became very sociable and extrovert. They loved his imitations of Churchill, Gracie Fields and others. He always seemed happy with life.

But he had inherited from his father, Joe, a dislike of guns. Most inspectors had their own personal weapons they carried at all times, even off duty. Not so John. He even seemed to dislike being with people who were carrying guns. On one occasion at a bar, when a colleague leaned over to collect the drinks and his sweater pulled up over the gun in the back of his trousers, John recoiled and asked him to try and keep it covered up.

For the most part the Inquest followed the very professional stage management set out in Pelly's report—until the second day, when the prim Chinese juror just didn't turn up. The police were sent to the monastery where she lived to pick her up and the hearing started an hour and a half late, but not before the coroner had delivered an oration, of which she possibly understood about every third word, about the iniquities of jurors who did not respect their legal responsibilities.

Though the case was almost entirely concerned with the police, one particular unit of the police figured more prominently than any other. This was the Special Investigation Unit or SIU, a unit set up in mid 1978 under somewhat mysterious circumstances, ostensibly to investigate the procurement of youths and the involvement of government servants in homosexual activities with them, especially if there was a security risk.

These instructions were ratified by no lesser person than the Governor, Sir Murray MacLehose.

The unit was headed by Superintendent Robert Brooks, a bespectacled somewhat harassed-looking man in his fifties, who answered questions firmly, properly but guardedly, and with a good deal of authority. His deputy was Chief Inspector Michael Quinn, thickset, with a square pugilistic face. Elsie thought it looked as if it was permanently pressed against a glass plate; the sort of face she imagined on the wrong side of the interrogation table beyond the Berlin Wall. "I wouldn't want to be seated opposite him at an interrogation table," she whispered to Aileen.

Quinn spoke with a smooth Irish lilt and smiled almost all the time, though not an amused smile. Perhaps he was more used to being behind closed doors or in the shadows. Both Brooks and Quinn denied the SIU had been engaged in a witch-hunt against homosexuals, though it came out in evidence that he was widely known as 'Quinn of the fairies'. By March 1979 the abortive attempt to dismiss Inspector MacLennan was only three months old and the file had been kept open. Quinn had been working on it. He wrote on it that he thought MacLennan brass-necked and arrogant for having the temerity to appeal against his dismissal. He now denied this, leaving him in some confusion when that comment was shown to him.

MacLennan, however, had not proved an easy fish to catch. They had convinced themselves of his sexual inclinations, but every road they went up seemed to lead to a woman. It was becoming quite frustrating— up till July 1979 that is. Within a month they had eight charges of gross indecency buttoned up, with as many male prostitutes prepared to give evidence against him in court. Admittedly all the "youths" but one was over 21 and hence the relevance to "Youths" in the SIU's terms of reference was a bit shaky, but that did not seem to dampen the enthusiasm of Brooks and Quinn.

Aileen turned to Elsie. "They were really after him, weren't they?"

"Yes, weren't they? Now do you think he killed himself?"

"Well, I'm beginning to think he might have had good reason to. But I don't understand the eight charges of gross indecency. They seem to have appeared from nowhere."

"I think it was a frame-up. Did you notice that by July 1979 the SIU had been investigating him for half a year and their suspicion was based upon him having been seen talking to what they describe as 'a witness'. Then, suddenly, within about a month, they have a whole lot of male prostitutes ready to support eight charges against him, all by definition tainted witnesses, none of them incidentally being charged themselves. Besides, if he was that indiscreet why didn't they have any witnesses before? On the other hand, if he was so discreet that by July they had no more than suspicion, then how is it he suddenly goes haywire and has so many assignations that no less than eight come to the notice of the police? No,' she had a very knowing twinkle in her eye, 'I think you will find he was well and truly framed.'

Chapter 11

As Aileen made her way home it was not so much the SIU that occupied her mind as the prim Chinese juror. Her behaviour was so extraordinary. Next day she rang the Registrar of the Judiciary, who apparently was responsible for choosing jurors, and arranged an interview. She went along with her tape recorder and was asked to wait a moment. After about ten minutes his office door opened and his head appeared hanging sideways, suggesting that he was carrying out a contortion to ensure that the rest of him was not seen.

"Er, Aileen?"

"Yes."

"Er . . . I'm terribly sorry to keep you waiting but my zip has broken. Would you mind hanging on a little longer?"

"Not at all," she said. What else could she say?

After another few minutes the door opened tentatively.

"You can come in now."

"Have you fixed it?"

"Er, I think so. But I have no confidence in it."

He was standing awkwardly holding his jacket around himself in a slightly bent position and he obviously couldn't wait to sit down beside his desk.

In the interests of changing the subject as quickly as possible, Aileen asked him how he knew, when he chose a juror, whether he or she could speak English.

It turned out that he had the utmost confidence in the jury selection system; considerably more, she gathered from his fidgeting, than he had in zip fasteners. A carefully selected list was given him by the Commissioner of Census and Statistics and the selected people had three opportunities to object. Besides, the summons to jury duty was all in English and so they would have to be pretty good to read it.

Aileen played the interview on her program next day and immediately a woman rang and told all Hong Kong how her amah had been summoned for jury duty. She couldn't read English at all and she had asked what it was all about.

"So I had to explain," she said. "You go place plenty people, OK? Man come. Other man say 'He bad man.' Third man say 'First man good man.' You then say whether he good man or bad man. OK?"

The listening public must have wondered if the Supreme Court registrar really knew what went on in the world under his jurisdiction.

The next day of the Inquest was concerned with the actual death. Much of the evidence was recited in strict accordance with the Pelly report. Quinn and Trotman described the entry to the flat and the discovery of the body. Quinn, however, was surprisingly hesitant. He was not sure whether there were four or five bullet wounds. He, with his wealth of experience of handling guns, thought this one was a Smith and Wesson, even though the Hong Kong Police didn't use Smith and Wessons. When he was shown the exhibit he recognised it perfectly well as a Colt, with its external cleaning rod and prancing horse on the butt. He explained to the Coroner how upset he had been—he a tough cop fresh from the carnage in the Malayan anti-terrorist campaign.

Dr Wong, a well dressed young enthusiastic doctor with round face and shining cheekbones, had performed an autopsy on Thursday 17th January. He discovered the paths of the five bullet wounds, one through the heart and the aorta. There had been a great deal of internal bleeding. The alcohol content of the blood was relatively low.

Dr Wong was not able to say whether it was suicide or homicide. But he added that it was very, very, rare for a person trying to commit suicide to choose to inflict wounds in the abdomen. He admitted he had never himself had experience of a suicide by multiple gunshot wounds, though there had been recorded instances of such with smaller calibre weapons such as a .22. All he could say for certain was that it was *not* an accident, although there were no signs of powder traces on the hands. He had not, however, protected the hands with plastic bags nor taken swabs from them for powder traces. After 20 months as a forensic pathologist, however, this was only the fifth case he had handled of gunshot wounds, and only the second involving multiple wounds. Previously he had been a houseman in obstetrics and gynaecology. It emerged that Ballistics hadn't asked for powder tests or precautions either, and nobody had thought to call the forensic chemist.

Elsie turned to Aileen. "Are they seriously expecting us to believe John MacLennan did all that to himself?"

"Elsie, when I was covering the aftermath of the emergency in Malaya there were little pockets of terrorists still around, so the manager of a rubber plantation lent me a gun for protection. I had never used a gun before so one evening I went into the plantation to take some practice with it. When I fired it I was so surprised by the kick, it flew out of my hand. Doesn't a police revolver give a kick?"

Later in evidence Mr Cimino, the ballistics expert, when asked a question about the kick of a revolver replied "Oh yes, the recoil is considerably greater with a .38 than with a .22, and it takes ten and a half pounds force to pull the trigger." Evidence was also given that when MacLennan fired a revolver on the range he used two hands for accuracy. So perhaps he might have done that again out of habit.

Aileen tried to imagine holding the gun backwards, pointing it at herself, without leaving finger-prints or powder burns and firing a shot through her heart and aorta. Then, having the bullet smash into a vertebra (presumably affecting the spinal cord) and, still holding this gun after the recoil, firing four more shots in the same general area. Surely to pull that off you'd have to be some sort of superhuman masochist.

However, the witnesses called at the inquest had a different view. When asked how long anyone could stay conscious after having a bullet through his heart and aorta and buried in his spine, Dr Wong said "Anything from a few seconds to ten or twenty minutes."

"He could have lived for five minutes and could have been conscious and capable of purposeful effort for up to two minutes," said Professor Gibson, professor of pathology from the University of Hong Kong. Professor Gibson thought the first shot was the well-directed one through the heart such as might have been fired by a man in full control of his faculties. The remainder gave the impression that the man firing them was losing the ability to fire a straight shot. "I cannot see any explanation for these five wounds other than that they were self-inflicted."

Dr Ong, who was the consultant resident pathologist in charge in the government and had been in the field for twenty one years, said: "It's my opinion all these bullet wounds could have been self-inflicted. From the post-mortem report the shot penetrating the right ventricle of the heart could have produced immediate death that is in three to five minutes. It would be possible to fire the four remaining shots in that period." He agreed, however, that the shot through the abdomen was consistent with an accident while withdrawing a gun from a holster and that, incidentally, such a shot would knock the victim back somewhat.

However, both experts were at pains to point out that their opinions were based on the facts presented to them, namely that the locked doors precluded the possibility of the presence of another person, and this could change if new circumstances were revealed. They both agreed it was very rare for a person to choose the abdominal area to commit suicide and very, very rare for multiple gunshot wounds to be self inflicted.

Chapter 12

A very strange thing happened during the delivery of forensic evidence by the pathologists. Dr Wong was on the stand. Suddenly Counsel, Andrew Hodge, representing the Commissioner of Police, rapped out a question in a loud clear voice: "I put it to you that in your examination of the deceased in the anus does it confirm that he was a chronic bugger?"

Surprised by the question, the Coroner, Mr Leonard, immediately stopped the proceedings and disallowed the question because it had no direct bearing on the inquest.

It appeared, however, that the Police were keen to ensure a focus on homosexuality.

Aileen had first become concerned about that subject in the early days on the talk-show. She discovered the devastating effect of outdated laws on homosexuality in Hong Kong, even between consenting adults. Blackmail was widespread. It had been a subject brought up frequently on the talk-show. Aileen knew many gay people in the entertainment business, but in Hong Kong they were furtive because of the repression. At one point she presented a program on the subject with a psychologist and a Chinese homosexual. Her listeners were thus able to speak to both on the telephone. At the time the SIU was investigating MacLennan, Niel Duncan, the general manager of the Hong Kong Arts Centre, set up a Movement for Homosexual Law Reform which prepared a petition to the Attorney General asking that the law be changed. Niel argued that it was impossible for a homosexual to take part in such a movement because he would be immediately clapped in gaol. Indeed, any single man would be in jeopardy. It had to be pursued by someone happily married, preferably with children, who could be seen to be above suspicion. So he took the matter up himself. He underestimated Hong Kong.

He argued that if a Hong Kong man had a mistress it was not a crime. It might even do a bit of good for his image. But should he live with another man he could be charged and imprisoned, and earn the title of 'queer'. His campaign received support in some influential places. The Dean of the Anglican Cathedral was quoted as upholding the Christian principle of tolerance and deploring a law which encouraged blackmail and intimidation. So the battle waged, but it was a sporadic, often suppressed battle because of the large number of people concerned with it who were afraid to speak. It wasn't long before rumour and innuendo started about Niel, particularly in the Chinese press. One story claimed that he was taken to task by the Arts Centre committee for making himself vulnerable, and in spite of the fact he denied all the innuendo, he was asked to leave.

It was at this point in the Inquest that Paul Stevens, MacLennan's solicitor, was called to the stand. All went smoothly till he was shown the alleged suicide note on the brown manila envelope. He looked shocked. "This is not the note I saw." He was as shaken as the rest of the Court. "I may be wrong," he said, "but my recollection is the note was on a small sheet of yellow lined file paper, though the content was similar." The experienced counsel had no difficulty in playing on his uncertainty and discrediting his evidence, but he had sewn a doubt that would later grow like a hardy weed. Subsequently Ronald Edgeley, the Government Chemist was called. He stated he had 12 years experience of handwriting examination and testified that MacLennan had indeed written the note, using a biro, but that he, Cimino, had not been asked to analyse the ink or identify the pen used.

In a quiet way the star of the show was Mr Bernard Downey, Counsel for the deceased's family, a pleasant elderly man in a tired grey suit. He caught the witnesses out in all sorts of ways. His main objectives appeared to be to cast doubt on the impregnability of the flat, the suicide note, the motive, the circumstantial evidence and the reliability of the police.

As to the state of the windows, he questioned several witnesses, who all confirmed that the rooms were in absolute darkness, the curtains drawn and the windows secure. For example, CI Kong said he checked the windows, which were locked, but he did not touch the curtains. His confusion, when he was asked how he checked the windows without touching curtains that were so well drawn as to achieve total darkness, was a sight to see.

With an obvious reference to the possibility of someone hiding in the wardrobe, Downey got Trotman, Pelly and CI Kong to state they saw two doctors, while Ballistics' Alistair Cimino said there were three doctors present at the same time as the other witnesses. Cimino answered questions quite clearly on what each of them was doing, leaving everyone in the Court wondering where the third man had come from and why no one else had seen him. The large number of people involved perhaps could have masked the presence of an extra person. There were a dozen present to witness the breaking down of the front door and more and more kept turning up, yet CI Kong said that when he entered the flat at 1220 the only two people in the flat were the two doctors. When Pelly arrived at 1230, however, there were so many people in the flat that he described a state of chaos.

Downey tied the armourer up in knots, because he hadn't written MacLennan's time in the Beat Register, as was normal, and had put in the change of shift stamp at 0645, after which he had issued another firearm at 0630. How was that possible? The armourer incorrectly described MacLennan as DDI because he didn't know, after 14 years in the police, that DDI meant Divisional Detective Inspector and not Detective Inspector. The armourer was, however, quite clear that MacLennan had signed the Register at 0600, checked against the clock. His attention had been drawn to this fact by MacLennan having first put 0500 and then having to correct it. Afterwards he gathered up the gun and the loose ammunition and walked out. Later it was stated that the watch photographed on MacLennan's desk showed the right time.

This really set Downey off. How long did it take to walk to the flat? SI Grant took just over 10 minutes at a leisurely pace. Other officers checked it by different routes. They all took over ten minutes. Even the arresting party in cars took over ten minutes. Yet MacLennan was supposed to have collected his ammunition, gone to his flat, unlocked the door with his keys, found an envelope, written neatly an unhurried note on it, stood up and looked at his watch prior to signing the note—all in ten minutes. He must have walked because his Volkswagen car had not moved from the flats' compound.

Despite witnesses stating that MacLennan rang at 0200, asking for a wake-up call and then coming into the station at 0555 to draw a gun, Downey discovered that in reality a man claiming to be MacLennan phoned and asked for a wake-up call (no one in fact recognised him) and that a man claiming to be MacLennan came to the station to draw a gun, showing his warrant card to both the Station Sergeant and the Armourer. That warrant card was never seen again and in particular was not on the person or clothing of the real John MacLennan.

Then there were the shots. The pathologists all concurred that a man committing suicide in the manner described would be capable of purposeful action for at least 20 seconds. Yet a neighbour, Sandra Hills, testified she was woken up by a bang and the bangs then continued for five or ten minutes or, on being pressed by Council "it could have been less". Not quite the same as 20 seconds.

Downey further established that, while the arrest had been planned days in advance, the photographer was only added to the arrest party three hours after the actual time of death. Trotman and others tried to phone MacLennan in his flat and, on receiving no reply, decided to go and search the flat, though MacLennan might have been anywhere— fleeing the Colony for example. No one attempted to pursue any other explanation than that he was in his flat and not answering the phone.

When the arrest party reached the site, evidence was moved while the photographs were being taken. Some photographs were taken three weeks later, in one of which there were black marks on the window pane which nobody remembered seeing. Several witnesses freely handled the alleged suicide note and tried door handles with bare hands. Dr Wong stated that someone had brought the note in to him in the bedroom to convince him it was suicide. CI Kong, appointed 'evidence officer', later seized the note and put it in his pocket with no protection.

Downey probed MacLennan's claim that he had been investigating "queer hawks". SI Grant, his boss, assured the Court that this was not so, but that his cases were much more mundane such as investigating forged $500 notes. Downey also questioned the motive for suicide, which had been given as knowledge that he was about to be arrested on eight charges of gross indecency. It soon became clear he knew nothing of such charges but thought the interview with the SIU was about the previous incident in 1978. "I thought all that was finished years ago." Furthermore, he had fought those charges, successfully, in 1978. Why give in so easily this time? Also he cashed a cheque for $250 the evening before and after his death the money was still in his wallet. What was he intending to do with it when premeditating suicide?

Quinn had forgotten to take his glasses to the scene, though he knew he was carrying out a search for documents. MacLennan's bed had not been slept in and he was still in the clothes he had on the night before, apart from having changed his shoes. There was no dirty crockery or glassware, nor cigarette ends in the ashtrays. In the photo of the body taken before the doctors arrived his sweater was turned up revealing the bullet hole in the shirt, but nobody remembered this. The fingerprint expert only took prints from the gun and the door (both of which subsequently proved useless), because he was asked to, but not from anywhere else because he wasn't asked to. The senior officers claimed they expected him to act on his initiative and considerable experience. The fact was that the presence of such senior officers clouded the issue of who was actually in charge. They couldn't examine the bedroom doorknob later as the police said they had lost it. Janet Gafoor, however, explained that it was never lost, and in fact had been fitted in the new door and was still there.

Downey established that MacLennan was on the watch list and under surveillance. Where were the tails? Why were they not called as witnesses?

As the initial on-site investigation closed, Trotman, Pelly and CI Kong had collected up all the belongings and taken them into police custody, a little surprised that there was no typing paper, carbon paper or other brown manila envelopes, or even a band to show the suicide note had used the last envelope of a pack.

It was at this point in the inquest that Elsie and Aileen became aware of a strange thing. Of the forty or so witnesses heard, only two were not paid directly or indirectly by government.

"Maybe," said Aileen, "that's because so far we have only heard the case for the prosecution, in the sense that John MacLennan is on trial accused of shooting himself. Perhaps next week we'll get the case for the defence."

"I hope so," replied Elsie. "I have asked to be called. I think I can add a lot about the 1978 incident."

Chapter 13

The Court was naturally adjourned over the weekend. On the Monday Aileen arrived a little early and had to sit outside for a few minutes. An Australian gentleman came and sat next to her. Obviously he didn't know who she was. She recognised him though for she had been sitting behind him all week. He was the foreman of the jury.

He made some remark about the weather and then said: "I am a bit worried about this law on homosexuality. It seems to encourage crime. Do you know what the law in England is?"

She said she thought that there was no law against consenting adults in private. As a matter of fact there was no law even in Hong Kong forbidding females doing what they liked.

"You mean here it's absolutely discriminatory and obsolete."

Aileen said she thought so.

At that point they were all called in and waited expectantly to hear the other side of the case. But it was not to be. The Coroner suddenly announced it was all over and, without any case being made for the 'defence', began to sum up. Elsie looked shocked and indulged in one of her stentorian whispers: "What about the evidence from all the rest of us?"

The Coroner was unmoved and proceeded with his three and a half hour summing up, which briefly went something like this.

"First of all," he said to the jury, "you must stick to what is relevant. However interested you may be in other things, we are only concerned here with how Inspector John Richard MacLennan died. We are not concerned with whether he was innocent of the charges in 1978, nor similarly of the more recent eight charges. You should not be distracted into considering whether the law on homosexuality should be changed nor on whether the SIU's methods were acceptable. It is of no relevance whether rumours of Special Branch files about senior officers were true, nor whether a police officer should be issued with a revolver while under investigation."

Elsie turned to Aileen. "He seems to have listed all the matters which the government requires him to cover up."

"Yes. Are we only to know he died and not why he died?"

The Coroner continued. "There are only four possible verdicts in this case, homicide, suicide, accident or open.

"There is no evidence of Inspector MacLennan being killed by someone else or that he died as the result of an accident. This leaves two alternatives, suicide or open. An open verdict is a last resort. You must if possible reach a decision. You may, if you wish, make recommendations to prevent a recurrence of similar fatalities.

"Almost all the evidence points to a verdict of suicide. Three forensic experts, two government and one from the Hong Kong University, have testified that the five bullet wounds were consistent with being self-inflicted. The windows were closed and both the front door and the bedroom door were locked from inside and had to be broken down. Inspector MacLennan was upset and worried. There is no doubt that he drew a .38 revolver from the armoury, the one that killed him, and it has been confirmed that the bullets matched the gun. Police officers who knew MacLennan recognised the handwriting on the death note and this has been confirmed as genuine by a handwriting expert.

"It is true that Mr Stevens was in some doubt about the note, seeming to recollect that it was on lined file paper, but he did admit that the room was dark and that he could not be sure. Everyone else, however, recognised the note. It is up to you to decide whether Mr Stevens' first impression was right or whether everyone else was right. You should note that Mr Stevens was in some doubt about the time of a telephone call he had received. The extent to which you can rely on his recollection of detail is something about which you will have to think very carefully.

"Remember that Inspector MacLennan was to be arrested later that day on eight charges of gross indecency."

Mr Downey rose to say there should always be a presumption against suicide in an inquest. The Coroner conceded this was true. He added that how long everyone was to be kept hanging around now depended entirely on the jury.

But they weren't about to be rushed. They came back after another three and half hours. The foreman rose: "We have decided unanimously—I beg your pardon—by a majority vote we have decided to return an open verdict."

A hush settled over the court room.

The coroner looked shocked. Members of the police who were in court, especially Superintendent Pelly, looked stunned.

"Have you any riders?" asked the Coroner after a long pregnant silence.

"No."

"Then would you please retire once more and consider any riders you may feel pertinent, and I do urge you to reconsider your verdict once again. It is most desirable that you reach a definite and unanimous conclusion."

So the jury went out again and in half an hour were back to confirm their open verdict. They gave four riders, two of which the coroner dismissed as irrelevant. The remaining two were that the method of charging police officers ought to be investigated to prevent a recurrence of what had happened in this case; and that the law relating to homosexuality in Hong Kong should be updated at least to accord with those in Britain. Aileen shrank low in her chair.

The inquest was over. If it had been intended to be a cover-up it hadn't worked, thanks to the courage and conviction of a young Australian architect and two even younger Chinese girls who had somehow overcome their original distaste of the subject and had buckled down to do a thorough and responsible job. But what was to be done now? They hadn't found out what really happened. Actually they hadn't even found out "who died" because strictly speaking they had carried out the inquest on the wrong man.

Chapter 14

Police Headquarters were located in a 20-storey building on the boundary of the Red Light area of Wanchai—for a good golfer just one shot from the *Pussy Cat* and several other equally notorious hostelries, lustily frequented all the year round by hordes of American sailors on R & R. Round the HQ was a high square wall incorporating mini turrets at the corners with slit windows, a leftover from the turbulent days of the riots of the late 1960s.

The Commissioner of Police, Roy Henry, tall, extrovert and charming but concealing a ruthless, perhaps even brutal reserve, occupied a spacious office on the top floor with a picture window displaying a broad panorama centred on the Ocean Terminal across the harbour in Tsim Sha Tsui. The day was blessed with bright sunshine and a large cruise ship was docked at the terminal; evidence of the considerable tourist interest shown in Hong Kong by people largely ignorant of the sinister undercurrents. Standing by the window in his khaki summer uniform, Commissioner Henry had the bearing of an orchestral conductor about to launch into the opening bars of a world symphony,

"Come in Ron, thank you for taking the trouble to come over." (As if his subordinate had any choice in the matter). "Sit down," indicating the sitting area as if he were directing the percussion.

Henry's Deputy (Jack Trotman's boss), stepped over to the chairs by the coffee table, relaxed and confident. This was not a boss/subordinate meeting; it went deeper than that. Clearly these two were close.

"I didn't like the way our image emerged from this inquest. I also didn't like the verdict. Couldn't we have done better?"

"I share your concern, Roy. There was a lot of sloppiness. I'm not sure why."

"That's what I'm talking about. It hasn't gone unnoticed at the top. I have been asked to look into it. That's where you come in. Someone I can trust not to be involved. I want you to have the drains up. Find out why there have been all these cock-ups. I want two reports. One the official confidential one to be sent up the line and kept on file, but between you and me I want to know more than that. We haven't worked all this time so carefully to have it all blown open by a lot of incompetence. So no mention of triads or anything that will compromise our infiltrators, Rodney and Sandy. There are too many people, some as high as even your level, who might be pretty unhappy if they knew about it. So we've got to quieten this whole thing down. And we certainly don't want to be leaned on from upstairs."

"OK, Roy. Got the point. How long have I got?"

"Can you do it in a week?"

"Sure".

"Good. Let's fix it in my diary now. I'll see you here this time on the 22nd. OK?" By the way, didn't MacLennan work for you once?"

"Yes he did. But that was a long way down the line. I didn't know him very well."

"But you did know him. What did you think of him?"

"Odd character. Good reports. Gave a good impression."

"But . . . ?"

"Did go off the rails once. Not too seriously. It was the Queen's visit. He was supposed to watch the crowds, facing them. Just as the carriage passed he did a smart about turn and saluted Her Majesty, which was the one moment when he was supposed to have his eyes glued to the crowd. I had the job of ticking him off. No harm done, as it happened, so we couldn't make anything of it. Just youthful enthusiasm I concluded. That was the only problem that came to my notice . . . But to get back to the subject we were on before, I wonder if there's any security risk from outside the police. This talk show woman and Mrs Elliott. Is there any danger they might unearth something, even inadvertently, and make it public?"

"You're right; I've already given it some thought. I agree they are dangerous women. But there's not much we can do overtly. Just take the usual precautions, have them watched, listened to, warned off if the opportunity arises. Monitor all the radio programs and let me know if anything comes up we can thump them for.

"Right. See you next week." As Henry waved his Deputy out one almost expected him to bow to an imaginary audience.

Chapter 15

Aileen arrived home a few days after the inquest to find her husband staring out of the French windows. He clearly wasn't admiring the view, which was magnificent, as was usual after dark with millions of pinpoint lights scattered all over the hillsides for miles around and twinkling reflections in the sea between.

"What's the matter, Boff?" Clearly a moment when she thought he had to be reminded he was professional scientist by using her pet name for him.

He came back to earth, jumped up and without a word kissed her and hugged her for a full minute.

"What were you dreaming about?"

"No dream I'm afraid. I'm being leaned on."

"How do you mean?"

"Sit down. We need to talk. G and T?"

"Thanks. What about?"

He said nothing. The only sounds were some gurgling and the tinkling of ice. He joined her on the settee, put an arm round her and started: "I've had a warning. Very casual—over coffee. They don't like what's been said on your program and they don't like the verdict at the inquest. From what I gather they hold you in some way responsible, though it escapes me how."

"Who's 'they'?"

"Ah, you may well ask. I can only say 'government'. It came from my head of department, but obviously he's not the source."

"What do you want me to do about it?"

There was a long pause and a few deep breaths. The firm hold on her shoulders said more than words could about his support. But finally he said, tentatively, "I suppose nothing. Your job is no less important than mine."

"I don't know. You earn more, and neither of us could afford this government flat."

"I can't believe the threat is that serious. Just be a bit careful. Try not to say things to upset them."

"That's all very well. I can't stop the listeners. Most of the gossip comes from them. Besides do you think I should let the authorities get away with a cover-up?"

"I don't think you have. The inquest was an open verdict. That means they haven't succeeded in a cover up. You've done your job. Just drop it for a bit and see what happens."

"I've got Elsie coming in the studio next Saturday."

"Oh Jesus! Well—just let her do the talking."

The next day's program was set. An eminent Nephologist, Dr Walter Turk, was the studio guest. His subject was the great need for people to donate their organs and how difficult it was in Hong Kong because of the culture. He explained how the Chinese believe the body must remain intact, and at one time did not even want their photograph taken, believing that a part of the soul would be taken away. Walter explained how difficult it had been to persuade people to give blood for transfusion let alone donate kidneys. Even the relatives refused to give permission for a deceased to have their eye corneas removed as the belief was that in reincarnation their loved ones would be blind. In fact 98% of the eye corneas used came from Sri Lanka, where the thinking was exactly the opposite. In that country the belief was that if you donated your eyes you were given great blessings and new vision in the next world. Walter Turk was asked by a caller how you could tell from a corpse whether the deceased had intended his kidneys to be donated. Another caller suggested a tattoo in a suitably obscure place. Many others then rang in suggesting the most absurd places. Walter said attitudes were changing, especially amongst the younger Chinese.

Then the interview took an unexpected turn. The callers raised the subject of coroners and how vague the rules were on the necessity for an inquest. "There are many strange cases of people," Walter said, "particularly policeman, supposedly committing suicide, which look exceedingly suspicious yet never become the subjects of inquests." He went on to state that the situation concerning the duties of coroners was very unsatisfactory as they were only seconded into the post for three months and were often called back to their own job in the middle of a case. "Hong Kong," he said, "must be the easiest country in the world in which to commit a murder and get away with it."

Aileen couldn't resist the opening and asked him how long someone could remain conscious after having a bullet through his heart and aorta and buried in his spine?"

"A few seconds," said the renowned specialist.

It was just what Aileen's listeners wanted to hear and for the first time, but by no means the last, came the general outcry from them: "we must have a full, independent inquiry."

Chapter 16

Saturday was the day of Elsie's return to the talk-show studio. Her opening line was "Can a man shoot himself five times in the chest when the first bullet has gone through the heart?"

Within half a minute a call came on the line from a very well known chiropractor, Dr Bruce Vaughan, who said "If the first shot went through the aorta and then embedded itself in the ninth thoracic vertebra, as we have been told, paralysis would be almost immediate. It would be almost impossible to stand up and continue firing."

Elsie went on "The law on homosexuality encourages blackmail and intimidation and is not applied impartially. The SIU are thugs and have been conducting a series of witch-hunts. Also the laws aren't strict enough and half the murders in Hong Kong are never investigated."

Elsie was in full swing. She said the police were slipshod and slovenly and didn't test for powder burns or fingerprints. The inquest was one-sided and biased. Only thirty eight witnesses were called out of a total of eighty five available and almost all were government-inclined, providing less than half a story.

Worst of all, they didn't call Mrs Elliott, who knew MacLennan had been set up and wanted to say so.

By this time the listeners were clamouring to contribute. They poured onto the air waves with emotional comments about the death of John MacLennan and the inquest. The accusations ranged from government cover-up, and police cock-up to legal mess-up and homosexual witch-hunt. Aileen could see her producer's anxious face through the glass partition. They were insured against libel, weren't they? She spared more than half a thought for Kevin. What would they do to him? She made a mental note to be sure to use the disclaimer . . . . "the views expressed on this program do not necessarily reflect the views of the station" . . . .

Then the cool considered tones of Professor Lethbridge of Hong Kong University came over the line. He had rung up only a month before, staunchly supporting the law on homosexuality as it stood and recommending it remain unchanged. His argument was that the law was the same as in Scotland which had not adopted England's Sexual Offences Act. However, in Scotland there was normally a requirement for two witnesses, which virtually made consenting adults in private safe from conviction. Hence, as long as the law was only applied to criminal offences such as offences against minors, he could see no reason for changing it.

It was a very different Professor Lethbridge who came on the air that morning. It appeared, he said, that the SIU had dealt almost exclusively with consensual or victimless crimes. In order to obtain evidence in such cases one of the two parties involved had to be 'persuaded' to give evidence against the other. Hence it seemed the SIU had obtained a troop of informers, male prostitutes, who were guaranteed immunity from prosecution if they kept up a good supply of evidence. The professor pointed out that such characters were not noted for their truthfulness, hence would be likely to give the answers the police wanted.

The Professor went on "There is clear evidence of a witch-hunt and misuse of the law. They are tracking down people and there is no social utility in it. I now recant what I have previously said on this subject and give you my considered view that the law should be changed to come into line with English law to prevent such malpractice."

Another caller introduced himself as Ishmail and pointed out that the legislators had got it wrong. "Sex is inherently selfish, clearly so in rape, prostitution and masturbation. Love is inherently unselfish, clearly so in love of country or of a dog or in extreme friendship or between parents and children, when one might sacrifice one's life for another. Ecstasy is when you combine the two. No love is involved in breeding by a bull or a horse, whereas it is between two swans who mate for life. I see no reason why two homosexuals cannot love each other just as much as two heterosexuals. As I see it, the only reason why the law was originally involved, namely to preserve heterosexual marriage, was to establish the rights of the children and give them stability. There are no children with homosexual love so no law is required. The only reason why the law has become involved now is because it has become politicised and the politicians don't understand love."

"I'll have to think about that one," said Aileen.

Elsie commented that it was a very profound view.

Aileen thought it better to get the topic back on the rails. "Elsie, I gather you are calling for an independent inquiry."

"Certainly I am. First of all, Aileen, I know the background. I know John MacLennan was framed in 1978, but the Coroner would not allow evidence of that nature to be given. Can they really claim that is not relevant to how he died?"

"Elsie, what about the inquest itself? In what way did you feel it fell short of being an independent inquiry?"

"In every way, Aileen, it just wasn't independent. It was all very one-sided. It was full of discrepancies and inaccuracies. And fancy not taking proper fingerprints or powder burn tests on the hands. And then those five shots in the chest. Nobody stopped and said, 'which is more likely, murder or suicide?

"And what about the motive, Aileen? They were at pains to stress that John MacLennan was worried, with eight charges of gross indecency hanging over him, but all the evidence points to the fact that he didn't know anything about them. He said he thought he was being interviewed because of the 1978 Yuen Long affair."

"Yes, what exactly happened then, Elsie?"

"Well, I was first involved when two magistrates asked me to come and see them. That's when I first met John MacLennan. What had happened was that a friend of the father of the boy, not the boy himself as the police said, had made the complaint. That friend had some relationship with another policeman. John MacLennan said it was absolute nonsense and asked that he be taken to court so he could prove his innocence. He went to the two magistrates who questioned him for three and a half hours, at the end of which they were convinced of his innocence. That's when they called me, and as you know he was reinstated. But, if he had been so successful in clearing his name at the time, he would hardly commit suicide at the thought of having to clear it again a year or so later."

"So what was the motive, Elsie?"

"Well, I don't know. The Coroner never attempted to find out. I do know John MacLennan had access to files on homosexuals and triads when he was in Special Branch and he made no bones about the fact that he had seen very senior names on the list. So I would have thought that was a much more fruitful direction to look in for a motive."

"Yes, I guess he discovered more than was good for him. But it sure is tough to be dismissed under Section 10 which enables a civil servant to be fired without disclosing the reason why."

"Yes, I thought it was very unfair. I went home, wrote out the whole story and took it by hand to Government House the next morning. He was reinstated the same day. But he said to me at the time, 'I'm afraid this is not the end of it. Some policemen are not very happy about the reinstatement and I have been told that I have not heard the last of it and there will be no promotion.' He did expect more trouble. The first thing they did was to transfer him from way out in Fanling to the city, Homantin in Kowloon."

The next call came from a lady called Margaret Thompson, who said Johnny MacLennan was like a son to her. They came from the same area in Scotland. She was another involved person who wasn't called as a witness.

Aileen asked her: "What sort of man was he?"

"Oh, a lovely young person, so considerate of other people. Well brought up and he loved his parents. He always spoke well of his mother and father. Oh, he had a very fine upbringing. They are strict Presbyterians."

"Margaret, did John have any suicidal tendencies or depressions?"

"No! Never. He was always very cheerful. They never have suicides where we come from. I spoke to him on the Sunday and invited him to supper on the Monday. He said he couldn't come on the Monday but would be with us sharp on Tuesday."

"The day he died?"

"Yes. He was in good spirits when I spoke to him on Sunday. When he didn't come on Tuesday we waited for a wee while and then we turned on the TV news and heard that a young policeman had been shot in Johnny's area. My husband said: 'Maybe that's why he's late. There may be an inquiry going on. They'll all be upset—knowing one another.' So we had our meal. Later Alex said it's funny he hasn't called.

So by next day we were worried and Alex rang up a friend who said John MacLennan was the policeman who had died. It really shook us.'

"How do you feel about the open verdict, Margaret?"

"It was the only possible verdict, Aileen. But I still don't think it takes away the stigma of those obviously trumped-up charges."

Another caller came on air and said they should give an award to the parents of John MacLennan because he stood up for the truth and died for honesty.

Aileen turned to Elsie:

"What are your feelings about the SIU?"

"The SIU has misfired so much that the sooner it is disbanded the better. We need to set up a crime squad that is really going to deal with crime."

"Is there any evidence that John MacLennan was being persecuted, apart from the very strong evidence from Pelly's conversation with him the night before he died?"

"Yes, but don't forget Pelly was talking about the 1978 charges. When John MacLennan spoke to me on the telephone in 1978, after he was reinstated, he said, 'They'll never let me alone now. They never do in cases like this.' It was because of that we agreed not to contact each other. Association with me is not always good for people, you know, Aileen, as you may find out. He also told the magistrates he expected more trouble. Then I was told by an independent source that 'they were still after John MacLennan's blood.' That was as late as October last year, only three months before he died."

"So you feel someone or some people were out to get him?"

"I haven't any doubt whatsoever, Aileen. There may be doubt in my mind about how he died, but no doubt at all about the persecution."

"When you say there is doubt in your mind, do you not feel that the police enquiries were sufficient?"

"Certainly not. They should have immediately brought in outside people, since it was a police death. They should surely have brought in others than those directly involved in the case. People like Quinn doing the investigation was not the best, even for his own good."

"You mean he laid himself wide open to being caught out, like he was over his 'brass necked and arrogant' remark."

"Exactly. I don't know why the coroner did not make more of that. He jolly soon discredited Stevens for nothing much more than hesitancy, but he seemed to completely excuse Quinn for denying the truth."

"Do you not think it strange that you were not called to give evidence?"

"I think it was strange quite a lot of people were not called to give evidence, because although we couldn't give evidence about the actual death, we could give quite a lot about the circumstances surrounding his death and about his character."

"And there is the fine point, Elsie, that if a man is driven to suicide is it murder or suicide?"

"I would call it judicial murder."

Just then the phone lit up and a caller came on who sounded like an army sergeant with a hair lip.

"Do you know how it was done?" the caller asked.

"You mean how it might have been done."

"No, don't muck about. Just listen to this."

"Go on."

"There was this person or persons unknown, see, in the bedroom with MacLennan. He goes out of the bedroom, locks the door with one of the keys supplied in all government flats, puts the key back in the living room drawer where the keys are always kept and goes over to the front door. He wrenches off the loop of metal the bolt goes through, with a screwdriver, and drops it on the floor. He then throws the bolt and goes out. He locks the front door with a spare key. He then puts a bit of plastic from a plastic bag over the end of the key, stuffs it in the lock, pulls out the key and legs it.

"When the housekeeper 'as a go to unlock the door, 'er key won't work because of the plastic, but she doesn't know that—she thinks the door is bolted. So when they force it open and see the loop for the bolt on the floor wrenched out of the wood, it looks just as if it was locked from inside."

Elsie couldn't suppress her excitement and jumped in almost before he was finished.

"That's a very interesting theory. Very interesting indeed."

"Yes, Mum."

"And did you know they collected the housekeeper to unlock the door before they had even tried the door."

"No, Mum."

"You see, it's almost as if they knew there would be no answer before they got there."

"Yes Mum."

Aileen seemed to feel she was not going to get much more out of their amateur detective, so she thanked him and continued her interview with Elsie.

"It was a terrible way to go, Elsie. But he's dead and we can't bring him back. Now, if the law remains unchanged, if the SIU remains in existence in its present form, if we don't improve our whole judicial system, this boy will have died in vain."

"I wrote to his parents, Aileen, and told them that, if it was any comfort to them, he may have done more with his death than the rest of us have done with our lives. A friend wrote to me from London and said that only a masochist would fire five shots in his own chest like that. If he killed himself, he must have been saying 'John MacLennan, get out of this world—get out—get out—get out.' The agony of it haunts me. I wake up in the night thinking about it." Tears began to appear.

Aileen was sensitive to the strain on her elderly guest.

"I only hope, Elsie, your call for an independent inquiry comes to fruition."

Derek had tiptoed in with the news headlines. Aileen read out a report that the Senior Member of the Governor's Executive Council, Sir Yeut-keung Kan, had unexpectedly resigned five months before his scheduled retirement in August. No reason was given. Aileen had just time to tell Frena to ask for an interview before there was an urgent telephone call from police headquarters demanding a tape of the program.

Then the pressure started.

Chapter 17

It began with a few anonymous letters and phone calls, often with no more than heavy breathing at the other end. Then there were strange clicks on the telephone lines. One morning Aileen arrived at the station to find a singularly unpleasant letter which read:

> *Drop this MacLennan case or you'll be sorry. Just watch out as you pass the alley ways, watch out when you stand close to speeding traffic or the water's edge. We will be watching and waiting.*

She couldn't wait to get to the studio. With due drama, suggesting she was exposing some sinister plot, she read the anonymous threat out on air, adding: "So folks, I'm going to put it in an envelope with a note on it to say if anything happens to me give this to the police." She didn't bother to do so, since she thought that's where it probably came from.

This was the morning, however, when she devoted the last half of the program to the ever popular Radio Doctor. A handsome gay Scot named Graeme Ross, rather a shy man with even less charisma than the Oxford Book of English Verse, though he shared some of its depth and sensitivity. He was actually a government doctor, though on air he was strictly anonymous. The listeners loved to ring in with their ailments, and even asked him how to treat their pets. This time, though, they had other matters on their minds. Could anyone shoot themselves five times in the chest? Graeme fielded the questions quite expertly, leaving plenty of room for doubt.

Since the listeners had raised the subject, Aileen asked him about the psychological state of someone intent on shooting themselves. John MacLennan would have needed the lights on to write the suicide note and to load the gun. So he must have deliberately switched off the lights. It was as dark as it could be. It was night, the curtains were drawn. He could not have actually seen what he was doing. Why lock himself in so absolutely, not only the front door but also the bedroom? Then there would be a very loud bang and possibly a bright flash, even blinding in that darkness. Could he have repeated it another four times? The discussion was lively, entertaining and got nowhere, until the head of the Samaritans rang in. He was a leading expert on suicides and proclaimed that after the first shot MacLennan would have been psychologically shattered and it would have been almost impossible for him to continue firing, irrespective of his physical state.

The program ended as usual with the News Headlines, brought in by Derek, which this time packed a surprise. The Attorney General had announced that he would hold a press conference to put the public's minds at rest over the MacLennan case.

As they were leaving the studio, Graeme suggested they go to a quiet restaurant for coffee. Clearly something was wrong. It took all Aileen's interviewing expertise to prise it out of him.

"Aye, there is something wrong, but I would be breaching the Official Secrets Act to tell you."

"Not if I didn't tell anyone else."

"That's silly. You're a broadcaster."

"Graeme, there's no safer place to tell your secret. I know more about protecting my sources than most people."

There was a long pause. "Every so often I have a very unpleasant duty to perform. . . . No I shouldn't burden you with this."

"Don't be daft. Get on with it."

"All right, if you insist. I am the duty doctor in the police interrogation centre. Sometimes they do some very unpleasant things and I have to do a patch-up job and certify that no harm was done."

"But that's impossible, Graeme. This isn't Russia."

"Don't you believe it. I don't think the Russians could teach them anything. It's so bad they call the place the Zoo. I wake up in the night still hearing the shouts and screams."

"Well, tell them you don't want to do it any more."

"I can't. I'm under orders. The only way I could get out of it would be to resign. That would mean leaving Hong Kong and everything I love about the place. Besides it's only about once a fortnight, and I'm usually alright after a couple of stiff whiskies when I get home."

"Well, I don't think you should put up with it. Before you know where you are you will become an alcoholic."

"Oh, nonsense. That's hereditary."

Aileen was worried about Graeme, not least because she knew him so well. Since Kevin was in government Graeme was their doctor and he was brilliant. What a waste to give him such a distasteful detail. Still, when he had got it off his chest he seemed better. Perhaps her best ploy was to remain his confidante so she could be the first to detect if things started going wrong. Besides, she had a lot to do before the press conference to make sure she got a good recording from which she could broadcast excerpts.

Chapter 18

The Deputy Commissioner reported to the Commissioner exactly on schedule. They sat across the coffee table as usual and the eleven page confidential report changed hands.

Roy Henry took it with some of the deference he might have afforded the manuscript of a new concerto and placed it on the table. "Thanks Ron, now tell me in a nutshell what it says."

"I took as my terms of reference the first three riders to the verdict on the inquest on Inspector John Richard MacLennan, concerned with charging police officers, the need for a checklist to aid thoroughness of investigation and the weakness in giving orders to subordinates. I interviewed about thirty witnesses.

"I have found nothing fundamentally wrong with the arrest procedure, but I do consider Jack Trotman might have been more circumspect in warning MacLennan he was to be interviewed by the SIU.

"The idea of a checklist is not practicable because investigations differ too much. However, I do think the jury had a point about the lack of thoroughness of the investigation. Though there was no evidence of anything other than suicide, it is clear that the investigating officers too readily came to the conclusion that it <u>was</u> suicide. As a result several tests were not carried out that would have been resorted to under more suspicious circumstances. I refer of course to the lack of fingerprinting and chemical tests on the deceased's hands and the suicide note.

"But the main criticism is that the action at the scene was not well coordinated. Because of the presence of unusually senior officers it was not clear who was in charge and hence, for example, orders for forensic tests were not properly given.

"I have made five recommendations to minimise these weaknesses in future."

Roy Henry nodded. "You haven't questioned the suicide?"

"Not at all."

"So this report is OK for me to pass up the line?"

"Sure."

"Good. I'll go through it myself, but I accept your judgement on that. Now let's get down to the real business. What did you find out?"

"I'd like to start with the DWs."

"DWs?"

"Yes, the Dangerous Women."

"Ah. Not Damned Witches?"

Ron laughed. "No, but it could be. In a radio program a few days ago they were together again and certain points were made which could be matters of concern if they are allowed to develop. For example, the SIU was ostensibly formed in mid 1978, but by the time of MacLennan's death in 1980 they had only brought one case and that was thrown out of court. This clearly doesn't satisfy the public, or at least not our DWs.

"Then there is the sexual inclination of MacLennan. There is absolutely no evidence of homosexuality before mid 1979. Even the strict Special Branch positive vetting came up with nothing. But suddenly he has eight charges of gross indecency with boys. How can that be?

"Thirdly I have had a strange experience. Most police officers I have interviewed have been quite open, but some have reacted very oddly, even clammed up. I didn't get the impression they were hiding anything individually, more collectively, though I would be hard pressed to support that feeling with evidence.

"Is there something I don't know? Exactly why did you ask me to look beyond?"

There was a pause. Roy Henry pressed the button on the table to summon his secretary. "Coffee, Ron?"

"Thanks."

"Bring us coffee," he told his secretary, "and then I don't want to be disturbed this side of lunch."

"Do you think the AG will be able to handle this press conference?" Roy asked.

"If he can't nobody can, especially with David Ford at his side."

"I can tell you I am depending on it. Because I don't know what other line of defence we have to shut them up."

The coffee was served in the colonial government's thick crockery, beige with green rims, crowns and letters 'HK' on each piece. When it was poured out and the door closed Roy Henry took a deep breath. There was a shade of pianissimo about his expression. "Some of what I am about to tell you must never be breathed outside this office. I wouldn't be telling you at all if you had not undergone the stiffest possible vetting yourself before you were appointed to the Triad Infiltration Working Group. Now I believe there are things you ought to know.

"I am going back in history a bit first, some of which you will know. In the 50s I was in intelligence in the emergency in Malaya along with Michael Quinn. He was a great guy then, full of loyalty and courage, took enormous personal risks. From there I did a tour in Fiji and came here to meet up with Michael Quinn again and also met David Ford, now Secretary for Information, who was fresh from an intelligence tour in Northern Ireland. We were tasked with looking at triads. Between 30 and 40 percent of the police were triad members—not just Chinese, but Europeans too. You will remember the trial of Superintendent Godber in the early 70s, where his mate Taffy Hunt turned Queen's evidence to put him away for bribery.

"What the public couldn't understand was that, only about eight years before, Godber had been awarded a medal for gallantry. It was during the riots that coincided with the start of the Cultural Revolution in China. There was a lot of turmoil. A huge crowd of Red Guards poured over the border at Sha Tau Kok. We sent a quick signal to the Foreign Secretary, a drunk called George Brown, asking for instructions. We must have caught him at the right time in the morning because he promptly signalled back "Throw them out." A battalion of Gurkhas did just that, armed to the teeth, yelling and waving kukris. Must have been an awesome sight. The Chinese just fled like rabbits. Similar thing happened in Macau except the Portuguese couldn't throw them out and they took over. But Mao Zedong wasn't ready, so by way of a compromise the Macau government was reduced to a puppet and has been ever since.

"But I digress. There were two sorts of riots in Hong Kong. One stirred up by the communists and one by the triads. The communist riots were nasty and a lot of our chaps got hurt. The triad riots were a charade to make their presence felt, and we believe to strengthen their position in the police. All the indications were that Godber, himself a triad member, won his medal displaying great courage in a few such charades, where actually nobody got hurt.

"After that he was given special treatment as a high flyer and became head of Traffic Division, where he exploited taxis and minibuses to the tune of millions of dollars to his personal account. It was one of your DWs, Mrs Elliott, who shopped him.

"Unfortunately for her she reported him to the Head of the Triad Bureau who happened to be Taffy Hunt and also a triad member."

"Wait a minute. The Head of the Triad Bureau was himself a triad?"

"Unbelievable isn't it? But yes, that's how it stood. However, when we got on to it we posted Michael Quinn to be his deputy, so we got quite a lot of useful feedback. As a matter of fact I became a triad member myself, nominally at least, for infiltration purposes. It was surprisingly easy. You see, the police triads had their own hierarchy, their own Dragon Head and incense masters and so on. The reason was they had to remain to some extent aloof or it would have become too obvious. There was a certain reserve between the real triads and us. As long as our lot remained substantially corrupt we retained a strong and workable relationship.

"You see, with such large numbers of triads in the police we had to tread carefully. We had to start by turning inwards. We decided not to aim too high, but to tackle the lower ranks first. The upper echelons, in government and the police, would be left to phase out by wastage, mainly retirement. That's incidentally what I am sure you encountered when you say some of the senior officers were uncooperative.

"Anyway, the next step as you know was to form the Independent Commission Against Corruption, or ICAC under Jack Cater. That was 1974, and their first job was to get Godber. He had been targeted by the police but, no doubt with a good deal of internal help, he managed to escape despite being on the "stop list". So the ICAC had to get him extradited, which they did with some difficulty. The most important weapon in their armoury was the new law which made it illegal to have unexplainable assets disproportionate to one's earnings. This is very powerful. If you hide your assets so the investigators can't find them it's very difficult to use them yourself. Then we started to make progress— such good progress we actually had a revolt within the police, as you know only too well, when hundreds marched on ICAC Headquarters. It was nasty. I felt very sorry for Brian."

"You mean Brian Slevin, your predecessor?"

"Yes. The Governor decided to give them an amnesty and let them phase out too; they were mainly station sergeants with not too long to go. That at least kept the police intact as a force. I don't know what else you could do about a rank and file revolt on that scale, when an unknown proportion of senior officers right up to the top are of doubtful allegiance and might even be on their side. It's the sort of thing you have nightmares about.

"Anyway, when we had made sufficient inroads into triad infiltration in the force itself, the next step was the main body in the private sector. Successive heads of the Triad Bureau had issued shattering reports, though there was little more we could do at that time, in particular we seemed unable to keep the Triad Bureau clear of triads. That's when David Ford had the idea of forming a special unit; we called it the Special Investigation Unit or SIU, to get at the roots of the triads covertly. Its cover was to tackle homosexuality. Quite clever really, because that's where you can find a lot of very productive leads, through the male prostitutes, procurers, pimps and so on who are mostly triads. The weakness, as you and your DWs have pointed out, was that the SIU were so busy doing the job they were formed to do they neglected their cover."

"I see." Said Ron. "So we had to establish the infiltrators Rodney and Sandy because you couldn't trust the Triad Bureau."

"Exactly."

"Does the SIU know about Rodney and Sandy?"

"No. They are two separate exercises. You are one of six people who know, apart from the two lads themselves."

"And the risk with the DWs, and indeed the media generally, is that they could blow it?"

"And set us back years. After all the lads have only just resigned from the Police. It is going to take years to spirit them into positions of trust in the Triad Societies. Till then absolute total secrecy is imperative."

"But wait a minute. The SIU has been going for nearly two years, and if they don't know about Rodney and Sandy what have they been doing?

"Oh, don't misunderstand me. They are in the infiltration game too, but on a smaller scale. For instance, they have just finished a case on the island of Cheung Chau. The island beyond, Shek Wu Chau, is the rehabilitation centre for drug addicts as you know. The SIU periodically send a couple of men in the guise of addicts to sniff around for tips about sources. Even the doctor in charge doesn't know. As a matter of fact it's rather funny, because he interviews the addicts when they arrive and asks them where they get the drugs. He discovered that an undue proportion of addicts came from Cheung Chau and that their source was a woman who operated outside the Dragon Theatre. So he wrote to the Chief Super in the island of Cheung Chau, eventually several times, and got no reply. Our boys found something similar and raided the Chief Super's office. They found the doctor's letters filed away unactioned. They soon built up a case for the ICAC and he's gone now, his Dragon Theatre lady with him. The SIU have had several cases like that. In fact they've been pretty busy."

"Going back to MacLennan, why did you dismiss him?"

"You have guessed, haven't you?"

"I think so. He was tackling the triads head on and you were afraid he would blow it."

"That was with my intelligence hat on. The others, however, with their Police hats on thought there was too little evidence and when Brian came back off leave I was overruled. But we could have dumped him under Colonial Regulations, without giving a reason, and incidentally saved his life."

Chapter 19

Aileen arrived home to find Kevin already on the balcony with his brandy dry and peanuts, contemplating the myriad pinpoints of light that stretched as far as the eye could see. It was a quarter to seven.

"Hi, I'd almost given you up"

It was their standard arrangement. They had found they were both so busy that they arranged to meet every evening at a quarter to seven. If one of them couldn't make it that was alright, but they had to inform the other.

"Actually, my love, if you weren't such a high priority I wouldn't be here now. But I am." She kissed him hard and long, then went off to fix herself a gin and tonic.

Kevin called after her "You've been at it again, I hear."

"Oh dear, have they been on to you?"

"Not exactly, but it was mentioned."

"So I'm being warned off in all directions."

"Where else?"

"I got an anonymous note in the post this morning saying if I valued my health I had better lay off asking for an inquiry."

"Jesus! Have there been others?"

"Oh, yes."

"How many?"

"I don't know—several."

"No, come on. How many is several? Five? Ten? Twenty?"

"About ten I suppose."

"And what have you done about them?"

"Put them in the bin. Or if they were phone calls, hung up."

"Have you told anyone?"

"Of course not. What can anyone do? Most would have been from the police, I expect."

"Somebody's got to do something. Supposing just one of the ten turned out to be more than a threat. Then what? What about the one you got this morning? Did you put that in the bin?"

"Oh yes. But I broadcast it first."

"Broadcast it! You must be mad!"

"I think it was quite smart. It gives me a certain protection."

Kevin pondered while he took several sips at his brandy dry. "Yes, I can see that. Were you scared?"

"Not scared exactly. It gave me a strange feeling in the pit of my stomach. A sort of apprehension mixed with excitement."

"Like when I undress."

"Oh shut up . . . . Now you put it like that the feelings did have certain similarities."

Aileen and Kevin had a wondrous intimacy. They knew every freckle on each other's bodies as a result of years of romping in their bedroom and even on hillsides and deserted beaches, still plentiful in the Far East and even in Hong Kong if you know where to look.

"I also had coffee with Graeme. That's got nothing to do with being warned off, at least I don't think it has. But he's worried too."

"What about?"

"Working in the Zoo."

"In the what?"

"The Zoo. Apparently that's what they call the police interrogation centre over in Pokfulam. He gets all sorts of nasty cases to deal with and some of what he hears is bloodcurdling."

"I'm sure he should never have told you that. They'd lock him away for life."

"I know. He mentioned the Official Secrets Act, but I told him any secret would be safe with me. I never reveal my sources."

"You just have"

"Oh, you're different."

"Well, I wouldn't like to see Graeme go down the drain, he's too special."

"The only way Graeme's going down the drain is if he lets it get to him. He's already drinking too much. He needs to talk and I think we are the only ones he can talk to. Obviously his boy friends would be far too risky."

Chapter 20

Hong Kong was beginning to heat up. The sticky drizzle of March and April had given way to blazing sunshine, and the huge tropical leaves and banyan trees of Battery Path provided a welcome shade as Aileen and her team walked up the steep incline to the little bridge that took them across into the utilitarian, early 1960s block known as Beaconsfield House, largely occupied by Government Information Services or GIS. As they entered the press conference room they felt they were standing where a lot of offices used to be, and somebody had knocked the walls down, leaving a low ceiling, quite unsuited to an auditorium.

The assistant producer, had gone on ahead with the recording equipment and had saved Aileen and Frena two seats, which was just as well as the long room was packed. Aileen was struck by the number of familiar faces. Then it dawned on her that half the audience seemed to be government information officers, from the police, several other departments and of course GIS headquarters.

Seated at a low table on a dais was the Attorney General, a slim bespectacled lawyer, the backbone of whose career seemed to be betrayed by his constantly being on the defensive—which indeed he was brilliantly good at. On his left, surrounded by piles of papers and files, was no less a person than the Secretary for Information himself, David Ford, said to be one of the closest confidantes of the Governor, and the conceiver of the SIU. It was also rumoured he was the top representative of Military Intelligence in Hong Kong, based on his past record. He had been sent to Northern Ireland as a major in the Intelligence Corps to get experience in Psyops. He was seconded to Hong Kong in 1966/67 to join a group set up under Jack Cater (later to head the ICAC), which became known as the "Catering Corps", to collect intelligence on the communists. He was recruited as an information officer in Government Information Services, but had a meteoric rise to Director of Government Information Services (GIS) and now Secretary for Information. It soon became very clear that David Ford was both producer and stage manager. He had issued everyone with an official press release and a few photographs.

The AG himself had a slightly strained, though boyish face and a splendid voice. His English was beautiful, not so much the crisp slightly overdone speech of the upper classes but more the near perfect pronunciation of an actor. He was crystal clear and convincing, very cool, measured and unemotional. Close your eyes and you could picture him in full courtroom regalia as Council for the Prosecution.

"There had been considerable interest," he said (as transcribed from Aileen's recording), "in the inquest into the death of Inspector MacLennan (he always pronounced it MacLellan). Quite a number of you here have rung up asking what my decision about reopening the inquest or not was going to be, and therefore it seems a sensible thing to say, publicly, what I have decided to do and also to give the reasons why.

"I have decided not to reopen the inquest and my reasons for so deciding are that I am totally satisfied that Inspector MacLennan committed suicide and I will explain to you the reasons for my coming to that conclusion in a moment.

"That being the conclusion I have come to, there is no power in me to reopen the inquest. The reason for reopening an inquest would be if it were suspected that new evidence might become available, but none has and I don't think there is likely to be any now.

"Now I think one of the reasons that made me so sure on the evidence that I have read of what took place, and from the other forty statements that I have also perused, is that Inspector McLennan's body was found inside his bedroom, the door of which was locked, and I'd like just to show you in a moment a photograph of the lock to that door in the condition that it was seen to be and photographed at the time. The nature of the lock was such that it could only be operated from inside the room and there was no means whatsoever of operating it, either to lock or unlock the door, from outside."

He then directed everyone to the photograph of the bedroom doorway. On the floor among chips of wood was the lock, with both the part operated by the handle and the mortice operated by the snib at the centre of the inside handle, in the shut position. It was clear from the photograph that the outside handle was plain and had no key hole or mechanism at its centre to permit operation of the mortice in either direction. He went on to say the only other access to the bedroom was through the window and he showed us a picture of the bedroom window shut and with the bolts in the locked position.

"The flat is on the fourth floor, there is no means of getting into it therefore save from above. If you got in from above, how you could leave, leaving the window locked behind you, would pass I think one's imagination. And the curtains were drawn and the windows were seen to be shut by, I think it was, a total of four witnesses who gave evidence at the inquest.

"The other circumstances that I thought were material were these; that Inspector MacLennan himself had telephoned the police station, I think one o'clock in the morning, in order to have a wake-up call at five thirty and when the number, which was the number of the phone in his flat, was rung he answered it. He went then to the police station, where he was recognised by the station sergeant who knew him and by the armoury sergeant who also knew him, and he drew from the armoury a revolver saying that he was going out on a police raid. That revolver was signed for and his best friend, in fact at the inquest, identified the signature in the armoury books as his signature. That revolver which was drawn at half past five was the revolver which fired the shots that killed him, because there was evidence from a ballistics expert that two of the bullets could be matched with rifling in the gun."

He then drew attention to the photographs of a note lying on the desk.

"Now that note as you see has a signature on it and handwriting, and evidence was called from a handwriting expert at the inquest that the handwriting was that of Inspector MacLennan, and in addition others that know his handwriting said they too recognised it as his.

"When the police first arrived at the flat the front door was in fact locked and it took a period of time before they managed to break that down."

"The photograph of the broken door clearly showed two locks, a chain and a bolt in the locked position. He pointed out that while the police were waiting for a crowbar they looked for another way into the flat and could find none.

He went on to the subject of the bullet wounds. "I'm sure you wondered as I did when I first read it. But I have now had a chance to look at some of the evidence that was given at the inquest and also to do some research into medical textbooks. And there are a number of documented cases of people who have put several shots into their heart and chest and the area round the heart and have lived for a considerable period of time."

He quoted two cases, a man in Italy who put two bullets through his heart and lived for an hour and a quarter and was conscious for most of the time. Also an 80-year-old woman in Minnesota who put nine shots into the area around her chest.

"You may wonder why such cases are possible, and the medical reason for it is this, that what causes you to lose consciousness is not the injury to the heart but the starvation of oxygen to the brain, coming from the fact that the heart has not pumped sufficient blood to oxygenate the brain. And that's why it is that it is well recognised, indeed it was seen in the war too, that people could get mortal wounds in the area of the heart and continue for a variable period of time to perform functions and certainly remain conscious.

"There are a number of other reasons which impelled me towards my conclusion, but this might be an appropriate moment to answer any questions that you may have."

He was asked how it could be that he considered there was overwhelming evidence for suicide when the jury didn't. He replied that, while it would not be proper for him to comment on the finding of the jury, he would point out that he had been able to take a cold hard look away from the heat and drama of the courtroom and also to read all the statements not presented at the inquest. He repeated that he was now totally satisfied that it was suicide and that there was no-one else involved. He was at pains to point out that he was not overruling the jury but merely putting forwards his own opinion, formed under different circumstances.

Then came a critical and obviously anticipated question. "Since the cause of death had not been established in a court of law, why was the body of Inspector MacLennan cremated so soon after death?"

The AG produced a note. He had indeed anticipated the question.

"The date of his death was the 15th January. On the 16th January a telegram was sent to his parents requesting their permission for an autopsy to be performed. They cabled back giving permission for an autopsy and adding two things: first they said please cremate the body and secondly they said see there is a service in accordance with the Presbyterian Church. And I would just point out that it was not at the request of the police that they said that; all the police had asked for was permission to conduct an autopsy. Now under Section 9 of the Coroner's Ordinance it is the Coroner and only he who has the power to say what shall happen to a body. It is not a matter for the police, it is not a matter for my chambers, it is for the Coroner who is an independent judicial officer.

"Now, at that stage, and I can't speak for the Coroner and why he decided to do it, but if I were guessing I would suggest that he knew, as he did, that there had been two forensic pathologists who had inspected the body and had been associated with the autopsy and, when you come down to it, assuming that they are, as one of them is, Professor Gibson, who is a leading expert in this area, when people like that have made their inspection then, as it were, they don't require to go back again, indeed in some cases you can't go back again because what you have done during the course of the inspection cannot be undone. That's the true history of it. And it was not, I think, ordered to be cremated with any different speed than any other. It certainly wasn't unduly hasty or anything of that sort."

A member of the press immediately pointed out that Professor Gibson had never seen the body and had only worked from photographs.

"In that case, was it Mr Ong? I'm very sorry, I've got the wrong one." (Lots of whispering between the AG and Ford.) "Thank you very much indeed."

Aileen then asked him whether Mrs Elsie Elliott's evidence would not have been relevant since she knew so much about the background to the case.

"Mrs Elliott provided a statement to the Coroner, and I have read that statement, it is one of the statements I mentioned at the beginning.

I have taken into account what she said in her statement. The Coroner would I am certain have called her to give evidence if he had thought she had had relevant admissible evidence to give. You see, I could say all sorts of things about anybody in this room but, at the end of the day, what matters is having people who have personal knowledge of what goes on, not gossip or tittle-tattle about what goes on."

Another questioner asked why powder burn tests were not carried out on MacLennan's hands, nor adequate fingerprints taken. The reply was:

"I would prefer you to ask the Commissioner of Police that because it is his responsibility not mine. But I can say this, just as a human comment. I suggest that if any single one of you had been in charge of that police party and had walked into that room under the circumstances I have shown you in these photographs, I think that you would probably have concluded that the overwhelming probability was one of suicide. And in those circumstances you might well not have done some things that in a more debatable case you might have done. You know, the police can never win, can they? Because if, in every single case of suicide, they go through every scientific test that possibly could be relevant to it, people are going to criticise them and say 'why do you waste the public's money doing these expensive scientific tests when it was quite obvious it was suicide?' If they don't do them people round them say 'Well, there you are, why didn't they do them?'"

Then they got on to the bullet wounds. A reporter asked him to comment on the relative calibre of the weapons in the documented cases he had referred to earlier and in the case of Inspector MacLennan.

"I don't think there was any description in the book of the weapon used by the Italian, save that it was a revolver. The lady I think shot herself with a .22 who had the nine bullet wounds in the chest. And MacLennan only had a police revolver."

Aileen was on her feet again pointing out that MacLennan's gun was a .38. She went on to say that the area of damage by a .38 was many times more extensive than that of a .22.

"I think the important point to realise is that first of all what causes loss of consciousness and thus the ability to do things is not damage to the heart. It is the starving of oxygen to the brain so that you lose consciousness from that. If you get a .22 bullet or whatever through the ventricle of your heart then that is, I would suggest, likely to be as damaging as getting a slightly larger hole with a slightly larger type of bullet. The point is that you have affected the mechanism of that delicate organ."

"Was any evidence given as to whether Inspector MacLennan was standing, sitting or lying down?"

"No. One could guess, and say this is what we think would have been the position, but obviously there was no-one there, was there? So we couldn't call anyone to give evidence at all about whether he was standing, sitting or whatever."

"Can you tell us, sir, exactly what the telegram to the parents said, informing them of their son's death?"

The Attorney General started by saying "Yes." Then he hesitated. Then he had a long whispering session with David Ford. Then he simply said, "No, I'm sorry, I can't remember."

There were several questions about the possibility of a change in the law on homosexuality which were well fielded and passed on the newly-formed Law Reform Commission, but a rather interesting one concerned the possibility of immunity given to homosexual witnesses. It was a question that turned out, later in the year, to have vital significance.

The Attorney General at this stage merely promised to look into it when the time came.

"If you are so sure that the Inspector MacLennan died of suicide' (forgive the direct transcription, but it was one of those delightful bits of Chinese English grammar) 'and you are referring to the Law Reform Commission, the laws on homosexuality at this particular time, are you implying that Inspector MacLennan was the victim of the laws relating to homosexuality in Hong Kong?"

"No, I am simply doing it because the jury so recommended."

Throughout the press conference one reporter asked around eleven questions concerned with the possibility of suing Elsie Elliott and supporting the SIU. The AG on various grounds refused to answer any of them.

As Aileen was rising to go, Andrew Hodge, who had been Counsel for the police at the inquest, came up to her and said "You know, the police revolvers in Hong Kong are very underpowered. It really is quite possible for John MacLennan to shoot himself five times in the chest." She noticed another familiar face hovering behind, another from the official side of the inquest. As she turned to leave he pounced.

"You know, what really happened was that the police got a terrible shock and panicked. They just flipped. Everything everybody says about not investigating it properly was absolutely true. Naturally we can't say that publicly, but nothing is going to change so we've just got to accept it."

Aileen saw that nearly everybody else had left. Why was she the only one that was being picked out? Hovering behind was the Attorney General.

"You must be Aileen of Commercial Radio's Talk-Show. I recognised your very attractive voice."

"Yes. I'm Aileen." He just looked at her. She thought, what does he want? She said, for want of anything else:

"You said you aren't empowered to reopen the inquest. Then who the hell is?"

"Nobody."

She had to admire the man. It had been a masterly performance. She felt as if she had seen a good actor in a play. She had surely been for a brief moment convinced that John MacLennan had committed suicide and that the evidence to that effect was overwhelming . . . till she played the tape of the Attorney General's press conference back in the studio.

Chapter 21

Aileen had often noticed that the absence of vision with radio so highlights the voice that it is much more difficult to get away with insincerity on radio than it is on TV or the stage. It is the same with tape. As she and Frena listened to it they began to have doubts. Especially over the whispering between the AG and Ford. What were they saying that they did not want the public to hear? Aileen decided to let her friend Anthony Polsky listen to the tape. He had as good as admitted he was a CIA agent, and now he volunteered to use his technology to interpret the whispering.

Meanwhile Aileen decided to play it a bit cool on the program the next day and see what public opinion was, though she could not resist getting Elsie on the line and playing her the bit about her evidence being gossip and tittle-tattle.

No-one reacts better than Elsie to such a spur. "What does he mean, I did not have personal knowledge of what went on? Wasn't I there when the magistrates interviewed John MacLennan? Did I not meet him, talk to him and correspond with the Governor about him? And what about the Attorney General's eight male prostitutes! Tainted witnesses. What is their so-called evidence if it isn't gossip and tittle-tattle? I shall continue to fight for an independent inquiry."

"Don't you think you should get realistic and drop it?"

"Never."

But everyone else seemed a bit cool about it. The press reports were fairly factual and seemed to accept the Attorney General's decision, though perhaps reluctantly. Even Aileen's listeners seemed to think God had spoken and there was a kind of helplessness about their comments.

She went to Nick Demuth after the program. "What do you think is going to happen?"

"Nothing. No-one can overrule the Attorney General. Elsie is whistling to the wind."

For the next few days there was not much reaction, apart from a vitriolic letter in the press from Elsie, addressed as a public letter to the Attorney General. 'So far I have always addressed my remarks to the Attorney General personally, in letters or on the phone. He has seen fit to discredit me in public, so I owe him no courtesies and will therefore address him in public."

Her blood was up. Could she take him on? Was she whistling to the wind? Apart from a few sporadic letters in the press and comments on the program, it was clear the subject was in its death throes. One comment made everyone think a bit. Someone wrote that being shot by a .38 bullet was rather like having a red hot 3/8 inch diameter round-ended steel rod clean through the body. It was a bit difficult to imagine five. Even Polsky's report on the whispering did not help much. It merely confirmed that the A-G had made a boo-boo as neither Professor Gibson nor Dr Ong had seen the body and that there was in fact doubt about the parents' intentions and they had better change the subject.

So another week went by and Aileen thought: he's done it with his technique, legalistic English and histrionics, and Nick was right.

For just twenty four hours she thought that.

On Sunday 1st June something happened that was so unexpected, so unimaginable, so totally without precedent, that when she first looked at the Sunday paper she thought she must be still asleep. After all, she was still in bed. So, hesitatingly, disbelievingly, she started to read.

"Jury foremen challenges AG."

There it was. A long letter from the courageous Australian architect, Tony Pannel, who had faced he knew not what when his jury brought an open verdict, and clearly wasn't going through the previous trauma for nothing. He systematically and professionally shot down the Attorney General's press conference on seven major points, ending with the cry 'long live the jury system.' He incidentally disclosed that the jury had voted on three different aspects of the case and the results had been two—unanimous, one—two agreed and one unsure. Hence his majority open verdict was eight votes out of nine and not two to one as everyone had thought. It was almost like five bullet holes in the chest, except that this time everyone suspected foul play—somewhere.

A silence fell over Hong Kong. War had been declared. What could the Attorney General possibly reply to that?

He dealt with it very easily. He simply refused to reply.

Chapter 22

As soon as Aileen had read Tony Pannel's letter she knew she was not alone in having doubts. Not that there was anything indicating doubt or hesitancy in Tony's letter. He was most positive and forthright. To the Attorney General's reported statement 'The window of the bedroom of MacLennan's fourth floor flat was locked from the inside' the foreman of the inquest jury commented, 'This is an absolutely false statement.' Strong stuff.

Aileen got out her tape again and began to notice some very interesting things. One in particular was that the official press release differed in certain major respects from his actual words. For example, the press release said ' . . . the windows were locked from the inside and they had not been forced or broken.' But Aileen discovered the AG did not say that. Indeed what he said was not a false statement at all.

She rang Tony Pannel that evening and discussed it with him.

'Well, of course I only saw the newspaper report,' he said.

'Quite. But it could be that one of the reasons he is refusing to reply is that he has a trump card up his sleeve. Namely, that if it comes to the push he can simply show that he was misreported.'

'Well, I wish he'd do something,' said Tony. 'I am being rung up at all hours of the day and night by every amateur detective in Hong Kong. The place is riddled with them. They all think it was murder and they all have a different theory about how it was done.'

The following day she opened the Talk-show as usual and brought up the MacLennan affair again with the words:

` Hi, there folks, hope you're going to stay with us for the talk show today and give us a call during the next two hours. We read in the papers that Tony Pannel, foreman of the three-member jury at the MacLennan inquest, has accused the Attorney General of being not absolutely truthful in his recent press conference? Think of that. You know that's a very serious accusation to cast at one of the top legal authorities in Hong Kong. A grave charge to make against a man who said soon after he was sworn in that it was his job to see that justice was done and to stand between the government and the citizen, to protect the citizen also on occasions from the government. He said he would brook no interference from anybody and would do what was fair, just and in the interests of the people of Hong Kong and the individual who was being charged. Fine phrases, the sentiments of which should be applauded by every decent citizen. Fine phrases from the voice of a clever man—and he is a very clever man.

'Some may have doubted his cleverness when he went voluntarily a few months later to Western Magistracy to act as a character witness for a man who was charged with being drunk and disorderly outside the Foreign Correspondents Club in the early hours of the morning—a man who, it was said, was shouting and using vile language and was being charged with assaulting the young police officer who tried to restrain him. Some felt it was not the action of a clever man, especially if he were Attorney General, to go and be a character witness for a drunk.

'But there is no doubt in my mind that he is very clever indeed. For example, when asked at the recent press conference why the body was cremated in such haste he replied . . .' at which point Aileen played the whole section of tape where the AG had based his argument on the expertise and experience of Professor Gibson doing the autopsy and ending, ' . . . that is the true history of it.'

She continued 'That is the true history of it. But it wasn't. A member of the press immediately pointed out that Professor Gibson had never even seen the body.' Then she played the part of the tape where the AG said:

'In that case—was it Mr Ong then? I'm very sorry. I've got the wrong one. Thank you very much indeed.'

Then she pointed out 'All right, so he made a mistake. But having based his explanation on the professional reputation of Professor Gibson, who didn't see the body at all, he never went back and gave us a new explanation. He never mentioned, for example, that Mr Ong had never seen the body either. The false statement remained as . . . (the Attorney General's voice) "That is the true history of it."

'Again, a couple of weeks before the press conference an army caller pointed out on my program that using the formula that every schoolboy knows, the area of a circle equals πr^2, it was simple to show that a .38 bullet made a hole three times the size of that of a .22, of which all the evidence of multiple self-inflicted gunshot wounds was based. I put this to the Attorney General. His answer was . . .'

She then played the tape of him talking about the loss of oxygen to the brain causing loss of consciousness and suggesting that a .22 through the heart is likely to be as damaging as getting 'a <u>slightly</u> larger hole from a <u>slightly</u> larger bullet.'

She went on 'From three times the size to slightly larger. Who is one to believe?

'But the one that really fooled all of us was the locked window. Listen to this.'

' . . . how you could leave, leaving the windows locked behind you would pass I think one's imagination.'

She drew the listeners' attention to the word 'locked.'

'The Attorney General didn't say the window was locked. He only said it would pass imagination to leave through it if it was. Listen how he went on . . ." . . . and the windows were seen to be shut, by I think it was total of four witnesses . . ."

So you see the Attorney General never said the windows were locked, only shut. And yet we all went away thinking that he had, and the newspapers reported just that.

As I said, in my opinion the Attorney General is a clever man, a good orator, a man of convincing arguments. It's a great gift and our vulnerability to good orators is centuries old.'

She then put on a recording of Marlon Brando playing Mark Anthony in <u>Julius Caesar</u> and doing the 'Friends, Romans, Countrymen' bit, all about Brutus being an honourable man, but implying something quite different.

There was the crowd being swayed by the power of oration.

'You all did see, that on the Lupercal

I thrice presented him a kingly crown

Which he did thrice refuse:

(crowd noises start to crescendo)
Was this ambition?
But Brutus says he was ambitious;
And, sure, he is an honourable man.'
Aileen faded out the roaring crowd and said:
'The Attorney General says MacLennan killed himself; and sure, he is an honourable man.'

She then faded in a suitable bit of music, and immediately there was a flurry of listeners' calls. Frena in the outside studio indicated that there was one for 'off-air'. During a commercial Aileen picked up the phone. A husky voice came over the wire.

'Baby, you're a honey. But for God's sake, be careful. Be careful how you drive. Be careful how you walk down the street. Because they'll be out to get you—won't they just!'. Aileen swallowed hard. The threat was not just against her. It was just as bad for Kevin. What danger was he in?

The program, however, fairly buzzed with excitement. Speculation was rife. How could you shoot yourself without leaving fingerprints on the gun? How could you turn a .38 inwards in a weak grip and not drop it with the recoil? Why didn't they test the hands for powder burns?

Elsie rang in. She had checked out the powder test, that the Attorney General had classified under the general heading of 'expensive scientific tests'. The test did in fact cost twenty Hong Kong dollars (US$3).

Chapter 23

The next day at work Aileen found an anonymous letter on her desk. It was a short story called 'The Inspector who knew too much' by Simon Blake. Frena had spent the previous hour going through telephone directories, ringing up a few puzzled and sometimes irate Blakes, and even consulting the telephone company, all to no avail. Simon remained as fictitious as his brother Sexton.

When Aileen read the story, it made her flesh creep. It was just too close to the evidence to be comfortable. She knew there was no way she could broadcast it without legal advice. She stowed it away for the future.

Just before the program she thought she would get the latest on the affair from PPRB.

'Police Public Relations Bureau. Can I help you?'

'Yes, what's the latest press release on Roy Henry?'

'Ha, ha, ha. Very funny. Anybody can have our job at the moment. The questions have been piling up from the media all week. Roy Henry promised us some answers by five o'clock yesterday. You've got no idea of the pressures on this office at the moment. We rang him at five and he promised them first thing this morning. It is now ten o'clock. If we get anything we will ring you straight away. Don't hold your breath'

By the end of the program at twelve there had been not a peep out of him.

After the program Aileen visited her lawyer's office. He read the story, whistled and after a few moments silence said 'If you say it is just a story and throw cold water on it, it should be O.K.

That evening Aileen had a call from another lawyer friend.

'I'm having a little dinner party next Wednesday. Can you come?'

'Thank you, but I'm not sure if I can make it. Can I let you know?'

'The Attorney General will be there.'

'Oh, I see. I'd better go then, hadn't I?. I'll take out insurance.'

Meanwhile speculation was rampant. There was even a sort of club formed in the Hong Kong University which was dedicated to producing theories on how the murder was done.

Then somebody broke into MacLennan's empty flat. It was shown on TV. A TVB reporter found that the bathroom window was very close to the corridor window and he demonstrated the possibility of climbing in or out by thrusting his head and shoulders through the former. He was a big fellow and it looked unlikely he could. The Star newspaper later claimed a reporter had actually climbed through the window. It didn't make any difference really because the bathroom led on to the hallway, not the bedroom. It still didn't get round the locked bedroom door. The next day Aileen said a little bit about all the speculation that was going around and how she thought the authorities should stop the uncertainty by having an independent inquiry. She said she had just received an example of it, which she would read. Mimicking the introduction to the old Children's Hour story, she said:

'Are you all sitting comfortably? Good. "The Inspector who knew too much", by Simon Blake.

Inspector McNaughton's knowledge that a very senior police officer was on the list of suspects of triad activities was dangerous. When he was so indiscreet as to admit the knowledge to other members of the force it became fatal. He had to be got rid of. This is how it was done—maybe.

For the purposes of this account we need to identify an unknown police officer. Let us call him "X".

At the beginning of January X casually mentioned to McNaughton that his turn was coming around to be called upon for raiding duties and he had better be sure to do his monthly firing practice.

At 1.45 a.m. on 15th January X rang the police switchboard and said:

'I would like a wake-up call at 5.30. My name is Inspector McNaughton.'

He gave McNaughton's number.

At 5.40 X rang McNaughton: 'Morning, John."

"Oh, it's you. I thought it was another joker. Some idiot's just given me a wake-up call. I was fast asleep."

"Yes, I laid on calls for the whole party. We've got a raid on this morning. Pop over to the armoury and get yourself a gun. I'll meet you at your place in twenty minutes."

"Twenty minutes! You got to be joking."

"I'm not. No time to lose. See you."

"But I've got to be in the chief's office at ten."

"Oh, you'll be back in plenty of time for that—if you move it."

So McNaughton quickly dressed and hurried to the station, arriving at five fifty five. He spoke to the station sergeant in great haste:

"I'm-on-a-CID-raid-and-I-need-a-gun-move-it."

"Pardon?"

"Raid—R.A.I.D—CID raid."

So the sergeant phoned the armoury and told them a European, Inspector McNaughton, was on his way down and should be issued with a gun. The haste of McNaughton made them both forget the CID raid log book.

McNaughton rushed down to the armoury, filled in 05.00 instead of 06.00, put his name in the wrong place—after all, he didn't draw a gun very often, he didn't like them anyway, and he was in a hurry. The armourer got him to correct the time.

Meanwhile X went to an adjacent empty flat, let himself in as only policemen know how, and threw a rope to McNaughton's bedroom window, which was open—as you would expect with a healthy young man in a small bedroom in January. He secured the rope and went round to McNaughton's flat. He met outside at 0607 and they went in together.

"I must just get my keys,' said McNaughton as he went into the bedroom. X followed him.

"That's not a CID revolver," said X. "Let me see it."

McNaughton passed it to him. A few moments later as he turned round the muzzle was pressed to his chest and the gun fired before he had a chance to react. He fell. X dropped the gun on the floor and left him for dead.

First X put on gloves and went to the front door. He locked everything he could find to make it look impossible to get in. Then he produced from his pocket book a suicide note he had carefully forged. He was a bit concerned about this. Naturally, anyone writing a suicide note in his own flat would choose a piece of normal writing paper. It would be a subconscious action. X could not do that because to have carried it he would have had to fold it, and that would have been inconsistent with a man writing a note and leaving it on a table. So he had chosen with some care a piece of lined file paper from McNaughton's office of a suitable size. It was yellowish. He had forged it by tracing words of McNaughton's actual handwriting.

Although he had made quite a study of handwriting and was pretty good at copying, this time he had had his problems. For example, he had managed to compose a note entirely using words that he actually had a copy of, but McNaughton was not always consistent. The P in the word "Please" he had intended to copy was formed quite differently from the P in "Police". Was this because they were written at different times or would McNaughton have been that inconsistent in such a short note? He didn't know. He had taken a chance on it and copied the words exactly. Only a world class handwriting expert would pick that one up, he thought, and we haven't got one here. So he had produced a master copy on tracing paper and then written on to the chosen paper over the top of a glass sheet with a light underneath.

Now, in McNaughton's flat, he pulled out his pocket book with the note between the pages. It had slipped a bit and the sides had become creased. That was bad. It would need explaining. Still, he smoothed it as best he could and left it on the desk. He checked to ensure the windows and the hatch beside the front door were locked. He then went back to the bedroom to find to his horror McNaughton regaining consciousness and groping for the gun.

For the first time he lost his cool. He grabbed the gun and fired four more times. He remembered to hold the gun close to the body, but because McNaughton was on his knees the tracks of the bullets were now downwards. Then, when he wiped the prints from the gun, he forgot to press McNaughton's hand on it. He was worried about the extra shots. He had not bargained for that. It was inconsistent with suicide, but it could not be undone.

He then locked one bedroom window and climbed out of the other. He closed it from outside and using the rope he climbed into the empty flat.

He went home and decided to write another suicide note. Unfortunately he hadn't any more of McNaughton's file paper so he had to use the nearest he had, a brownish manila envelope. Using the master he produced a new suicide note. He had plenty of time before he was on duty.

Just before he left he had an idea. Now that he knew exactly what time McNaughton had died it would be corroborative evidence if he put the time on the suicide note. But he had let himself become short of time. So he filled in the time "0610" above the date with less than his previous care, and without noticing that he had used a different slope and formation of the "1", had formed the "0"s in a different way—his own way—and had written the figures smaller then on the date.

As a member of the party to go to McNaughton's flat that morning, he had two jobs to do if he could. One was to swap the notes, the other was to bolt the bedroom window from inside. The first was by no means plain sailing, because McNaughton's solicitor picked up the first note and read it before X could get to it. However, he was there second and effected the swap unseen. He had much less difficulty with the window because nobody went near that for a couple of hours.

There were a few nasty moments at the inquest: when the solicitor didn't recognise the manila envelope; when the fingerprint expert couldn't find McNaughton's prints on the gun (fortunately he didn't check the manila envelope); when the pathologist examined McNaughton's hands and couldn't find any power burns; when they had to try and explain the five bullets; and when the jury returned an open verdict.

But he breathed again when the authorities stepped in and declared it suicide, because as soon as this one blew over there was another he had to get rid of.'

Chapter 24

Aileen didn't give the listeners a chance to react because it was time to close the show. She wondered what they would do with that. The fact is, the press had all been given a photograph of the note at the Attorney General's press conference and the '06.10' <u>was</u> written differently, there was no doubt about it.

On 7th June the Bar Association met behind closed doors. The Attorney General attended for the first part of the meeting, then left. This may or may not have been significant. As a result of the meeting the Bar Association issued a 356-word statement. Who on earth bothered to count the words? Perhaps the number of words was the only thing about it most people could grapple with. It read:

'Section 29 of the Coroner's Ordinance, Cap 14, expressly provides that "Notwithstanding that an inquiry had been concluded, the Attorney General may, if it appears to him that further investigation is necessary, require the Coroner to re-open such inquiry and make further investigation.

"Whether it so appears to the Attorney General must be a matter for him to decide; and the Committee has no doubt that the Attorney General's decision was made in perfect good faith, after sound deliberation and with the best interests of the public foremost in mind.

'If the Attorney General is to carry out his most difficult job properly and well, he is entitled to expect and receive from all members of the public their trust, and wherever possible, their support.

'Having said that, the Committee feels bound to express its concern that a situation arose where it may have been thought that the Attorney General was impugning the jury's open verdict.

'While it is correct that the Attorney General did indicate that it would not be proper for him to comment on why the jury reached that verdict, his conclusion might nevertheless appear to suggest that the jury had come to an incorrect verdict.

'The Committee believes that the Attorney General did not intend to make such suggestion, but in the Committee's view, it was most unfortunate that the reports of the press conference gave that impression.

'The Committee feels that in general any public pronouncement which tends to undermine the public's faith in a jury's verdict or to affect adversely the attitude of future jurors and quality of their deliberations ought to be avoided.'

Carefully constructed, the statement must have taken a lot of working out, good grammar and in the process had become, to Aileen, totally incomprehensible. Both TV stations reported it that evening and interpreted it in exactly opposite ways. One said the Bar Association supported the Attorney General, the other said they censured him. In the end the media sought legal advice as to what it meant. If they ever found out they didn't say. That was the situation as Aileen put on her best bib and tucker the following Wednesday to attend her friend's dinner party— total confusion.

She was usually at work at least an hour before her program, but when it came to social occasions she felt the lady should arrive second. That night she was fifty-second. The party was in the United Services Recreation Club, part of the green oasis in the centre of Kowloon where several clubs were located together. The USRC was very pleasant at night. You walked from the car park through plenty of overhanging foliage, otherwise almost nonexistent in Kowloon, until you came out in the pool area surrounded by a long string of coloured lights. The pool was large, floodlit and very blue. All round were grassy areas with stone tables and rattan chairs surrounded by hedgerows, but this night the area at the far end had tables neatly laid with gingham cloths, each with a lighted candle. There was no need for an orchestra, the cicadas chirruped all evening

Being rather late, Aileen went apologetically up to the other fifty-one having pre-drinks, expecting a few raised eyebrows. No such thing. There were some perceptible sighs of relief. How odd, she thought. Her feeble attempt at an apology was immediately swept aside with 'Not at all. The AG hasn't come yet.'

It was not long after that he did. He greeted his host, mingled a little and apparently quite accidentally drifted into Aileen's group, where they were deep in discussion about some obscure religion that had been discovered to have various attributes likely to save the world from impending disaster if anyone ever found out about it. It seemed the AG knew all about it and told them the deeper significance of it.

Then, just as accidentally, Aileen found him gently taking her arm and leading her towards the buffet.

'We mustn't jump the queue,' he whispered. 'I might find myself with five bullet holes in the back.'

He was elegantly dressed, but when they had collected their food and he had led her to the only table laid for two, away in a dark corner, he became more relaxed, transferred his jacket to the back of his chair, sat down and said:

'Why did you cast me as Brutus?'

'I didn't. I cast you as Mark Anthony, the great orator who could sway the crowds.'

'Oh? It sounded like Brutus to me. I wondered whom I had stabbed in the back.'

He was an interesting person, cultured, widely read, and knew his Shakespeare intimately. He had actually been an actor at one time, performing with such eminent persons as Michael Hordern. He asked her which Shakespearian character she identified herself with. She had never thought about it, but it was too interesting a challenge to pass up.

'I think I am most like Lady Macbeth. Full of determination but never following through. How about you?'

'I'm Malvolio. The most misunderstood character in Shakespeare.'

But John MacLennan couldn't be kept out of it for long. It was as if his spirit was sitting at the table with them, prompting them and causing the candle to flicker.

The AG could be very blunt and to the point.

'Do you think it was murder or suicide?'

'I honestly don't know,' she said. 'Certainly suicide has not been proved beyond reasonable doubt. And the very fact that the authorities, and you in particular, are so keen to declare it suicide has just had the effect of increasing the doubts and suspicions in everyone's minds, including mine. My lord, you do protest too much.'

He smiled. 'I put it to you that you are largely to blame for those doubts and suspicions.'

'Why me? What have I got to do with the evidence?'

'Because the ghastly thing is your audience trusts you. Normally you act as mediator, allowing the opinion to sway this way and that. But in this case you have come down heavily on one side. You have even resorted to the most outrageous histrionics.'

'What on earth are you talking about?'

'I'm talking about what you do all the time. "It's a sad day for Hong Kong . . ." when some little decision doesn't go the way you want, or "The government has ground to a standstill . . ." when they don't immediately take some action you think they ought to take, or likening a cold logical press conference to one of the most emotive orations in the English language. In this case you have let sincerity go to the four winds and you have come down on the most sensational side just like the lowest form of journalist.'

Aileen felt the blood running to her checks and the anger swelling behind her tongue. She held onto the arms of her chair. He could see it all. But she held on. She thought, this is what he is trying to do, probing for a weak spot, testing my limits. After a fraction of second in which her eyes flashed, she smiled as devastatingly as she could:

'But you've got it all wrong. I'm not a journalist at all. I'm an actress. My job is to entertain.'

'Well, you should be more careful then. Do you realise I could get you three months behind bars for what you have done, for libel, contempt and defamation?'

'I know. I consulted a lawyer before I did it.'

Now it was his turn to hesitate. The wheel of fortune had turned.

'Then why?'

'Because I knew you would take no action.'

'Why not?'

'Because if you had taken me to court I would have subpoenaed at least five witnesses who are too scared to come forward any other way. And you wouldn't like that, would you?'

His rueful smile told her he was ready for a truce.

'I won't give you the chance.'

They talked and talked. Sometimes about her job, sometimes about his, both past and present. It developed into a friendly and relaxed conversation. He told her about his wife and family. She envied them because he was very attractive in a sort of smooth, sophisticated, hard way. As for his children, they were obviously the most important part of his life.

But John MacLennan kept bringing them back to him.

'That story you broadcast. That was positively improper.'

'What, "The Inspector who knew too much"? I thought it was rather good.'

'Bizarre and ridiculous.'

'And shooting yourself five times in the chest isn't bizarre and ridiculous?'

He had the greatest skill of anyone she had ever met in not answering the question. You would think he had answered and yet, without knowing it, you were suddenly off in a different direction.

'You see, that sort of story could mislead your public.'

'You obviously didn't listen to how I started it. I said something like "Now listen carefully, children, I am going to tell you a story. Are you sitting comfortably?" How could anyone take that seriously? But you should have done, because it is symptomatic of the speculation going on all over town.'

'You see, it's quite wrong. It <u>was</u> suicide, you know. You were getting warmer a few weeks ago when you said on your program it was murder by suicide. Since then you've gone right off the scent.'

She thought she did cast him wrong. He should have been Julius Caesar, bestriding the narrow world like a colossus. She could just hear him saying:

'But I am constant as the northern star,
Of whose true-fixed and resting quality
There is no fellow in the firmament.
Thus I am sure MacLennan killed himself and constant do remain to keep it so.'

She looked up. He was smiling at her again, his eye twinkling behind his glasses. 'Would you like another drink?'

'If you have poison I will drink it since I see you love me not.'

He twinkled again and a gin and tonic was duly placed before her.

Night's candles were almost burned out and they were joined by the head of the Consumer Council and her husband, a senior administrator in government and as such one of the strongest opponents of 'rocking the boat'. He saw the whole process of the media questioning the MacLennan suicide as rocking the boat and had no time for it. He and the AG discussed the TVB film where they purported to show a reporter climbing through MacLennan's bathroom window. Ridiculous, impossible, they both said.

'And did you hear that bizarre story Aileen broadcast?' said the AG.

'No.'

He turned to her. 'Go on, tell it to them.'

'I don't know if I can remember it.'

'Of course you can. Tell it to them.'

Well, she tried. She couldn't remember the details, but every time she made a mistake the AG corrected her. Clearly he knew it off by heart. Looking back on the evening she realised he knew a great deal of what she had said on air off by heart. It was extraordinary. She made a mental note that, in future, if there was anything she wanted to bring to the attention of the Attorney General, all she had to do was to broadcast it. It was obviously the quickest and most effective way.

Suddenly they looked around and found they were the last people there. A lone waiter was hovering, thinking of home. It was half past midnight. There was even a certain hoarseness about the cicadas. They all got the message at once and rose to go. They walked quietly and thoughtfully to the car park and parted with some sweet sorrow. She thought, what a charming fellow. She liked him. And now they were to become antagonists again. She wondered, when it was all over, if they could ever become friends.

Because, you see, she had this subtle and indefinable feeling that he was acting under orders

Chapter 25

The speculation simmered, boiled and often overflowed. The Hong Kong University detective club thought of lots more theories on how it was done, by whom and why. In every bar, club, restaurant and lounge the same questions were being asked: murder? suicide? cover-up? whitewash?

The Attorney General replied in a very long-winded statement on 5th June that the public must trust him to do his job honestly and fairly.

Then Elsie decided to step in and blow the lid off. She announced that she would give a press conference on 17th June and reveal a deep, dark secret. Naturally this got a bit exaggerated to imply that 'Elsie will tell all', but certainly everyone was agog to know what she knew that the public didn't. She rang Aileen the night before and didn't sound like the usual Elsie at all. At first she just talked a lot about the technicalities, about how she had had her statement analysed by her lawyers and so on, but her real concern started to come out. She wasn't worried about libel, she was afraid for her life.

"Elsie, for goodness sake, come over here and stay with me for the night."

She hesitated. She was tempted. She nearly did. But she was, after all, in charge of a school. It was not the sort of place she could just walk out of.

"No thanks, Aileen, I'd better stay here. I'll be alright. And anyway, I have told all my household that if a robber comes they are to give him anything he wants. So if anything happens to me everyone will know it is not a robber. But you will come to the press conference won't you? I shall feel so much better if I know there is one friend out there."

"Of course I'll be there. Why don't we have lunch together beforehand?"

"No, I won't, thanks all the same. But I would like a cup of tea afterwards."

Aileen felt a little neglectful because 17th June was a public holiday and normally she and Kevin would have gone out somewhere. So at breakfast, to try and pacify him and let him think she wasn't deserting him, she said:

"Why don't you come to the press conference?"

"What on earth for?"

"I thought you might find it interesting to see Elsie Elliott in action."

"And what the hell do you think that'll do to my image? No, I've got a lot of Institution work to do. We are redrafting the code of ethics."

"Oh for heavens sake! Get your nose out of your wretched engineering just for once and come and see how the other half lives and works."

"To be quite honest I am afraid Mrs Elliott will eat me."

"Oh don't be ridiculous. You're just making excuses. I believe you are really afraid to be seen in public."

"Why, I don't look that hideous, do I?"

"I sometimes believe you think you do. You never will come with me on interviews and press conferences. It's as if you don't want to know what I'm doing."

"I guess you're probably right. Your work is all gossip and tittle-tattle, just like the A-G says, and mine is all precisely factual. You can't really mix the two, you know. But just to show there's no ill feeling, I will come and if Mrs Elliott eats me you can live with that gnawing regret for the rest of your life instead of me.'"

Aileen didn't think it was the best of motives for going to Elsie's press conference, but she had won the argument and didn't want to press her luck.

The press conference was held in the *Fung Shui* room of the Hong Kong Hotel and since Fung Shui means wind and water Elsie had probably done that deliberately. As soon as Kevin saw the TV cameras he said "I'll sit at the back". Aileen had promised to sit in the front to give Elsie moral support. So husband and wife parted. Aileen collected the press release and started reading avidly to see what the great disclosure was. After a while she was conscious that someone was sitting beside her, breathing heavily. It was Elsie.

"Oh, you're still alive, I'm so glad."

"Don't look now, but they're here." Elsie whispered.

"Who?"

"The SIU."

"Oh, lord. How do you know?"

"I saw him. I could tell the way he looked at me. Typical policeman of the worst sort. Don't look round, Aileen, that's what he wants. But after I move away you just glance round and you'll see this tall European at the back in a blue safari suit. Very sinister."

"Elsie."

"What?"

"That's my husband."

"Oh dear. Is he one of us?"

"Uncommitted."

Elsie was clearly in a twitter, seeing murderers behind every pillar.

But the hour struck and she rose, faced all the microphones, enemies, vultures, onlookers and friends and made her statement firmly and resolutely. She covered the whole of her acquaintance with John MacLennan since 1978, but most of all she pitched into the SIU, knives bared and banners flying.

She said that Howard Lindsay, a crown counsel, had phoned her in late 1979, at great risk to himself, to inform her that certain members of the SIU had intimidated another senior police inspector to try and 'set up' John MacLennan by introducing him to male prostitutes, so laying him open to homosexual charges. However, despite this intimidation, the inspector had refused to take part in any set-up.

She had suggested that the inspector should report the entire matter to his superiors, or at least make a sworn statement about it for his own protection.

"I know this set-up attempt," she said, "had been related to the Attorney General by Mr Howard Lindsay well before the death of MacLennan."

She said that during a meeting with the Attorney General on 20th December 1979 she too had informed him that she knew of a set-up being planned by individuals of the SIU, and that an inspector had been asked to take part in setting up a colleague, that colleague being John MacLennan. The inference was clear that, had the Attorney General acted on this information, John MacLennan might not have died.

Of course, once having started on the Attorney General, she couldn't resist adding: "I should now like to ask the Attorney General whether my allegation was followed up. Or did he dismiss this serious allegation as mere 'gossip and tittle-tattle', as stated in his press conference?"

Aileen wondered whether the AG was perhaps beginning to regret having made that remark.

Then, just to twist the knife in the wound, Elsie brought up the Attorney General's mistake at his press conference, where he had referred to Professor Gibson carrying out the autopsy and then changed it to Dr Ong. "This was a double mistake," she said, "Dr Ong had never seen the body either."

And so Elsie went on. She hinted, just without going over the edge, at intrigues, attempts to pervert the course of justice, and cover-ups. The message was clear. She didn't care for the SIU.

When she had completed her statement she invited questions and they poured in for an hour. Some were friendly, some not. Aileen tried to fill in with a few friendly ones, but some were just obvious invitations to libel, loaded questions, treacherous questions, death traps. The wily old lady parried them all with the complete confidence and competence of a warrior in a children's playground.

She rounded off the press conference with an almost Churchillian sense of drama: "The Attorney General has asked us to trust him. In the light of what I have stated and in the context of the MacLennan case, can the Attorney General be said to have inspired public trust?

"Since the Attorney general is answerable only to His Excellency the Governor, I call upon the Governor to speak out on this matter."

Then she invited everybody to tea.

Aileen introduced her to Kevin. He seemed a bit subdued. Elsie apologised most profusely for having suspected him of being in the SIU. Since he had no idea she had, he said very little except, "Oh, er, that's alright."

As they stood by her taxi, she shook hands and thanked them for coming. Then she gave Kevin a little kiss and slipped into the taxi.

He was rather quiet on the way home. Aileen asked him if he had enjoyed it.

"Yes, I did. It wasn't what I expected."

"What did you expect?"

"I expected a Gorgon, with snakes for hair, eyes that turned you to stone, and breathing fire. Instead I find a dear old lady, a really lovely, sincere, caring soul who wouldn't hurt a fly unless she thought it was her bounden duty to do so. She didn't want to give that press conference. What's more, when she stood up in front of all that array of prying electronics she was scared stiff and almost didn't show it. She's got great courage, that lady, great courage, the more so because she is not without fear."

Aileen thought it was marvellous what a little kiss could do.

Chapter 26

Elsie's tactics had been superb. If she had named the inspector she might have been in trouble, but much more important, there would have been no mystery. As it was, all the tongues were wagging trying to find out who he was, did he really exist, or was it just a figment of Elsie's imagination?

Two days later a very small item appeared in the press, saying there was to be a meeting between the Governor, the Attorney General and the Secretary for Information, Mr David Ford, "in order to examine the implications of Mrs Elliott's allegations". Aileen wondered if it was significant that the Commissioner of Police had been left out. But one thing was for sure, Elsie wasn't whistling to the wind any more.

She now had a lot of backing. One newspaper tabled a series of questions including "Was Mr Henry one of the top police officers investigated by MacLennan during his special branch duties?" The official answer was "No", but the press couldn't get much closer than that.

Aileen did her bit. She pointed out on air that the Attorney General had said he would reopen the inquest if any new evidence was presented to him. "But he has a lot of new evidence," she said. "A reporter has climbed through MacLennan's bathroom window, showing exit from the flat was possible. The <u>Star</u> newspaper has pointed out that no expert witness was called to verify the handwriting. Since Mr Ronald Cimino, a member of the government forensic team, who was claimed to be an expert, had not taken them to court he seemed to be admitting that he was not sure he could establish he was an expert. And now there was evidence of a set-up. What more did he want?" She asked.

"Since he is still refusing to reopen the inquest in the face of all this new evidence, it is clear that either he has been told not to reopen the case or he is trying to tell us in an obtuse way that to reopen the case could be so damaging to the administrative structure of Hong Kong that it would be better to live with the mystery."

The Attorney General's office immediately rang up the Commercial Radio general manager and complained.

"I have no control over her," said Nick.

"But you must have."

"Have you ever tried to control a redheaded woman?"

But he came down to Aileen after the program, twisting his hands like Shylock.

"When you land us all in court I can just see me genuflecting before the magistrate and pleading "But I can't control her, your Honour, it's the Irish in her, your Honour."

A leading TV interviewer was in Aileen's studio the next day and said during a musical break: "How o you stand up to the pressures of this program?"

"It's having Nick upstairs. He bawls me out daily and accuses me of endangering the station, but if anyone complains about me from outside or tries to get him to lean on me, he tells them what they can do."

"Yes," came the wistful almost envious reply, I doubt if anyone else in Hong Kong has that kind of support."

Meanwhile the Attorney General had issued a long-winded reply referring to the allegations of Elsie and his meeting with her. He kept referring to the mysterious inspector as XYZ, which increased the mystery so much it made everything else he said seem quite unimportant. But one thing was rather significant. He expressly denied that XYZ had at any time been asked to frame MacLennan. Some people wondered if it was all a put-up job by Elsie, others if the AG was a liar.

Elsie was not at all satisfied that she had the Governor and half his staff running around, she tackled some British Members of Parliament and John MacLennan made his debut at Westminster in the House of Commons in London. The Minister of State at the Foreign and Commonwealth Office, Mr Peter Blaker, had to reply. True, he said nothing, but she was getting places, she really was. Who was left?

Margaret Thatcher and the Queen. Aileen remarked to Kevin, "Give her time."

The media, however, could not resist the mystery of this Inspector XYZ. The name was just too inviting. They dug and they delved, determined to find out who he was. By this time Aileen knew, but she didn't want to get Nick into any more trouble, so she left the disclosure to someone else.

Elsie put pressure on the Commissioner of Police by writing an open letter demanding XYZ be allowed to make a statement confirming or denying the truth of her allegation, and be guaranteed protection against victimisation. The latter remark touched a few tender spots, but the pressure was too great and by the 30th June his name was out. He was Inspector Michael Fulton and he immediately sought legal advice and asked permission to make a statement.

With near perfect timing a letter to the press arrived from Europe, dispatched by former crown counsel Howard Lindsay, and was duly published on 1st July. It named Michael Fulton and confirmed the story. It also went on to say that he, Lindsay, on hearing the statement from Fulton that he had been threatened by officers of the SIU if he did not co-operate and set up MacLennan, considered that such officers were guilty, inter alia, of criminal intimidation, conspiracy to invite the commission of crimes involving indecency, and attempt to pervert the course of justice.

Lindsay described how he met with the Attorney General on or about 22nd November 1979, repeated Fulton's allegations and asked him to take some action. No decision was made at that time.

So Lindsay wrote to the Attorney General asking for action to be taken against the SIU officers, adding "It will be a pleasant change for the prosecution to use witnesses who are not prostitutes, blackmailers, etc., and who do not need immunity from prosecution."

He saw the Attorney General again in December and repeated his request for action, but he was told that this could only be done after an official complaint.

After MacLennan's death Lindsay dictated a note to the Attorney General's secretary, reminding him of the previous warnings and requests for action and adding "Congratulations on the result of your inactivity."

In August 1979 Gordon Huthard, the operator of another gay bar and relative of the Lane

Crawford family, was arrested and soon after that Lindsay was himself investigated by the SIU for

homosexual activities and taken to court. The SIU were unable to support the charges against him and the

case was dismissed, because as a lawyer he cross questioned the witnesses (all male prostitutes) proving

them all liars. But he lost his job anyway and had to leave Hong Kong.

After this disclosure Elsie became more hopeful about the mystery. "I think we're beginning to crack it," she told Aileen, "and I hope that it's not going to be just the MacLennan case."

Fulton duly made his statement and confirmed Elsie's allegation. The gossip and tittle-tattle was true this time anyway. But one very interesting point arose in a telephone call to Aileen's program. Apparently there is a precise legal difference between setting up and framing. One is encouraging a crime to be committed, the other is saying a crime has been committed when it hasn't. So that when the AG denied that Fulton had been asked to frame MacLennan, he was not only telling the truth regarding that fine technicality, he was introducing a complete irrelevancy. Elsie had never used the word 'frame' in her press conference, only 'set up'. Yet the AG fooled the masses into thinking that he had denied Elsie's allegation.

Indeed, the general feeling in the media was that the Attorney General's appeals to trust him were an indication that there might be good reasons not to. The press became increasingly daring. There were remarks in editorials like "The more we hear about this case the more we are led to believe that MacLennan did not kill himself." The MacLennan fever even began to spread to England, where the magazine <u>Private Eye</u> said MacLennan qualified for the <u>Guinness Book of Records</u> by shooting himself five times with a .38, and described the Attorney General and British Minister of State Peter Blaker as 'modern-day King Canutes' for their roles in the case. Certainly the public were left wondering how long the authorities could go on ordering the tide of its opinion to recede.

On 4th July Tony Pannel, the foreman of the inquest jury, publicly called for the resignation of the Attorney General. The next day the Chairman of the Hong Kong Branch of Justice called for a full judicial inquiry. One newspaper took the opportunity to print a long discussion on who might replace the present Governor, Sir Murray MacLehose. Elsie wrote to MacLennan's parents advising them to take legal action against the Attorney General on the grounds of his inactivity, and against the Commissioner of Police for withholding their son's effects.

Then she wrote to the Chief Justice, Sir Denys Roberts (many had wondered when he was going to be brought into the fray), requesting an independent inquiry.

But the government had the answer to it all. They simply refused everything.

Chapter 27

Although Aileen had challenged the Attorney General on air to reopen the inquest, because he now had new evidence, she was rather conscious that the new evidence was a bit thin. A reporter climbing through the bathroom window didn't really prove very much because it didn't explain how the bedroom door was locked from inside. The fact that the handwriting 'expert' had ignored his own discrediting in the press didn't disprove that the alleged suicide note was in John MacLennan's handwriting. Whether there was an unsuccessful set—up attempt on John MacLennan or not didn't really answer the question as to whether it was murder or suicide.

What was clear was that the Attorney General was appealing to the public to come forward with new evidence, when it was quite obvious that the man with the power to seek out new evidence was the Attorney General himself. He was the one who could bring in international and independent forensic and handwriting experts from outside Hong Kong if he wanted to get at the truth, but clearly, for reasons known only to himself (maybe), he was disinclined to call on such advice.

So Elsie and Aileen decided to do it for him.

Elsie sent the full medical report from the inquest to a Home Office pathologist in UK who had agreed to analyse it for her. Aileen tried a more superficial approach, hoping to get a wider set of opinions which might at least point them in the right direction. She sent basically the same letter to the Central Scotland Police, the New York Coroner and the Forensic Science Laboratory in Australia.

First of all she gave the background to the case and included photocopies of the press reports of the pathologists' and ballistics evidence at the inquest. She went on to ask if they could obtain an authoritative statement from a real expert on the possibility of a man putting a .38 bullet through the right ventricle of his heart and then, over a space of minutes, firing four more shots into his chest and abdomen. What was the possibility of doing this, she asked, without leaving fingerprints on the gun or visible powder burns on the hands?

The Central Scotland Police replied very quickly and gave her a name and address to write to in the Home Office pathology department. Since this was a different address from the one Elsie had written to, she sent another letter there.

Then she tackled the handwriting. At the Attorney General's press conference David Ford had distributed to the media several photographs, one of which was a close-up of the alleged suicide note. She didn't know how useful that would be to a handwriting expert, but she thought it worth a try. She got a friend of the MacLennan family to get a sample of John's handwriting for her. This they did and she found herself in possession of a letter written by him to his parents in November 1979. She took this to a photographer and asked him if he could take full-sized photographs of the letter and blow up the print of the alleged suicide note to full size and try and straighten it up a bit—it had been taken on a slant.

Meanwhile she made some enquiries and found that the most renowned handwriting experts in the world were in Switzerland. So she went to the Swiss Trade Commission. They were most interested to learn of her request, and after a short while found her an address. She was thus able to send a set of photographs to Dr Edgar Haldimann in Lenzburg.

For extra measure she sent the whole lot to the diplomatic correspondent of the London Sunday Times, who had given her a memorable interview on her program the week before.

They then sat back with their fingers and toes crossed and waited.

Only, of course, neither she nor Elsie were the type to sit around and wait. They had to be doing something. So Aileen said, let's have a bit of gossip and tittle-tattle, and invited Elsie, Graeme Ross and Tony Pannel to supper.

They went from rumour to tattle, back to tittle and flavoured it all with gossip. What a supper it was.

Tony said he was being rung up many times a day, and often far into the night, by members of the public he didn't know from Adam, with views, theories and questions. Journalists would pester him for statements, telling him he had a duty to the public. Since he had refused up till then, Aileen suggested he did an interview with her. He gave her a rather gratifying reply.

"I think you are the one person I would give a statement to, because with you it goes out exactly as a caller says it. It is live and nobody can edit it or slant it. The trouble is I don't trust myself to say exactly what I want to say first go."

She suggested they go into another room, conduct the interview, and then he could edit it himself. He rather liked the idea and that's what they did.

He started the recording by saying how very concerned he was that the Attorney General had overruled a jury. He felt this cast grave doubts on the judicial system in Hong Kong. He said the evidence was presented to the jury as a suicide case right from the start, and they kept waiting for conclusive evidence which never came. He described it as a case of John MacLennan on trial for shooting himself, and they were only given the case for the prosecution and not the defence. But even the case for the prosecution was unsatisfactory. He knew about guns and he was certainly not convinced anyone could shoot themselves five times in the chest with a .38. The windows had not been checked, fingerprints were not taken, there were no tests for powder burns—no conclusive evidence at all. Even the note could be explained in other ways, such as being written under pressure, if the so-called expert evidence was accepted.

As they went back to join the others, she asked him about the other two jurors and their problems with English. He said he couldn't have wished for more thoughtful and intelligent colleagues. They had understood everything perfectly and Aileen's earlier fears had been quite unfounded.

They arrived back to find the gossip in full swing. "I heard John MacLennan died the night before,' declared Elsie.

"That's funny!" Aileen had suddenly remembered something she had heard a few days earlier. "I have a friend who lived in the next block of flats to MacLennan, and she had an Indonesian neighbour who heard shots around midnight, but her husband told her not to get involved."

"There you are." Elsie was getting into top gear. "What did I tell you?"

Greame wondered if the body temperature would have been consistent with that.

But Tony was much more interested in the bullet wounds. He said the shock of the first bullet would have knocked John MacLennan unconscious and, in any case, holding a .38 such an awkward angle, the recoil would have spun it out of his hand at the first shot.

Aileen told of an incident that occurred a couple of weeks earlier, when she had asked a spine specialist what happened when a bullet lodged in the ninth thoracic vertebra. He had told her that it would cause displacement and severe shock to the spinal cord. The result would probably be paralysis from the waist down, there could be excruciating agony which, coupled with the shock of the bullet, could cause rapid unconsciousness or possibly numbness from the waist down, upsetting the balance. The force of the bullet would almost certainly have knocked the recipient over.

Elsie was incensed. "And he was supposed to fire four more shots after that! Why didn't they tell us all that at the inquest?"

Then Aileen told them about her excursions into the handwriting business. She first showed them the enlarged photograph of the note.

Tony was most interested. "I have never seen this before."

"But surely you must have been shown the note at the inquest?"

"No, we never were. We were only shown very big enlargements of selected phrases with comparable phrases from handwriting known to be MacLennan's. For example, we were never shown the numbers at the bottom."

Then Aileen showed them the genuine letter. The effect was dramatic, because the handwriting looked completely different. True, the letter was written with a pen on airmail paper while the note was written with a ballpoint on an envelope, but nevertheless the differences were startling.

"It's a forgery," declared Elsie.

"Looks like one to me," said Tony.

Now, Aileen took a closer look. What struck her was that there were two clear characteristics in the letter which were not in the note. One was that John MacLennan, when writing the figure 1, always drew his pen away to the right at the bottom. This characteristic did not appear in the note.

"Perhaps that's why they didn't show us the figures at the inquest," remarked Tony.

Secondly, John's writing waved up and down all the time along the line, whereas the note looked as if it had been written over guide lines.

"I would have thought," said one of the assembled company, "that a chap would waver more if he was about to commit suicide, not less."

One odd characteristic was that in the note the word 'Police' was spelt with a letter much more like the letter at the beginning of 'Ron' than at the beginning of 'Please'. Why should he spell 'Police' with a capital R?

In the end they came to the conclusion that the authorities had dealt with the MacLennan case so ineptly that it amounted to a kind of death wish of an ailing administration turning in on itself.

As they were leaving, Elsie turned to her host: "Thank you very much, Aileen, I can't remember when I enjoyed an evening more. I haven't had roast beef and Yorkshire pudding for years."

Chapter 28

Aileen played Tony Pannel's interview the next day on her program. His measured, thoughtful, mild Australian accent obviously came as a surprise to many who were expecting a tub-thumping shop steward demanding the resignation of the Attorney General if he couldn't clean up his act.

The reaction was very favourable. The listeners thought he was a great guy who deserved a medal for courage and they wanted to know more about fingerprints, powder burns and bathroom windows. Even Nick came in beaming, obviously very conscious that his Talk-show host had got a rather outstanding exclusive interview.

"Well, you've sent the Attorney General a little further up the river. As I said all along, there's a lot more to come out about this business."

As Aileen paused to pick up her jaw he puffed out his chest and walked out, and she was left whistling to the wind.

That evening Aileen noticed that the film <u>All the President's Men</u> was being shown on TV on a night she had an appointment. She wanted to see it. She thought the MacLennan case was already showing distinct similarities to Watergate and she felt she might learn something. Graeme Ross had recently bought a video recorder, so she rang him up and asked him to record it. A week later she rang him again.

"Graeme, when can I come and see that film?'

"How about the day after tomorrow?"

"I could come at five thirty."

"That'll be fine. It lasts three hours."

Aileen mentioned the arrangement to no-one. There was no reason why she should.

Two days later she drove round to his flat close by in Barker Road.

"Come in, Aileen. Forgive me if I don't watch it all again. I'll go round to my club for a swim. Nobody knows you're here, so you won't be disturbed. Help yourself to anything in the fridge." She poured herself a glass of beer and settled down.

He came back soon after eight and watched the end of the film with her. At eight thirty there was a ring at the doorbell. They looked at each other in surprise.

"I thought you said we would not be disturbed."

"I'll see who it is.

As he opened the door a short, thin plain-clothes policeman with a mop of fuzzy hair pushed by him and made straight for Aileen.

"You must stop demanding an independent inquiry. You don't know what you are getting involved in. The way you are persecuting Mr Quinn is very wrong. He is a very kind person, very polite, and the finest detective in the world. All the SIU are very polite and they are doing a fine job."

When she recovered from her initial shock the anger started to rise. I've been set up, she thought. I'll have this out with Graeme later.

After the initial catharsis the policeman, whose mercurial qualities caused her to think of him as Quicksilver, became calmer and accepted her invitation to sit down, though he never took his eyes off her. It was as if Graeme wasn't even there.

He prattled on about the SIU and their methods. He admitted he was gay and that the SIU had him under surveillance.

"You see, there are two kinds of surveillance, the sort where you know and the sort where you don't."

"Which was yours?"

"Mine was pathetic. I could see them all the time. I knew I was being followed all the time, I knew my phone was tapped. That's the worst kind of surveillance. I have been driven to the brink of suicide several times. Three times I have stood on my balcony and looked down, but I simply haven't had the courage to throw myself off. But the SIU are very polite and very kind. It's not their fault. They have a job to do and they do it in a very friendly way. So you must stop harassing them. It is causing them a lot of distress."

Aileen asked why the SIU worked in the way they did.

"Because they are so professional. You see, David Ford, Commissioner Henry and Michael Quinn have all been trained in psychological warfare and have all had a lot of experience in it. So they know the right way of going about these things, and they see the SIU do it properly."

Quicksilver was a naturally strong minded type of man and Aileen was surprised at the rather intense, desperate way he spoke. When he had gone she said to Graeme: "What a dirty trick. How could you set me up like that!"

"Believe me, Aileen, I am as amazed as you. I assure you I told no-one you were coming here today."

They looked at each other for some moments, the same thought going through both their minds. She was the first to speak: "It's either my telephone or yours."

"My very thoughts."

The next day she contacted Professor Harris of the Hong Kong University and got him to come on air and talk about psychological warfare. He said the sort of man most susceptible to brainwashing was the insecure type with personal problems, no friends, perhaps a character defect, preferably already under strain.

"Such as a homosexual?"

"Most certainly. The procedure is to find out his weakness and play on it, to put him under overt surveillance. He will then undergo a conviction reversal."

"You mean like believing an organisation is good when you know it is bad?"

"Exactly."

"What if the victim is normally strong minded?"

"If he had the weaknesses as I have described, that usually makes it easier."

Aileen ended by saying it would be interesting to know if the SIU had ever used such methods.

Soon after that Elsie and Aileen started getting replies back from their experts. Elsie's forensic pathologist gave a wishy-washy reply very different from his earlier enthusiastic comments. "It's almost as if he had been warned off," she said. Aileen had a reply from her friend in the <u>Sunday Times</u> to say he didn't think the MacLennan case would have any interest outside Hong Kong. The Home Office replied that investigations of a suspicious death in Hong Kong came outside the jurisdiction of the Home Office and the matter to which she had referred was not one in which the department could intervene. Dr Haldimann said he couldn't do a thing without the originals of the handwriting, and neither the New York Coroner nor his Australian counterpart replied at all.

But she got what she was looking for from a very unexpected source. Someone gave her a paperback called <u>The Onion Field</u>, a true story written by Joseph Wambaugh, a detective sergeant in the Los Angles police department. It was the story of a policeman who was shot five times with a .38 revolver. One bullet 'enters left upper chest, goes through the heart, diaphragm, liver, spleen, kidney and nicks the aorta.' The pathologist's report on this wound at the inquest was: 'It was a fatal wound inasmuch as it was a through and through wound of the heart. It was just about as promptly fatal as any could be expected to be. I'm sure that unconsciousness would result quite promptly in a matter of seconds . . .'

Aileen was in no doubt that the Los Angeles police and forensic pathologists knew a darnn sight more about wounds from a .38 than anyone in Hong Kong, so she was now convinced that, if the first wound in the Hong Kong case was the one Professor Gibson said it was, John MacLennan was murdered.

She leaked to the press the fact that the services of a top Swiss handwriting expert had been sought; a friend of hers in very influential circles got hold of a few of the editors of the Chinese press and told them they weren't pulling their weight. Meanwhile Elsie had a few very searching questions tabled with the Speaker of the House of Commons. She worded them so as to probe the UK link and thus to make them acceptable to Parliament. Briefly they sought to know why and when the SIU was established. Why did MacLennan leave the Metropolitan Police after only serving for six months? Did they have any reason to suspect he was homosexual? What was the relationship between the Metropolitan Police and the Royal Hong Kong Police? Was the UK Government aware of triad infiltration in the Hong Kong Police and if so what were they doing about it?

On 9th July 1980 the Governor, Sir Murray MacLehose, ordered a Commission of Inquiry to investigate certain allegations and key issues related to the death of John MacLennan. Out of his sense of justice, no doubt, he had the Attorney General make the announcement for him in the Legislative Council. The AG made the announcement on the day Elsie's questions were to be asked in the UK Parliament in London., which made the latter *sub judice*. Elsie rang Aileen, "That's a sneaky bit of timing, if ever there was."

"Why?"

"Because to answer the questions would reveal UK involvement in the MacLennan case, which would have rocked the establishment. The establishment of a legal Inquiry makes each *sub Judice* and because of the time difference there is ample time to withdraw them."

PART II

Chapter 29

In May 1980 John Conway retired at the age of 65 from his position of civilian firearms advisor to the Scottish Northern Constabulary in Inverness. He could look back on a chequered career ranging from outstanding successes in forensic investigation to a conviction for petty theft. But then the life of a private investigator is riddled with the most extraordinary pressures, almost beyond the comprehension of normal mortals.

Conway had served with the Metropolitan Police in London, where he specialised in forensic science, because of his interest in photography. His work covered a range of jobs, scene-of-crime photography, fingerprint enlargement, restoration of numbers and symbols erased from watches and machinery, examination of questioned documents, forged ration coupons and the like. He learned it all on the job. There was no formal training in those days. During World War II he served in the Navy, advancing his interest in guns. On his return he completed fifteen years service in the police and left to join the Coal Board.

It was while he was in the police that he became friendly with a policewoman, Margaret MacKenzie. John thought police life was a man's life and often chided Margaret for invading a man's world. But the chiding led to understanding and to affection and later they were married. Margaret was strong-minded and became the driving force behind much of John's later career. But, with a significance neither could have foreseen at that time, she came from the Black Isle and was closely related to Katie MacLennan. So John Conway was already linked with the MacLennans when he made his first excursion into civilian life.

It was an enticing job. In the police his promotion had been slow, all the more for his outspokenness. But in the Coal Board he was in his element, conducting infrared and ultraviolet tests and high-speed photography, investigating accidents and fires for an imaginative and appreciative boss.

After three and a half years and a further change of boss Conway looked around again. He soon found himself an experimental officer in the forensic science department of the Royal Ulster Constabulary. There were three sections; chemistry, biology and O&S (politely translated as Miscellaneous). Conway was in O&S, which included scene-of-crime photography, examination of questioned documentation, firearms and ballistics. With unstable conditions in Northern Ireland being what they were, he was soon overloaded. He was in and out of court like a tradesman. In one week he made it eight times and on one particular day five times. Conway being Conway, he made no bones about it and no doubt let it be well known what he thought about the management.

The crunch came when he was prevented from attending his father's funeral. He could contain himself no longer. He stormed into his superintendent: "I can't go on like this. I'm in court in the morning giving evidence on questioned documents and in the same court in the afternoon on ballistics. It's only a matter of time before some counsel discredits me by asking 'what sort of a specialist are you?' If you can't spread the load better that this I'm leaving."

It's not the sort of thing you say to superintendents. Before he had time to put it in writing he was given a month's notice. It may have been in the heat of the moment, because it was later extended to three and after he left he was offered the job back. But he didn't take it. Instead he advertised himself in the <u>Photographer</u> and Gerald Gurrin, a London Handwriting expert, replied and called him to an interview. Gurrin had been in the English Law Society's Law list for half a lifetime. There were two ways of getting on the Law List. You could earn it and be awarded a free entry or you could pay for an advertisement. Gurrin was one of the three free entries under the heading of 'handwriting expert'. Now he was getting on in years and Conway seemed the right material to train up, eventually to take over the business. So he took him on. Margaret landed a job with a firm of private detectives so things seemed settled.

But they weren't. Before he knew what was happening Conway was giving evidence in court against a police detective sergeant accused of framing someone. It was the first of many such cases.

John Conway was delighted when Margaret was put on a job to investigate thefts in a department store just around the corner from where he worked. He used to go and see her every lunch time—until he himself was stopped by the store detectives, searched and found to have a stolen article in his pocket. He was charged and convicted. Gurrin took the sympathetic view, paid for a solicitor and told Conway to forget it. Certainly he continued to work for Gurrin for another seven years. Did he really steal? Or was it a plant? The store was not so lenient with Margaret. Perhaps that was what it was all about.

He rapidly earned the reputation of being anti-police, to which he would almost gleefully reply: "Yes I am. I am anti-bent-policemen." But naturally enough there was a reaction, in the form of discrediting, furious cross-examination in court and on one occasion he was even prosecuted for perjury. He had been to court in Sheffield to comment on the fingerprint evidence presented by the police. His comment was that fingerprinting evidence should be presented as photographs, not photocopies, and he proceeded to show characteristics of the fingerprints in the photographs which were not visible in the photocopy.

"How long have you been doing this sort of thing?" asked the counsel for the prosecution.

"Seven years."

Then followed a prosecution for perjury. The case opened with the judge himself questioning the witnesses. "How long has Mr Conway been giving evidence in court on the photography of fingerprints?"

When three of the witnesses replied: "Over seven years", the judge directed the jury to return a verdict of not guilty, which they did. No defence was called. The counsels did not speak. John heard from his counsel afterwards that the judge had seen the difference between being an expert on fingerprints (which is what John was accused of claiming) and an expert in photographing them, and had concluded it was a trumped up charge. But it added another blot to a chequered career.

So Conway continued working for Gurrin and as the old man got older Conway had to support him in court more and more, until towards the end he handled the cases almost exclusively. Then in 1968 the old man, now over eighty, retired and Conway took over the business. It was thriving. He was known himself. At first he paid for his entry in the Law List, but when in 1971 one of the remaining two experts, Henry Rhodes, died suddenly, John wrote to the Law Society and asked if he could be considered as the official replacement of Mr Gurrin. They no doubt examined his record, his long apprenticeship with Gurrin and the frequency of his appearances in court. Duly, in 1972, he was awarded a free entry in the Law List and thus became one of the only two 'handwriting experts' so listed in England.

In 1973 the Conways moved up to Scotland. The English Law List didn't apply there and there was not the same call for document examination. So John Conway went back to firearms with the Northern Constabulary in Inverness. But he wasn't forgotten, and cases did arise where he was asked to conduct examination of questionable documents.

On one occasion in 1978 he was engaged by the Hongkong and Shanghai Bank to go to Hong Kong and investigate a case where the local police, in the form of no less a person than Mr Ronald Edgeley, had given the opinion that a signature was a forgery. Conway proceeded to upset them too by going a stage further and pointing out evidence suggesting that the plaintiff, a Thai millionairess, had forged her own signature—typical of John Conway. Once more he was 'anti-police'.

But it caused a problem. If his evidence was accepted, not only would it discredit the Hong Kong police, it would put them in the position of having to arrest the plaintiff they were supporting, for forgery. It was a very delicate situation. Apparently a message was sent to the Bank that their handwriting expert had been convicted of petty theft, prosecuted for perjury and dismissed from the Royal Ulster Constabulary. No doubt if he was put in court all this would have come out. It was at this stage that the Bank of America became enjoined, which delayed the case while they introduced their own experts. John was asked to submit all his photographic evidence and was quietly sent home.

Chapter 30

Conway was approaching retirement in the Highlands when the news filtered through to that remote region about the untimely death of John MacLennan and some of the mystery surrounding it. At first the Conways could do little more that read the press, take an interest and talk about it. But the enigma of the five 'self inflicted' .38 bullet wounds in the chest was a little more than John, with his background in ballistics, could take. And then there were the stories surrounding the alleged suicide note—was it genuine? After all, the evidence at the inquest seemed to have been given by his old friend Ronald Edgeley, backed by the opinion of a few acquaintances, if one was to believe the Scottish press. That wasn't the way John went about questioned document examination at all. He didn't put much value on the opinion of friends and acquaintances in the matter of handwriting.

So when he retired in May and the commotion was still going on in Hong Kong, Margaret suggested John offer his services to the MacLennans.

"But I want to set up my own private business in questioned document examination."

"That can wait a few weeks, John. Joe's blind and Katie won't even travel on a bus without him. What can they do to defend their son's name?"

It was stirring stuff. So, partly because of the strong Scottish family ties (the word 'clannish' didn't get into the English language for nothing), partly because the two areas of doubt—ballistics and handwriting—were right up his street, partly because his son Lloyd was now an inspector in the Royal Hong Kong police and it would be an opportunity to see him, and partly because he saw a chance to have a good old stir, Conway went along to Joe and Katie MacLennan and offered his services. Naturally they jumped at it.

Conway started to make his preparations. He didn't hurry. It was the middle of the growing season and there was a lot of work needed in the garden. He started to work out, however, how he could afford the fare and the stay in Hong Kong. A retirement pension isn't designed to cover that sort of thing. He had seen a name in the paper quite often, a Mrs Elsie Elliott, who seemed to be closely connected with the effort to get justice. He located her and she told him that as the parents' representative the government should support his visit, but in any case she had a fund to support public justice and she offered to lend him the money for the fare as an interim measure. So he booked his flight for 2nd August. On 9th July, however, the Commission of Inquiry was announced. This rather changed things. Was he still needed?

"Yes," said Margaret. "Joe and Katie are never going to be satisfied with an official statement after what the Attorney General out there has done to them. But they will take it from you. You go and get the truth."

So John went over to see Joe and Katie.

"Supposing I go and I find out your son was homosexual and he did commit suicide? Won't you wish I hadn't gone?"

"No, John, we would really like you to go. We want to know the truth. We can take it, whatever it is, because it can't be worse than the uncertainty we have lived with for the past six months."

"Well, since it is now a Commission of Inquiry you had better give me some sort of authority. Then I can officially represent you at the hearings."

"Yes, of course. What do you want us to do?"

John had been in and out of courts all his life, while Joe and Katie had hardly been off the farm except to got to church. He had a good idea of the form such authority should take. So he dictated it. Katie guided Joe's hand on the paper so he could sign, and she signed it herself.

Then Ron and Anne joined in. "This is a family matter, Dad, we'd like to sign too."

So John went off as the family representative, with all four signatures in his pocket.

Meanwhile Elsie was going frantic. The Hong Kong Government had appointed a counsel to represent the family through a firm of solicitors in London always used by the Hong Kong Government. Elsie saw this as yet another cover-up. She asked permission to appoint an independent counsel and was refused. She then asked if she could attend the hearings herself on behalf of the parents and was refused. So when John Conway rang her on 28th July, to tell her he was definitely coming, she was on top of the world. She told him to approach the London firm of solicitors to get official permission. She was so excited she rang Margaret Thompson.

"At last we are going to get the case for the defense."

Early the following morning Conway rang Elsie again to say he had obtained the official permission.

Meanwhile Aileen was still busying herself with handwriting and at 9 a.m. that morning she rang Margaret Thompson to ask if she could keep John MacLennan's letter a little longer. Of course she heard it all. About the angel from Inverness descending on Hong Kong and everything. As soon as she put the phone down it rang. It was Elsie: "Aileen, your phone seems to be continually engaged, night and day. Listen, I've got the most exciting news."

"About John Conway?"

"How on earth did you hear about that! I thought your grapevine was good. I didn't realise it was that good."

She was clearly a bit deflated by having lost the hottest story in Hong Kong, but it didn't put her off for long.

"I've no idea where he is going to stay, Aileen. He won't be very well off as a retired policeman. He certainly won't be able to afford our hotel prices. I've contacted his son, and he is in a tiny police quarter that couldn't possibly take a second bed."

"That's all right. He can stay with me. I have a spare room that my Dad uses in the winter."

"Do you mind?"

"Not a bit. Perhaps I will be able to give him some protection. You never know who might want to prejudice his judgment."

So it was decided that Aileen would go with Elsie to meet him at Kai Tak Airport on Sunday afternoon and take him home. Lloyd Conway was to be there too.

Elsie knew Lloyd and introduced him to Aileen. He was a tall, wiry, serious-minded young man. He had nearly completed his first tour with the Hong Kong Police and was leaving. It didn't surprise Aileen. He struck her as too good to stay. He complained that he and his colleagues were disturbed and angry about the John MacLennan case.

"Who with?" she asked.

"Our senior officers."

"Not with the public or the media?"

"Oh no. The whole thing's been handled so amateurishly we are ashamed to work for our seniors. The public and the media have every right to be perturbed the way it has all been bungled. Besides, none of us believes he could have shot himself five times. After all, a .38 is designed to stop someone coming at you with a knife. If you can turn that on yourself five times, all I can say is that the Hong Kong Police have got the wrong gun, and none of us who carry it are in any way protected by it."

Just then he spotted his Dad, and went to meet him. The women held back a moment. John Conway was ebullient, sharp-featured, slim and rugged. He came down the ramp into the arrivals hall at the trot as if he had just come off a short bus ride. He greeted them all with an eager smile and in a strong North Country accent said:

"Right, let's get down to it then."

Aileen felt a bit self-conscious as she drove home with two policemen in the car. As she cut the traffic lights a bit fine there was a chorus of: "We didn't see that." But when an austere Jaguar in front overtook another vehicle over a double white line the chorus was: "Take his number!" She was a nervous wreck before they were halfway. However, they arrived unscathed and she took John Conway into her home.

But she didn't know at that stage about his criminal record.

Chapter 31

Most people who survive the gruelling flight from London to Hong Kong are content to put their feet up for the rest of the day, and often for the rest of the week. Not so John Conway. All he wanted was a cup of tea and the inquest notes. Ah Sun provided the first and Elsie the second. When he had asked for his third cup of tea Ah Sun, who couldn't abide English names and renamed everyone who entered the house, decided he should be called 'Chartong' which, roughly translated, means 'English tea'. So, Chartong he became from that moment onwards.

Elsie was concerned with much more serious things. Aileen had seldom seen her so happy. She had carried the burden of the defence of John MacLennan for so long, and now Chartong was lifting it from her. What's more, he was experienced in ballistics and handwriting, the two very grey areas. What a bonus! She talked non-stop, telling him all the background, handing him files, folders, scrapbooks—till he almost disappeared under the mass of paper. They were closeted together for hours. Then he sat up reading it till well after midnight.

What he most wanted to know was how far they had got with the inquiry. Had he missed anything? They were able to reassure him on that. Though the Chief Justice had appointed a commissioner, Justice Yang, and the inquiry had opened eleven days earlier, it had been adjourned at once because the counsel for the parents, Conrad Seagroat Q.C., had not arrived. When he did he had to be formally admitted to the Hong Kong Bar, so that Chartong was just in time for the reopening. But representation of the parents was a point Elsie was not happy about.

"Appointing this fellow Seagroat will do nothing to quieten public suspicion, which is widespread. He was selected through a London firm of solicitors, Charles Russell & Co. I happen to know they are nearly always used by the Hong Kong Government for this sort of thing. Their Hong Kong office is not only in the same building, but in the same corridor as Hampton Winter and Glynn who are the solicitors frequently used by the Hong Kong police. If he is to be accepted as independent he has got to prove it. In fact, I don't think he's going to be able to, and I have already approached Members of Parliament and asked them to press for an independent inquiry in Britain.

"I've got nothing against Seagroat himself. In fact I don't even know him. It is not a question of personalities. But this particular case has been so mishandled and the public so misled that it is essential now to prove to the public that justice is being done."

Chartong managed to quieten her down quite a lot. "Don't worry your pretty little head," he said. "As a matter of fact there is more to Charles Russell & Co than most people know. I've done a bit of detective work on them. Here, settle down and I'll tell you a little story.

"Russell is the family name of the Dukes of Bedford and you can see it in the names of streets and squares all over Britain and the Commonwealth. When the New Territories lease was first signed, Lord John Russell, who later became Prime Minister, was the Foreign Secretary, and it came to his notice that triads were buying up land there and, had this been allowed to continue, China might have got the whole lot back. During his investigations Lord Russell discovered a great deal about the secretive methods of the triads and how difficult this made it to counter their work. He was successful in thwarting them, however, as can be seen in the New Territories today.

"So when, in about 1910, the then Home Secretary, Winston Churchill, sought his advice about forming a team of watchers to keep tabs on aliens with criminal intent, Lord Russell recommended they be formed along the same secretive lines as the triads. This became the basis of the British Secret Service. They adopted the triad code of anonymity and secrecy. Under the third rule of the code, that of exemption from prosecution, all activities by the watchers were classified under a blanket term of either 'in the national interest' or 'in defence of the realm'. This was easy to fix since they were formed by the Home Secretary himself.

"In 1947 a descendent, a solicitor named Charles Russell, opened an office in Lincoln's Inn, strangely only a few yards from the spot where his ancestor, Sir William Russell was executed under Charles II. He employed a solicitor named Mr Glynn who was shortly to go to Hong Kong and form a firm of solicitors in the name of Hampton Winter and Glynn. This became the Government's virtual in-house solicitors, looking after all the civil servants, doctors, nurses, and so on, especially the expatriates. Charles Russell followed later and formed a dual venture with Hampton Winter and Glynn. Although they shared offices and staff they remained separate entities. No doubt with their connections to Lord John Russell the legal firm of Charles Russell had been retained in many civil cases involving the British Government.

"But China turned to communism. It bordered the Soviet Union. So the burden of spying considerably increased the workload of military intelligence officers deployed in the area, especially at the Little Sai Wan communications centre, where several members of staff were believed to have triad connections. The constant threat of triad-backed charges of homosexual conduct by government officials and intelligence officers had to be guarded against by Charles Russell & Company who, should the need arise, could invoke the Habeas Corpus Act to preserve the anonymity and achieve the swift release of any person so arrested.

"Of course it is too late for this in the case of Johnny MacLennan, but it is interesting that Charles Russell & Co. have supplied the counsel to look after his interests. With their traditional background in triad activities Seagroat could be a good choice."

Elsie looked puzzled. "Are you saying that Hampton Winter and Glyn are representing the police and Charles Russell is representing the parents and the two firms are linked?"

"Yes."

"Isn't that like getting counsel for the defence and the prosecution from the same firm?"

"Something like that."

Elsie was impressed. She obviously had a lot of faith in Chartong. He told them some of his past experiences, even about some of his brushes with the police in England. But he clearly knew his guns and his documents and he was bent on finding out a lot more in these areas than the police had up till then.

Chapter 32

When Kevin came home after a long meeting, expecting some sort of welcome, he stood for a while staring at the three collaborators huddled over masses of paper and all talking at once. So he went into the kitchen to find Ah Sun.

"Him drink plenty tea. Very thirsty."

"Well I'm very hungry. How about a sandwich?."

"OK Master."

He had almost eaten it when Aileen first noticed him. "Oh, Hi. Didn't see you come in." He was introduced to Chartong, who clearly seemed distracted to be dragged from his detective work, so the relationship got off to a bad start.

Chartong spent all next morning reading the inquest notes. Then in the afternoon he went to the Hilton Hotel to meet Mr Seagroat and his solicitor, Alan Harrison.

After the show Aileen received a curious phone call.

"Aileen, it's Steve, Steve Corrick." Aileen remembered him from a few years back when she had interviewed him about illegal immigrants. He was at the time Senior Inspector in charge of the border police post, and she had had a wonderful drive through the most rugged country of the New Territories to see him and his two dogs.

"Steve, it's been a long time. How are the dogs?"

"I am afraid I had to get rid of them when I joined Government House."

Aileen was aware he had been appointed ADC to the Governor, but had not seen him since. "What a shame. Anyway, what can I do for you?"

"Can I come to tea?"

"Yes of course. Do you know where to come?"

"Of course, I'm still a policeman. See you about 4, if that's alright."

Aileen rang home to warn Ah Sun and was surprised to find herself talking to Kevin.

"What are you doing home?"

"I was at a meeting in the University and it was quite short, so I thought I would call in for a cup of tea."

"Stay and join us. You remember I spoke of Steve Corrick from the border post in Sha Tau Kok. Well he's coming to tea."

"Why?"

"I don't know, but he's ADC now, so he must be up to something."

"I wonder. Anyway I can stay for a bit. See you soon."

When Aileen arrived home she dived straight for her miniature tape recorder and crawled under the coffee table with it.

"What on earth are you doing?" asked Kevin

I am trying to bug the room. Get me some sticky tape and come under here and help."

"No need. I've got a wireless bug I have been playing with. That'll be easy to fix with a portable radio/recorder in the next room"

The coffee table was one of their prized possessions. It was quite long, made of Blackwood, and had a startling design of inlaid mother-of-pearl with a huge phoenix in the middle. It attracted everyone's attention and Kevin thought it was a bit of a risky place to put a bug. Anyway, he fetched the tape and between them they managed to fix the bug under the table.

None too soon, apparently, as almost immediately the bell rang and Ah Sun ushered in Steve Corrick, adorned with a huge handlebar moustache. As they were settling down Kevin slipped into the next room and set the tape going. They both had a strange feeling of conspiracy, He because he suspected he was doing something illegal, especially to the ADC of the Governor, and she because she had interviewed Steve before and he clearly now regarded her as above board with no funny business.

At first it was just niceties, but sure enough Corrick soon raised the topic of John Conway. "I hear he is staying with you."

Almost before Aileen could say "Yes" the door bell rang again and this time it was Chartong. Kevin couldn't resist "Talk of the Devil."

Steve seemed quite pleased and soon was questioning Conway about his experience and reasons for coming to Hong Kong. Steve did not overstay his welcome and within the hour was gone, leaving Aileen and Chartong to conclude that within another hour he would be making a full report to none other than the Governor, Sir Murray MacLehose himself.

"Fame at last," was all Chartong could say.

"I hope it's not just notoriety," said Aileen. "Anyway, how did you get on with Conrad Seagroat?":

"Oh, it was very friendly. They seemed very grateful for my past experience and said it should be helpful. Though I'll bet you they are telexing the Metropolitan Police in London at this very moment, checking up on me," he told Aileen.

But he was soon back among his papers and starting to ask awkward questions. "Did Sandra Hills really hear a shot, or was it a window banging after somebody had climbed out of it? Why did John MacLennan take his typewriter home? Why on earth write a suicide note on an envelope, why not on a piece of note-paper? What was the temperature on the night of January 14/15th? Would he have had his window open or shut?"

Of course, Aileen didn't know any of the answers, but it augured well for the lengths he was clearly prepared to go to get at the truth. There was, however, one question she could answer. "Aileen, I keep seeing references to an organisation they call the ICAC. Something to do with corruption."

"Yes, it stands for Independent Commission Against Corruption. It goes back to the early 70s when the government in general and the police in particular were so riddled with corruption, much of it triad inspired, that law and order was falling apart. Elsie was one of the leading protagonists, trying to get the extent of it recognised and something done about it. I did a program recently and some pretty scary statistics came out. For instance in 1960 Police Commissioner Henry Haule revealed that of the then 3 million inhabitants of Hong Kong one in six was a triad member. Then in 1970 the heroin trade started in earnest, which hugely increased the corruption in the police to protect the dealers. During this time Elsie made a lot of it public so in 1974 Governor

MacLehose established the ICAC with a staff of about a thousand and some very sweeping legal powers. For example the age old principle of being innocent until proved guilty was abandoned in the sense that if you had assets disproportionate to your income it was up to you to prove your innocence. This enabled the ICAC to start making arrests all over the place, putting hundreds in prison, though they always had trouble finding witnesses because of the triad oaths of brotherhood. In the end, in late 1977, there was a violent rebellion by the police, when several hundred, mainly station sergeants who were the triad organisers, marched on ICAC headquarters and attacked the staff. It was so serious MacLehose had to declare an amnesty, which became known as 'the corrupt amnesty', allowing the existing station sergeants to remain in post till their normal retirement."

"That must be the toughest crackdown on corruption in the world." commented Conway. Is there anywhere else that has done that?"

"I don't know. Not that I know of. It's written up in this 1976 Year Book if you're interested. You can read it up for yourself."

"Thanks. And tell me more about this press conference the Attorney General held."

"You can listen to the tape if you like."

"You bet'yer."

She sat him down in a comfy armchair with headphones—she had heard it too often herself already. But in the silence he presented a most amusing picture. He sat there with a frown on his face, muttering "Nonsense!", "No, he's wrong there," "He ought to get his facts right", with an occasional out-burst of "Absolute rubbish!"

She couldn't help asking him afterwards what was 'absolute rubbish'.

"That drivel about a .38 being slightly larger than a .22. A.22 is a relatively harmless bullet. It is not intended for shooting at people. The whole idea of a revolver is to knock a man down. That's why they used a .32 in the First World War. And even that on occasions wasn't enough, and men wounded with a .32 sometimes were able to follow through with a bayonet after having been hit. So they developed the .38 with the express purpose of stopping a man, which is exactly what it does.

"And did you hear all that nonsense about unconsciousness being starvation of blood from the brain. With a .38 it's nothing of the sort. It's a thing called hydraulic shock. If a .38 hits a main blood vessel unconsciousness is almost instantaneous.

"And did you notice he even got the name wrong. All the way through he calls him MacLellan, not MacLennan. They really are a sloppy lot here."

Aileen was to have many more lectures like that as the weeks went by.

Chapter 33

The next day Aileen went with Conway to the reopening of the inquiry. He was an immediate success. Conrad Seagroat referred very correctly to his 'considerable experience in ballistics and handwriting'. He then presented his credentials to Justice Yang, who had been appointed to head the inquiry and gave him permission to carry out any tests he wanted and to be given access to all the exhibits for that purpose.

The media were impressed. At last someone independent had come who was going to dig up the truth. All those months of hammering at a stubborn bureaucracy had been worth it. Some of the papers went a bit overboard and described Conway as a Scottish policeman, and a ballistics and handwriting expert, which, some weeks later, was to prove very damaging. But at the time people accepted it was very right and proper. Chartong was 'Surprise cop for inquiry'. 'Expert to do tests on gun and suicide note'. At last!

Justice Sir T.L. Yang was an interesting choice. He studied law in UK and was called to the Bar there. He later emigrated to China where he practised Chinese law, with its rather different emphasis. On moving to Hong Kong he became a District Judge. In 1975 he presided over the trial of previously Kowloon's Deputy District Commissioner Peter Godber, accused of bribery, during which Yang came very close to the tide of corruption and triads prevalent at the time.

The re-opening day was mainly taken up with the Counsel for the Commission, Mr Michael Neligan, recapitulating the inquest. Aileen and Elsie found it a disappointing address, in that it was a reiteration of the

141

previous one-sided inquiry, but probably it was a correct starting point. At one stage they were so disgusted they got up and walked out, thus missing a critical moment. Just after they had gone Mr Neligan referred to a well-known broadcaster who had betrayed a knowledge of this affair, and urged her to come forward. No doubt she would have done so there and then if she hadn't just left. As it was she heard it on TV that night where, so as to make no mistake, they took the extra step and identified her. Several of her friends rang up immediately and asked her what she was concealing from the Commission.

She felt a bit cheesed off and decided to say so on air the next day. She wasn't sure of the legal implications, so she wrote out the statement and read it to Nick before the program. It went: "I heard on TV last night that Mr Neligan has accused me of betraying a knowledge of the MacLennan affair and urged me to come forward, as if I were some fugitive from justice. I was a bit surprised to hear it since I have been in the habit of broadcasting everything I have found out about the affair and I am well aware that all such broadcasts are transcribed by the police and passed to the Attorney General's office. I therefore contend that, far from betraying knowledge, I have already supplied it in full. However, if Mr Neligan should feel that I could still be of use in the witness box I have no objection whatever to appearing there. He only needs to give me a ring, I broadcast the number every ten minutes, or he can write to me. I believe the address of Commercial Radio is well-known. However, I have some cause for reluctance. I would hate to be accused afterwards of submitting evidence which might later he described as gossip and tittle-tattle."

She noticed Nick had put his hands over his face and appeared to be weeping. She said: "If you feel like that why have you just given me a bonus?"

"I don't mind you as a person. It's only on air that I can't stand you."

However, having had his playful dig he had to admit he couldn't see anything wrong with it so she duly read it out on air.

Down in the studio, Frena was pouring over a news flash that had just come in. Confidential material had been leaked to a UK magazine about a hitherto secret group known as the Standing Committee on Pressure Groups, or SCOPG, The magazine, The New Statesman, published an article under the headline 'Colonialism: a secret plan for dictatorship'.

"What's all this about?" Aileen asked.

"They've unearthed a lot of snoops who are keeping pressure groups under surveillance, including Elsie Elliott. They've identified Johnnie Johnston of Government Information Services as a member of the committee and reported he was Lieut-Colonel in charge of psychological operations in Northern Ireland."

"Oh, not another!"

Derek, Aileen's main link with the news room, brought in the news headlines which started with China buying Gammon House from the Carrian Group for over US$ 200 million. There was also a comment about Elsie.

"What is it with this Carrian thing," Aileen asked Derek.

"On the face of it they are cashing in on the current property boom," he said.

"What do you mean 'on the face of it'?"

"Well, on the face of it they have just shifted $200 million of Chinese money into Hong Kong. But its much more than that. I have leads that more is coming in from British Barclays Bank and even more, much more, from Malaysia, from the Bank Bumiputra. Not millions but billions. Where is all the money going? What's it for? I'm taking leave next week to see if I can follow some of this up."

"Well, you be careful. Nick can give you some protection here, but not in Kuala Lumpur."

The red light came on and she read the headlines on air. A caller pointed out that the Hong Kong economy was doing very well out of communist money and had been doing so for years. Then Aileen got Elsie on the phone. "How do you react to being described in the British press as Hongkong's legendary one-woman opposition, teacher and Urban Councillor, who always has been under heavy surveillance?"

Elsie burst out laughing. "Yes it's true. They waste an unbelievable amount of effort on me. They even follow me into restaurants when I go for a cup of tea."

Then Aileen read out her statement. She was told afterwards it made Mr Neligan very angry but since, it was suggested to her, his own statement had been improper, he couldn't do anything about it. Certainly he never did.

Chapter 34

Meanwhile the inquiry dragged on. The pace was painfully slow and the same old witnesses came out with the same old evidence. When the lawyer, Stephen Llewellyn, was called he again claimed client privilege, as he had done successfully at the inquest, and failed to disclose what MacLennan had said to him the night before he died. Since Llewellyn was the last witness to speak at any length with the deceased, his testimony might have been critical, so the Judge asked for application to be made to the parents to have the privilege waived. Otherwise, it all started to look like an expensive rehash of the inquest. Just the very point the media had complained about—namely that the Attorney General had made no attempt to seek new evidence—seemed now to be perpetrated by the Commission.

Clarification regarding the bedroom windows, however, came out for the first time, casting a very dark shadow on the four witnesses, who had testified at the inquest that they had examined these, apparently without noticing they were covered with black photographic paper to achieve total darkness. Aileen said on air it was funny that all four should have failed to notice that fairly conspicuous fact. Chief Inspector Quinn went all through his story all over again, adding this time that he had applied to the Attorney General to take legal action against Mrs Elsie Elliott for criminal libel and had been turned down. He revealed that the SIU code name for John MacLennan was 'Miss Piggy'. He said some devastating things against Inspector Fulton, otherwise known as XYZ, including a flat denial of the attempt to set up MacLennan. That might not have been so bad except that Mike Fulton was not given the opportunity to defend himself till the following year. When asked why the SIU had only brought three cases to court in two years he replied they were short staffed—he only had a man and a dog. This was somewhat contradicted by a succession of witnesses from the SIU, one of which described MacLennan as being considered 'disposable' and another, Inspector Graham, admitting that they tapped telephones.

At last the waiver of privilege came through for Stephen Llewellyn to reveal what amounted to the last significant words of the deceased. Everybody waited with bated breath. At least this was something they hadn't heard before. For some it was an anti-climax. Nothing came of it that everybody didn't already know, since only matters that had arisen elsewhere were discussed. Llewellyn did report, however, that MacLennan was sure that the SIU were concerned with the Yuen Long incident and he clearly had no idea of any other charges to be brought against him, though the name "Peter" did come out in the conversation.

There was slight relief from the boredom when the police ballistics specialist, Mr Cimino, was in the box and Chartong kept passing notes to Mr Seagroat with some very curly questions. But nothing really came out of that either. When asked about John MacLennan's posture at the time of the shooting, all Mr Cimino could say was:

"I can't say if he was standing, sitting or kneeling. All I can say definitely is that he wasn't lying down." On the phone that evening Aileen commented to Elsie "Not exactly Sherlock Holmes stuff!"

The Commission flew two 'experts' out from the UK to give supporting evidence on forensic matters. And that's all they did. One spent most of his time telling the court what a respected person Professor Gibson was and describing at some length the effects of multiple stab wounds—which appeared to the laymen in the court to be absolutely irrelevant. It seemed a strange decision to pay for a flight halfway round the world for a man who admitted he had no experience of multiple gunshot wounds with a. 38. In the same phone call Elsie remarked to Aileen "Why not get somebody who had?"

At least he was a bit more definite about some things. He concluded that John MacLennan had fired the first shot through the abdomen while kneeling near the foot of the bed. He had then stood up and fired four more shots into his chest! He also felt that the photograph of MacLennan's anus proved conclusively that he was a practising homosexual. However, when Conrad Seagroat asked him if the state of the anus could have resulted from the use of instruments for sexual excitement during natural sexual intercourse, he admitted it could, which seemed to undermine the 'conclusive proof' somewhat. As if to clinch the alternative explanation, a girl was produced who said John MacLennan had kissed her.

But on one point the expert was particularly insistent. Namely that the police had been most remiss in not doing the chemical tests on MacLennan's hands.

"That test would have proved beyond doubt whether MacLennan fired the five shots that killed him."

Then came the matter of handwriting. The note was produced and Chartong suggested to Seagroat that is should have been protected in a plastic bag. Everyone from the Judge down heartily agreed. A plastic bag was duly produced to protect a note that had already been handled by dozens of people on both sides of the world! The second UK expert gave an opinion on his examination of it. Aileen was amused to note that he meticulously went through every point raised in the story she had broadcast by Simon Blake, without admitting so of course, but failed to refer to vital matters which by then Chartong had mentioned to her—such as the question of whether there was anything inside the envelope when it was written. Why were there no more envelopes like it among MacLennan's belongings? And if it was his last envelope, why was there no indentation of a band on it to indicate it came from a pack of envelopes? The judge received none of this evidence.

The witness was also asked if he had identified the pen that wrote it and he replied that he was unable to do so as the commission had 'lost it'.

The next day there was an elderly amah, aged 78, in the witness box, a Mrs Lai. It was very slow going because it all had to be done through an interpreter. After a while she complained she was cold, so Justice Yang sent for a shawl. She then complained she was still cold, so he had the air-conditioning switched off and everyone sweltered. The Counsel for the Police, Andrew Hodge, was a bit irritated and kept saying, 'Bear with me, madam.' Conrad Seagroat was more expert. He started off by calling her 'Madam Lai', apologising for having to ask her a few questions, and quite won her over. One of the other counsels spent a long time asking whether she had ever seen any stains on MacLennan's sheets. Finally Conrad Seagroat interrupted and asked the point of this questioning. The judge clearly didn't know what it was either. Counsel said he was trying to get a line on MacLennan's sexual activities. The judge commented, "Well, let's not beat about the bush. If you mean semen stains, say so. But you could get them whether he was heterosexual, homosexual or just plain masturbating."

Chapter 35

Around this time reference was repeatedly made to a list of homosexuals that John MacLennan had claimed to have seen. One day it got such prominence that Aileen played on her program a recording of the Lord High Executioner in <u>The Mikado</u> singing "I've got a little list".

The next day came the only real shock of the inquiry. It was the sudden disclosure, surprisingly by the counsel for the police, Andrew Hodge, that MacLennan had claimed that the Commissioner of Police, Mr Roy Henry, was on a file of prominent homosexuals. Andrew Hodge went on to say that this was totally unfounded. However, it was later disclosed that Roy Henry was indeed on 'the little list' of suspected homosexuals, so the press felt free to put him in the headlines. Aileen couldn't resist playing the song from <u>The Pirates of Penzance</u> proclaiming a policeman's lot is not a happy one. She had an anonymous caller after the program urging her to beware, as her life was in danger, a conclusion that she had suspected for some time, especially in quiet moments, and to have it confirmed did nothing to allay the feeling in the pit of her stomach that it might be the case.

Chartong was horrified. "Anywhere else in the world a disclosure like that would have been hushed up."

Aileen didn't know whether to be proud of Hong Kong or not. The disclosure itself was pretty shattering, but the apparent freedom of the press was rather encouraging.

Till Justice Yang stamped on it.

There followed a series of anti-media pronouncements by members of the Commission, threats of contempt and references to the law of *sub judice*, which resulted in the MacLennan inquiry coming almost permanently off the front pages and the accounts reduced to emasculated summaries of the evidence. It was overdone. Members of the Commission were heard to complain later about the lack of publicity they were getting.

Certainly Commercial Radio took it seriously and engaged, in spite of many protests, a criminal lawyer to look after Aileen. As it turned out they were absolutely right to do so.

On 26th August Mr Neligan was taken ill and returned to England, and for the next few days his place was taken by his assistant.

But, on the whole, what went on outside the inquiry was more interesting than that within it. On 5th August, a well-known kung fu actor, Ko Kong, got into an argument with a policeman who shot him in the chest. There were two interesting features of the case. The first was that only one shot was fired from a Hong Kong police .38 and it killed him instantly, which did nothing to support the theory that John MacLennan had shot himself five times. The second was that the police immediately pronounced, before there had been any investigation, that the shooting was considered entirely the fault of Ko Kong. This demonstrated in most timely fashion that the oft-repeated statement 'No foul play is suspected' should always be taken with a pinch of salt. Aileen was able to support this by broadcasting two other authentic cases where the police had pronounced 'No foul play is suspected'. The first was that of a woman found sewn up in a sack at the bottom of the harbour and the second was of a body found with feet, hands and head chopped off.

But the bit that really renewed public interest was where the Governor gave a rare press conference and announced that in his opinion the law on homosexuality should be changed to come into line with that in Britain. One might have thought that, when the Governor made such a statement, it would presage precisely such a change. But not in Hong Kong. It started off a whole train of correspondence in the papers. The Attorney General decided to go into print and give His Excellency somewhat watery support, but this only seemed to stir things up.

It was obviously a very emotive and little understood subject. Certainly to begin with, the correspondents on both sides of the argument seemed somewhat naive in their approach. The Chinese opponents asked why they should suffer from a Western colonial affliction, claiming that gay demonstrators only occurred in other countries, and that all homosexuals in Hong Kong were expatriates. The expatriates countered that homosexuality occurred in every society in the world. It was also suggested by the opposition that legalising homosexuality would cause a wave of vice and would be quite wrong when prostitution was not legalised.

In the end it was a Chinese voice that brought common sense to the argument and pointed out all the muddled thinking in the previous correspondence. Of course, nobody was trying to legalise homosexual prostitution, merely to prevent witch-hunts against consenting male adults and give them the same freedom as consenting female adults. Indeed, homosexuality was referred to in Chinese euphemistically as 'Playing with the flower in the back chamber' and often with marked tolerance in many masterpieces of Chinese literature, such as The Scholars and Dream of the Red Chamber. In any case the matter in dispute did not relate to a Chinese law, but to a nineteenth century British law.

Sensibly, having received a rational letter on the subject, the editor closed the correspondence. The fact was that attitudes to sex were widely different in China and the West, and Hong Kong came somewhere between the two.

But an interesting fact emerged later, namely that the previous Attorney General had tried more than once to have the law changed and it had been blocked by an elderly Chinese, a senior Executive Councillor, who contended that it was not a Chinese deviation. One wondered what he thought now of the eight male prostitutes, all Chinese, appearing in the MacLennan case.

A really intriguing story was that of John Richard Duffy. He was a lawyer with a particularly notorious record of finding loopholes in police prosecutions. Whether it was a coincidence or not nobody seemed to know, but in mid-1978 they decided to prosecute him for homosexual offences. So keen were they to get him, they ostensibly founded the SIU in connection with his case. By October they got a conviction and he was sent to gaol. This was certainly effective in stopping his success record in defending his clients.

Now the protagonists were eagerly awaiting his release so he could give evidence to the Commission, except that out of the blue he lost his remission. So Elsie decided to seek permission to visit him to find out why. She got it and on arrival in his cell he showed her photocopies of correspondence written from the authorities to someone in England asking for information that could be used to discredit John Conway. Where else in the world would a convict be able to produce such a document in his cell?

But that was not the end of the connection with the MacLennan case. When Chartong looked at the inquest notes he found it had been held on John Richard MacLennan. Indeed this was the man that had been cremated and the name on the casket of ashes sent to the parents. But there was no such person. There had been John MacLennan and there was John Richard Duffy, but no John Richard MacLennan. The inquest had been carried out on a non-existent man. There was much commotion when the Judge ruled that every document relating to MacLennan's case, including the death certificate and the inquest transcription, had to be amended.

One evening, Chartong referred Aileen to the terms of reference of the Inquiry, which were to determine whether: the death was other than suicide; whether there were any shortcomings in the investigation; and whether the charges were properly brought; and investigations carried out with propriety and relevance and were properly motivated.

"These are limited," he pointed out, "to matters surrounding the death, whereas the title is an Inquiry into Inspector MacLennan's case, a much broader concept. That means that anything that is not immediately related to the death can be regarded as irrelevant, such as the impact on people in power of things he found out. It is interesting that they have already focussed and spent a lot of time on evidence that might indicate Johnny's sexual inclinations, but as soon as it was hinted that he might have uncovered the homosexuality of the Commissioner of Police it was immediately ruled irrelevant, so we can't enquire what effect such a disclosure might have had on Johnny's superiors' attitude to him. I think we should keep a close watch on that."

Chartong could not immediately follow up on this point because on 22nd August the inquiry adjourned so that Justice Yang could go on his two-week holiday. Chartong flew home on the same day. He didn't see that he could do much in Hong Kong during the adjournment and he wanted to give the MacLennans a progress report and get power of attorney from them to settle John's estate. His parting words to Aileen were: "You'll see. This affair won't stop at the end of the Inquiry. There will have to be a massive purge of all the top homosexuals. It's their very presence that prevents effective screening lower down in the hierarchy. They'll have to go. Not all at once, of course, but you'll see, they'll all disappear, one by one."

Aileen could foresee a steady disintegration of the Hong Kong Government.

Chapter 36

It was August the 22nd. Aileen was just coming to the end of an on-air call about the iniquities of pulling down that notorious piece of colonial architecture, the Hong Kong Club, when she noticed through the soundproof studio window Frena, her producer, pointing to her temple and rolling her eyes. She and Frena had a very rich vocabulary of signs and this one meant there was a nutcase on the line and Aileen had better have a word off-air first before she unleashed him onto an unsuspecting public. So they faded in some music and she found herself speaking to Robert, who claimed to be a homosexual and an intimate friend of John MacLennan. This clearly warranted much more than the between-call off-air time she could afford, so she arranged to meet him after the program the next day, at a restaurant in San Po Kong, though he was most insistent that she came alone. She left her technician to take down the address in Chinese and returned to the program.

As she was winding it up the head of news room himself, Jerry, came in with the headlines and sat down looking very shaken. As soon as they were off air Aileen said "Whatever is the matter".

"Derek's dead."

"What? Where? Whatever do you mean?"

"His body was discovered in a ditch in Kuala Lumpur with his throat cut."

"How dreadful. What's being done about it?"

"Apparently the Hong Kong police have offered to assist, but the Malaysian police have said no thank you. I gather he was following up a few leads on the Carrian case. He must have touched a nerve."

It was a very shaken Aileen who put her tape recorder in her handbag, gave the Chinese address to a taxi driver and set off into a seething industrial area virtually unknown to Westerners. The journey seemed to be through miles of housing estate. These were the early type of concentrated, relatively low-level, but huge blocks of single-room flats at Wang Tau Hom, interspersed with busy market-filled side-streets, giving way to the later model, higher—but thus even more concentrated—blocks of Wong Tai Sin. Masses of people flowed around like the currents of a whirlpool, chattering and shouting, energetic, tackling the incredible challenges of their life. Up till then there was a main through road. There seemed to be nothing beyond. But San Po Kong was at the heart of it all. You got the impression it led nowhere, that you had been sucked into the whirlpool of life. When the taxi stopped at a low-class Chinese restaurant, she appeared to have hit rock bottom.

Aileen wasn't sure whether to pay the driver off or hold to him for a possible getaway. She hesitated, swayed uncertainly towards the former, paid him off and fought her way through the pavement masses, trying not to tread on the sleazy magazines displayed by some hawker all over the path. She pushed open the restaurant's smeared glass door to be met by a blast of cold air, an ear-crunching clatter of plates, and the shouts of the waiters and *dim sum* (dainty morsel) sellers. Above it all came a plaintive but distinct "Aileen".

At a table near the door sat an insignificant but neatly dressed and groomed Eurasian boy of about 20. Though the restaurant was crammed he had saved her a place and she sat down. He spoke very good English with a slight American accent. He was fluent and obviously had a lot to get off his chest. He seemed quite happy that she should record the conversation so she did, though a Chinese restaurant is the last place on earth one would choose in which to make a recording because everyone speaks/shouts at once and expects to be heard.

Robert told her freely he was wholly homosexual, not like John MacLennan who he said was bisexual and went with both boys and girls. As he put it: "John was not a practising homosexual. By that I mean he didn't do it like a usual gay person does. If he did it would be once in a blue moon, or when he'd had too much to drink, or wanted company, someone to hold on to in bed. He never paid. He only wanted to go to bed with people for friendship, never payment. I have been to bed with John several times but I have never received anything, money or gifts or anything. These male prostitutes are telling lies. I think they have been paid to give their evidence against John."

His story was that he had known John MacLennan for about five years, since before the Yuen Long affair. They had become very friendly and John had confided in him about being harassed by the SIU. He described how they spent the night together on New Year's Eve in John's flat and the phone rang at 6 a.m., when a voice said "Happy New Year you big queen". He remembered it was a red telephone. John got very annoyed and took the receiver off so they could go back to sleep or whatever. At 8.30 am they got up and dressed. They decided to go out for a swim. They found Victoria Park swimming pool closed so went to the beach at South Bay on Hong Kong Island. Robert related how, on another occasion, John had become convinced his telephone was bugged and he took off the mouthpiece and earpiece, but found nothing there.

On 11th January, Robert said, he left Hong Kong with his parents and he and John promised to correspond. He did receive two letters from John, one dated 13th, one dated 16th. He assumed John had died on the 17th. Robert, in fact, never wrote back.

When he arrived back in Hong Kong in mid-August he was met at the airport by two Chinese and a European wearing clip-on warrant cards, who told him "Stay out of the MacLennan case or you had better be very careful where you walk." He was very frightened. About a week later he had been to the Park Cinema and afterwards went to a restaurant nearby. When he came out he was met by the same two Chinese, but a different European, who pinned him against a wall and searched him. They took one 500 dollar bill from him and two 250 US dollar bills plus 60 dollars cash. They also took his travellers cheques his parents had given him. Also some personal belongings, a gold chain and a ring. They said: "We want to get this MacLennan case over thick and fast. So stay out of it. This is what will happen to you if you get involved." He said he went home and cried for three hours. Always after that he felt he was being followed. She asked him if he had reported this to the police, but he simply replied: "How can you report the police to the police?"

It was very strange that at that moment two Chinese and a European came up to their table as they were talking. This European wore jeans and a Hawaiian shirt and carried a bag over his shoulder. They stared for a moment and then went out.

"Oh bloody hell, bloody fucking hell. There you are," he said. "It's them. They are SIU."

"How do you know? They could have been just as surprised to see me here as I was to see them."

"Can't you see? I know the buggers, I recognise them. They follow me. Besides, the jeans, teeshirt and the navy bag, it's practically SIU uniform, they always dress that way, believe me."

He said he had been very close to suicide, which gave Aileen the opening she needed to ask about the scars on his arms, crisscross scars up the inside of each arm and looking quite recent. He told her he had in fact tried to commit suicide by slashing his arms with a razor blade, but that he had been taken to hospital. "I'm not a male prostitute. I am gay but I don't sell myself. Nor do I advertise myself as being gay. Being gay has many meanings. Some people do it as a living. They have no choice. Some people have a background of too many children in the family, perhaps all boys. But I don't want to be treated like a one-night stand. I want something lasting. I don't go to bed with somebody because they pay me. I go to bed with someone because I want to. Also because I hope it is going to remain a friendship.

"But some guys take advantage of you. One called Gordon Huthart, related to the owners of Lane Crawford Department Store, took me to his flat and gave me drugs. He gave me Mandrex and then brandy. I was out of my mind. I would have done almost anything. In about fifteen to twenty minutes your body and your muscles feel so relaxed and your arm feels it weighs ten tons. You can't lift it and you can't seem to fight. You know he's doing it to you but you can't seem to push him away. You don't have the strength.

"The worst of the lot is Ian McLean. He's really evil and wicked. He's the owner of the antique shop in front of Central police station. He's a very fat European. He lives up Victoria Peak. They call his place McLean Mansion. A lot of Chinese know him. They call him Dai Yee Man. Translated it means big second mother, which is like <u>mama san</u> or brothel keeper, because he looks like one and is so feminine in how he speak and dresses. He's huge and fat and ugly. Something like bald but curly and all."

Aileen asked if Ian McLean employed male prostitutes.

"He's not a <u>mama san</u>. But he gets all sorts of kids, little kids. I for one know he carries grass on him 24 hours a day on his body. I've actually been with him and he carries it in his handbag, in his car, in his house and . . .'

"Heroin?"

"No, marijuana—grass. He even grows it. In his home. In flowerpots. I don't think it's fair the way they picked on John MacLennan. Why didn't they pick on some of the big boys, like Ian McLean? And why do they only arrest Europeans? I know a lot of Chinese big shots here in banks, studios, and so on. Why didn't they arrest the male prostitutes? I think it is very unfair they only pick on European people. In such a case I should be arrested."

Aileen watched him as he prattled on. The waitress came with more noodles, then merged again into the gloom of the restaurant and the grimy plastered walls. She couldn't make him out. Was he a phoney? Certainly he had told her a load of what could be lies, probably more than she knew. Yet a lot of what he had told her he could have read in the press report of the inquest. But he had come out with a few facts that took a lot of explaining. How did he know John MacLennan's telephone was red? Because it was, though that had never been in the press, or at least not in the English press. How did he know it was in the bedroom and not in the lounge? She had no doubt at all he had known John MacLennan. He was too fluent for it all to be imaginary. Yet John MacLennan died on the 15th January, not the 17th, so if Robert had a letter from him dated the 16th it should be a very interesting document.

As they parted she asked him next time to bring the two letters, but she had the feeling there would not be a next time. That weekend she and Kevin were to stay at the Royal Hong Kong Golf Club at Fanling, in the New Territories, close to the Chinese mainland border. Kevin had arranged to play with some friends and Aileen took the opportunity to be away from the telephone, alone with her thoughts.

If Robert was genuine, then the implications were pretty significant. It meant the male prostitutes produced by the SIU were almost certainly phoney; that Elsie's disclosure about the attempted set-up involving Inspector Fulton was probably true, and all that indicated there was a unit in the police operating Gestapo methods entirely outside the law. On the other hand if Robert was a phoney why did he make contact with someone in the media? He didn't seem to want publicity. He had dragged her out to a most obscure restaurant in San Po Kong. He kept on telling her how frightened he was of the police, especially the SIU. How he wanted her to go to Justice Yang on his behalf. He wanted to stay out of it. So what did he stand to gain if he was not sincere? Aileen's thoughts ranged over bizarre possibilities. Was it a set—up? Was he in the pay of the SIU to get her to broadcast things he had told her so they could have her for libel or just get her in the witness box so they could crucify her? At least that would explain the intimate details of John MacLennan's flat. She puzzled over these suspicions all weekend and came no nearer to a conclusion.

Chapter 37

She arrived home on the Sunday night to be told someone had been desperately trying to get in touch with her. He had tried her home, Commercial Radio and several of her acquaintances. At 11.30 that night he finally reached her. He sounded desperate.

"Aileen?"

"Yes."

"I have been trying to get you. I have been so frightened."

"Why, what has happened?"

"After I left you someone rang me and said there was a job going in Central. So I went there and was met by three policemen. They said that they told me not to get in touch with anybody, not to speak to anybody, then they beat me. They punched me in the face and in the stomach. I was taken to Queen Mary Hospital. I'm so frightened. Simon was with me."

"Who's Simon?"

"He's my friend from Hong Kong University."

"Robert, will you meet me again?"

They arranged to meet at the same restaurant in San Po Kong. He said he would bring Simon.

"And don't forget those two letters."

This time she did not pay off the taxi. She kept it as a getaway. She went into the restaurant, grabbed Robert by the arm, stuffed him into the taxi and directed the driver to the United Services Recreation Club,

Though not confined to the military, the club was one the SIU would probably consider off limits.

When they were halfway there Robert said: "What about Simon?"

"Where was he?"

"It wasn't quite three o'clock. He hadn't come."

"We can't go back now. I'm sorry about that, but you will be quite safe here, I promise."

Aileen took him into a small annex off the main club lounge, and for the first time looked at him carefully. Sure enough he had a bruise on his face. He pulled up his teeshirt and showed her some pretty florid abdominal bruises too. Clearly he had been in some sort of a brawl.

"Where are the letters from John MacLennan?"

"I haven't got them. When I got back after ringing you my flat had been ransacked."

In the quiet of the lounge she made another recording, partly because the first was so obscured by the clattering of plates it was of limited value, and partly because she wanted to double check the facts. She did. They double checked all right. Whatever motivated his story it was at least consistent.

Before they parted Aileen told him to ring up her friend, a young Irish American priest, Father Sean Burke, who looked after a shelter for the destitute elderly called Helping Hand. Aileen thought that would be a safe place to hide Robert while she got his evidence properly presented. But he didn't ring. He tried to commit suicide, again.

Meanwhile Aileen rang up Elsie. She was often approached by characters like Robert, but she couldn't identify him. Neither could Father Burke. Still searching, Aileen got a bit of a lead from a lawyer friend, to whom she told the story. When she mentioned the European who approached them in the restaurant in his Hawaiian shirt with a bag over his back, he laughed:

"Didn't you know? That's the SIU uniform."

"That's what Robert said."

"He's right!"

"What do I do with the tape then?"

"Take it to the Attorney General."

"You've got to be joking."

"I'm not. You may have misjudged the AG. He wanted an independent inquiry right from the start but he was overruled. You might find him a lot more receptive than you think."

But other people advised against such a course, and Aileen continued ringing around trying to make up her mind. There was a long silence from Robert. She began to get very worried about him. She was beginning to expect to hear about a body found floating in the harbour, with no foul play suspected. It was therefore a relief when the phone rang and she heard his voice:

"I'm in the Tang Siu Kin Hospital. I swallowed a lot of Valium. They are transferring me to Queen Mary Hospital in a couple of days."

"I'll come and visit you. We must get you protection."

"How can you get me protection from the police against the police? Besides, I'm very ill at the moment, and I've not given my real name and address. I'll ring you again from Queen Mary. Come and see me there."

She never heard from him again.

She meticulously tried to check out his story. The bit about swimming on New Year's Day was wrong. She discovered that John MacLennan had spent what he called 'Hogmanay.' at a small police station far up in the New Territories where they played tapes of Andy Williams through the night. But still much of what he had told her did appear to be accurate.

Aileen became increasingly concerned for the boy's safety and felt rather responsible.

She started asking about him all over town. She had no picture to go on but she was able to describe him accurately, for he was pretty distinctive. She talked to a psychologist about the scars on Robert's wrists, how there were so many. He told her this was a well-known symptom of schizophrenia, and that a lot of his story was probably imagination.

One morning she had a call off-air from someone who thought he had met Robert. She arranged to meet him in a little restaurant in the heart of Central district, by the side of the Hilton Hotel. It was a favourite meeting place for gays. She played some of the tape and he recognised his voice immediately.

"Oh, yes, no doubt about it. That's Slasher George."

"Slasher George?"

"Oh, yes. He's the son of a prison officer, who has disowned him. He's well known for trying to commit suicide by slashing him arms. His brother pulled it off I believe."

As they sat there another young Chinese came over and added to the story. 'Slasher George ' was well known in the gay world. It seemed that a few days before, a 'cruiser' picked up what he took to be a male prostitute outside one of the big hotels in Tsimshatsui. They got into a taxi and the boy started to brag to him how he had told his story to Aileen of Commercial Radio. The 'cruiser' was scared and said how he hated a loud mouth, then opened the door and threw 'Slasher George' out of the taxi onto the busy street.

It was during all these enquiries that 'Raven' came into Aileen's life. One morning when she arrived in her office she found on the desk a typewritten envelope with her name on, marked Confidential. Usually Frena opened and dealt with all the mail. Typically it consisted of invitations to attend a new act in one of Hong Kong's glamorous night spots, requests to judge a local event, or talk to Rotary or PR companies seeking interviews for their clients. But this one was marked 'Confidential' and it was unopened. Inside was the brief message, "RING 3564991 and say 'this is Claire'. Do this from an extension off the main switchboard, not a direct line."

She went into the canteen, which was busy at that time of day. Many of the Chinese did not have cooking facilities in their small apartments so they came to work for their breakfast which consisted of a bowl of Congee, a sort of savoury porridge. They sat on small circular stools at large round tables, chattering enthusiastically.

She dialled the number, which was answered immediately, and gave the name Claire. Then a voice that was to become very familiar to her in the weeks ahead said, "Where are you calling from.?" She told him she was in the radio station's canteen.

"That's OK. You have been asking a lot of questions about a young man who gave you information."

"Yes, do you know where he is? Is he O.K.?"

"You needn't worry about Slasher George any more, he is quite safe."

"How do you know? Have you seen him?"

"Yes. Trust me. Just don't worry any more. He is perfectly safe."

Aileen felt relieved, but when she tried to question the voice further the only reply was a 'click'.

After that Raven became an important part of her investigations. The voice was all she ever knew him by, but obviously he was a policeman in a pretty influential position, judging from some of the information and leads he gave her. Since they always turned out to be genuine she began to trust him, and because he always spoke in a quiet croaking voice she called him 'Raven'.

Finally, she discovered why Raven had told her Slasher George was so safe. He was in jail for two months for passing a dud cheque. Her faith in his story was waning. She began to think it was of little importance and probably the best thing for everybody would be to forget about the tape.

That turned out not to be one of the options.

Chapter 38

The headline in the <u>South China Morning Post</u> read 'Top British Detective Arrives'. The story went on to describe a top man from Scotland Yard who had resigned at the peak of his career, "The legendary Vincent Carratu, a former top Metropolitan Police fraud squad expert . . . used to the blood and guts of murder inquiries . . .", and now in Hong Kong in connection with the MacLennan case

Aileen's thoughts were on this new development as she left home, swung her car onto the road and accelerated towards the city. Within moments the car was careering from one side of the road to the other, almost out of her control and she narrowly missed one of the sheer drops on the right before she brought it to a halt. Very shaken she stepped out to see a flat front tyre and walked back to the flat to fetch Boff.

He took one look at the tyre and exclaimed "Oh my God!"

"What?"

"Look at this," and he extracted a new shiny nail. "This has never been used and has not been lying on the road because there is not a scrap of rust on it. Do you realise what that means?"

"It means someone has dropped a new nail."

"Or someone drove it into your tyre during the night so that when you started it would be hammered in the rest of the way and cause a puncture on this dangerous road."

"Don't be silly. That's what they call a conspiracy theory. For goodness sake put the spare on so I can get to work."

But Boff was not in such a hurry. He checked the other three wheels first and found another shiny new nail which had skewed sideways on the other front tyre so had not penetrated.

Then he fitted the spare, and as she jumped in to drive away said, "Can't you see you are in grave danger? I think you ought to resign the job altogether before you get killed."

Unable to provide a satisfactory answer, she drove off.

It was about this time that the London <u>Sunday Times</u> of 7th September filtered through to Hong Kong. The popular in depth feature article 'Insight' had a whole page devoted to the MacLennan case. Aileen had sent the facts of the case to the Diplomatic Correspondent some time before and the result was that the Insight editor, John Ball, himself the son of a senior policeman, had been to see her. He was an excellent journalist, deeply probing, intelligent, easy to talk to and Aileen had faith in his integrity. It must have been the same with everybody because the article contained confidential information that had not yet been submitted to the inquiry. It was a mini-inquiry of its own, complete with naming the Commissioner of Police as 'under investigation', evidence of a frame-up against MacLennan, evidence of blackmail and discrimination by the SIU, deep suspicion about the suicide theory, and an excruciating photograph of Quinn, that was almost a conviction in itself, with the caption 'We're going to drop you right in it'. It also introduced Gordon Huthard, the son of a prominent Hong Kong businessman, who openly admitted his own homosexuality and was an outspoken campaigner for gay rights. He ran an immensely successful discotheque in Central, "Disco Disco", which advertised Thursdays as 'Boys' Night'. The article concluded by stating that Gordon Huthard, and lawyers Howard Lindsay and John Duffy, were among the first victims of the initial crackdown by the SIU, although in Huthard's and Lindsay's cases this targeting had proved unsuccessful.

Reading the article, Aileen thought that Disco Disco was worth a visit. She rang Chartong. "Would you like to come to the club where many of the gays involved in the MacLennan case hang out?"

"You bet."

"I have to see a show in the Eagle's Nest in the Hilton Hotel. Eartha Kitt's the star and I'm interviewing her on the program tomorrow. What about meeting me afterwards? I should be free by midnight."

"Great, I'll wait in the coffee shop."

Aileen left the Eagles's Nest just before midnight and went downstairs. The coffee shop was decorated with photos of old Hong Kong antique markets around Hollywood Road and Cat Street, illuminated by spotlights. The table candles twinkled on her beaded black sleeveless shift dress as she made her way to a far corner. There she found not only Conway but a good looking personable young man with him, in short-sleeved open-necked cotton shirt and well cut jeans ideal for the warm muggy night. Conway wore something quite similar but managed to make it look scruffy. Aileen was excited when Conway introduced his companion as none other than the mysterious XYZ, Senior Inspector Mike Fulton.

Chartong was industriously piecing the evidence together as always. Aileen joined in with her questions.

"So it was you who was asked to set up MacLennan? I admire your guts in coming forward. Can you tell us about it?"

"Yes, I've decided to speak out but it has been a difficult decision. Because in the interests of the administration of justice, no police officer should comment publicly on a case. However the Attorney General issued a public statement stating that I have denied I was asked to frame anyone. I must put the record straight as that is just misleading the public. In fact I <u>was</u> instructed by Chief Inspector Michael Quinn of the SIU to take boys to MacLennan's flat, with the idea that they could catch him with them in his apartment red handed. I never complied with such an instruction, but the intention was quite definitely an unscrupulous set-up, though not a frame."

"Can you say how you became involved with the SIU yourself? Forgive my asking, but are you a homosexual who they have power over?" Aileen asked

Mike drew the line and said that he couldn't say any more. But he did add that his friend. former crown counsel, Howard Lindsey was waiting in Disco Disco. Aileen caught Chartong's excitement.

"Wow, Mike, isn't he the lawyer they tried to nail on homosexual charges? The one who defended himself and proved that all the evidence against him was given by paid male prostitutes and was trumped up? The one who tied them all in knots and got acquitted? The one who took the Attorney General to task for having no integrity?"

Mike smiled. "The very same."

"What are we waiting for? Let's go."

Chapter 39

They stepped out into the warmth of Queen's Road with its garish neon signs, glowing Chinese characters in red, blue, yellow and green, and went up a relatively dingy steep side-street. It became increasingly dismal as they plodded through the remains of a flower market and the street became darker and narrower and steeper. Just before it curved to the left, into the unknown, there was a dark but rather plush entrance on the left, going down into the depths of flashing lights, mirrors, and the reverberating thump-thump of the disco.

Gordon Huthard himself was at the door, presenting a slightly soiled, unkempt look despite his black shirt and well tailored beige suit. He was very pasty-faced, almost emaciated. He looked as if he had not seen daylight for years. He took them into his corner sanctuary, a pillared alcove modeled after a scene of some Roman orgy. He told them in a complaining whine about the constant police raids and harassment; how his phone was tapped; about his arrest and discharge; how he was accused of serving liquor to a minor and how the police trumped up evidence to get his liquor licence revoked.

"Quinn's behind it," he said. "How he has the gall, after the corruption scandals he was involved in! It is well known he was Hunt's deputy."

"Hunt? The one who was in the middle of the Godber corruption syndicate a few years ago?"

"Yes. He gave evidence against Godber in return for immunity."

Mike stepped in. "That's true. The Independent Commission Against Corruption, what we call the ICAC, was young at that time and they had to get Godber back when he absconded to save its face, in fact it's very existence. They couldn't get him on normal corruption charges because they were not extraditable offenses. So they had to get him for bribery. That needed a witness. Rumor has it they had to pay Hunt handsomely to do it."

Gordon wasn't used to being supported by a policeman. "So how could the deputy to a man like that be innocent?"

Aileen changed direction. "Gordon, from the descriptions I'd always imagined this place to be in some sort of constant disorder. I don't know, I suppose I thought there would be triads creeping out of the woodwork and brawny men beating up the gays."

He grinned. "I'm protected. Not like the Backdoor."

"The Backdoor?"

"Yes. The other disco. They refused to pay the protection money. On their opening night someone released fifty snakes on the dance floor."

Then he showed his visitors proudly round his brash club and left them sitting on the edge of the dance floor with drinks 'on the house.'

Mike must have thought some explanation was necessary. "Gordon doesn't have to pay protection money. He has a close relative who is said to be the mistress of the head of the 14K Triad Society."

The floor was full of male couples swaying seductively to the beat of the loud canned music. There was a strange energy about the place. Aileen recognised it as the same energy she experienced when Boff snuggled up close. But that was an intimate force. This energy pervaded the whole premises.

After a few minutes Mike got up and brought back a handsome well dressed macho type, holding a glass of beer. The casual but expensively dressed man held out his hand, "Hi, I'm Howard Lindsay."

"He's come from Gibraltar where he runs a thriving legal practice." chipped in Mike.

Howard sat down and took no time getting stuck into his story. He had been Crown Counsel with the Legal Department, who was himself one day arrested for homosexual activities.

Aileen interrupted and asked if he would have his say on tape, so that she could broadcast it on her radio program. Howard agreed with alacrity. The noise was overpowering by the side of the dance floor so they wandered off to find a quieter alcove. The small room they found gave Aileen the definite impression, from its liberal distribution of cushions and its sweet sticky smell, that it was more often used for activities of a distinctly illicit nature. It suited her purpose though so she turned on her recorder. Howard began to tell his story.

"I was arrested at 6.30 a.m., and said little or nothing to the policemen until 10.30am when they charged me. I just wrote on some of the charge sheets 'These people are blackmailers'.

"After that I had a conversation with Quinn, who said they had considered not giving me bail because they knew I had suffered a nervous breakdown. They were worried that if they released me on bail I might commit suicide.

I was then transferred to Central Police Station in Hollywood Road and left with the station sergeant. He said since I was under arrest I shouldn't be in that particular room because it was the public part of the office. I was directed into an adjoining room and left there, alone, for about half an hour. I was shocked because on one of the chairs were two police holsters with apparently loaded revolvers. I examined one out of curiosity. At the time I assumed it was simply a case of gross incompetence. It was fairly typical of the standards of the Hong Kong police to put a person under arrest into a room with loaded revolvers, almost inviting him to shoot his way out. In retrospect and in the light of the MacLennan case, I think Quinn's reference to suicide, followed by this exposure to the guns, could have been a deliberate temptation. It would be consistent with the kind of psychological pressure he used on MacLennan. At that time, however, I was convinced that it was simply sloppy procedure on the part of the police. Now I feel differently.

"In court I was confronted by male prostitutes of very questionable integrity, whose evidence was full of loopholes. The magistrate found no case to answer and I was duly acquitted.

It all seemed very familiar. Howard went on to say that he had got on the wrong side of both the Attorney General and Quinn, about whose conduct he had written a formal complaint. It was not difficult to believe Howard had been added to the target list.

After he left Hong Kong, he told her, he wrote a scathing letter to the Attorney General, who replied saying that he did not like Howard's suggestion that he had acted dishonourably. Howard said he wrote back: 'I don't think you acted at all. You are like Brutus.'

Aileen was amused at the thought that Howard should have been independently reminded of the same passage in Shakespeare as she was.

Aileen and Lindsey went back to the table on the side of the dance floor. Mike had introduced Chartong to several of the 'gays' and they had all opened up to him. Mike Fulton then suggested the two meet and have a long chat later in the week.

"I'll give you a ring."

"Watch it. Aileen's phone is tapped."

"Yes, so is mine. I'll ring you and ask if you are going bowling. That means meet me at the Star Ferry."

Chapter 40

Aileen wandered into the main part of the disco. She was greeted by several acquaintances that she had no idea were gay, but now they looked every inch of it in the dim flashing colours and their off-duty dress. As the loud thumping music numbed her ears the dancers, mostly Chinese males, danced together, rubbing against each other, in tight embraces. They lunged erotically, with hands caressing buttocks and thighs, kissing sensually as they did so. Most of the dancers were completely uninhibited to the extent that Aileen found herself wondering how many were on drugs. Certainly the sweet distinctive smell of marijuana filled the air. In a corner two very glamorous females sat holding hands and chatting coyly, giving each other a lingering kiss. On the dance floor too were a couple of attractive girls dancing together, arms entwined around each others necks.

Aileen said to Mike who had come over to stand by her side "Anything seems to go in this place Mike, what about a dance? Or will that ruin your reputation?"

"I've had worse offers," he grinned as he spun her onto the dance floor.

Under the flashing garish multi coloured lights they danced well together and soon were the centre of attraction. "I'll never live this down." Mike jibed.

"Somehow I didn't expect to see lesbians here too. The two sitting over there in that alcove are certainly great looking girls, look at those legs that just go on forever. I bet there are a few men who would think that a wicked waste."

"They would be quite wrong. Those two great girls are actually only one great girl and one transvestite."

"For heaven's sake. Which one is for real?"

"The one in the low cut white and yellow dress. The red satin 'lady' is actually a cross dresser, as they prefer to be called"

"But, forgive the expression, what's in it for white and yellow?"

"Sexually, you mean?"

"Sure."

"Everything. Cross-dressers are often great in bed. Nearly all of them are 'normal' heterosexual men who just like to dress up as women. Only thing is they get a high out of wearing women's underclothes when they have sex, but it is heterosexual sex for all that."

"Must take a special kind of girl to take that. Perhaps she has no choice. If he is her man and that's how he wants it, that's the way it's got to be and she puts up with it."

"Sometimes, but often the girls get a kick out of it too. A sensual male in a pair of black silk stockings under a sexy satin nightgown is a definite switch on for some."

Suddenly Aileen stiffened and a shock of recognition swept over her. She saw that one of the gorgeous looking dancing girls was none other than Kevin' macho golfing friend and a colleague in Government with a high position and heavy responsibilities to go with it. She realised how embarrassed he could be to see her there.

"Do you mind if we sit down now in that dark corner over there? How's the time anyway? Wow, I had no idea it was so late, nearly 3am! Somehow I have to drag myself into the station by 7.30 in the morning and sound on top of the world . . . . It's been a fascinating evening. I have learnt so much and got a terrific interview for the program. Let's see if Chartong is ready to go."

He wasn't. He was in full swing, chattering and exchanging views with a party of young men who had really taken him into their confidence.

Mike took her outside to get a taxi. At the door of the disco Aileen recognised another familiar face. It was Quicksilver. The strange young policeman who had turned up unexpectedly in Graeme's flat. Aileen was quite relieved to see him as she had the definite impression that he was on the verge of some sort of a breakdown when they had last met and might have done himself, or someone else, an injury. A few minutes of conversation however did nothing to allay her fears.

She badly wanted to interview him about phone-tapping and psychological warfare, but knew it would put him in danger. So she just said "You haven't revised your ideas yet about the SIU? When you do please give me the story. I'll be very discreet. We can even distort your voice these days so no one will know it is you."

"I told you the SIU are O.K. Everyone in town has a down on them, you've all got it wrong. They are only trying to protect, not to destroy. You should just see the care they take of me. They watch me every minute, follow me everywhere. See over the road even now. It's 3am for heavens sake and they are still watching over me. They are so hard working, never let up for a minute. Even when I am home they keep ringing up day and night to see if I am all right. You wouldn't believe how kind Quinn is. He came round the other night, brought me a bottle of whiskey and as we drank it he began to cry, explaining to me that he was only looking after everyone, no one understood him. Very sensitive Quinn is, cries a lot. He stayed five hours talking to me, didn't get any sleep. That's more caring than my own family."

Aileen was aware that Quicksilver's voice was rising hysterically, he was very distraught.

"O.K. Take it easy. I'm glad you aren't worried by the SIU. That's good. Just take care".

He grabbed her shoulders and started to shake her violently.

"I don't have to take care. Quinn and the SIU take care of me . . . why don't you bloody listen . . . . just listen?" She turned to avoid his outburst, but in doing so scraped her cheek against the doorpost.

Mike said very firmly "That's enough". She was bundled into a taxi and thankfully gave her address.

The London detective Vince Carratu went to Disco Disco a few days later and the gays just put the shutters down. He couldn't find out a thing.

As Aileen let herself quietly into the apartment she was surprised to see the lights were on. Her husband came storming out of the bedroom.

"Where the Hell have you been?"

"I should have called, Boff, I know . . ."

173

"Do you know what time it is? It's nearly four o'clock. I've been frantic."

"I thought you would have been asleep."

"ASLEEP! What with all the threats you've been getting. I didn't know what to do."

"I'm so sorry, but just wait till you hear . . ."

"No use ringing the police. I didn't know where you were."

"No need to shout. I'm back."

"Graeme didn't know either. Neither of us knew what to do."

"Don't keep on about it. I said I was . . ."

"You can't drop it just like that. You are under threat, for God's sake. Can't you see?"

"Can't you see I'm here. I'm perfectly safe and I'm not deaf."

"I imagined you in a pool of blood in the gutter . . ."

"Oh, cut the drama."

". . . with triads wiping their knives on your skirt."

"You're being ridiculous. I'm tired. I'm going to . . ." She moved towards the bedroom. He grabbed her arm and noticed her grazed cheek.

"My God . . . what happened to you . . . you've been in a brawl."

"A BRAWL! I've been in a brawl? Don't make me laugh."

"Well, if you haven't been in a brawl, where the Hell have you been?"

"Look. I've got the MacLennan answer."

"I said where have you been?"

"Just listen. It's Quinn. Don't you see? It's Quinn."

"You've been with Quinn!"

"No I've been in Disco Disco."

"WHAT !!!"

"Don't worry. John Conway took me there."

"That creep. I always knew he would get you into trouble."

"I haven't been in any trouble."

"Going to some sleazy dive 'not in trouble'. HUH !"

"It's not like that at all. MikeFulton was there and Howard Lindsey—he's a lawyer—and Gordon Huthard . . . I got some wonderful information."

"Unadulterated perverted sex, I presume."

"No."

"Can't you find better company than a decrepit moth eaten detective old enough to be your grandfather and a bunch of drug pushing queers?"

"It's not about that. It's about John MacLennan."

"MACLENNAN!!! For a year I've heard nothing else but bloody MacLennan. You've talked of nothing else, you've eaten with him, dreamed of him, slept with him."

"But . . ."

"And from all accounts he was one of the most perverted of the lot."

"You've got the wrong . . ."

"You're just a perverted slut."

She slapped his face very hard. Without hesitation he grabbed the neckline of her low cut chiffon dress and ripped it from top to bottom, scattering a hailstorm of tiny jet beads. She flew at him, cat like, nails bared.

"You're just shit. Just full of shit."

She stormed down the corridor screaming "Shit . . . Just shit . . ." and the slamming bedroom door reverberated through the twenty storey building.

The room was full of pain, the silence broken only by the clock in the hall chiming four. He moved towards the corridor, changed his mind and proceeded to the far corner of the room where he fell on his knees sobbing uncontrollably.

For a few minutes that was all there was—just sobbing.

Then she was standing behind him in what was left of her tattered clothing, placing a gentle hand on his heaving shoulders and whispering "He's dead. He's dead. He's dead."

Chapter 41

There was a certain chill about the home. Kevin was distant and he and Chartong simply didn't speak. The lounge took on some of the flavour of a report room, with ideas and theories being batted around, tested, stored away or discarded. Chartong was in fine fettle. His nose was down like a bloodhound and he was away. He wanted to know the circumstances of the death. He set out to verify, or otherwise, every detail of it.

First of all he wanted to check how long it took to walk from the Homantin Police Station to Johnny's flat. Johnny had written the time, 0600, in the armoury register and 0610 was written on the alleged suicide note. How was this possible? Inspector Grant had given evidence at the inquest on 5th March that he had walked the journey in just over ten minutes. But 'over ten minutes' is not ten minutes. Why wasn't it 0615 on the note? Trotman had confirmed that the watch on the desk in Johnny's flat was showing the right time.

So Chartong went over to Homantin to check it himself. There were three ways of making the journey. Either south to the Oi Man pedestrian bridge and back north to the flats. That took a good fifteen minutes. Or north to the flyover and back south to the flats. That took at least fifteen minutes. The third alternative was to brave crossing a freeway and leap over a high iron fence in the middle. That appeared to be a better way of committing suicide than five gunshots. Besides, you needed to be fit to do that, not putting on weight and going to seed like John MacLennan. A further snag was that it wasn't just the walk, it was the stairs and/or the lifts. In no way could Chartong, excellent walker though he was (ex-policeman who lived in the Scottish highlands), do it in under fifteen minutes. So the times just didn't tie up.

Then he found, in the inquest report, reference to the body temperature as measured by Dr Wong, the pathologist. At 12.30 p.m. on 15th January Dr Wong measured the body, rectal, temperature as 22° C (71.60°F) and the room temperature as 20° C (68° F). This showed a temperature drop of 15° C (25.2° F) since the moment of death. He went straight to the Hong Kong University library to look up the bible on the subject by Keith Simpson. Taking into account other factors these readings indicated death the night before and that the man who collected the gun could not have been John MacLennan, assuming of course the correctness of the inquest notes signed by the coroner.

Then he noticed that the locks on the doors in Aileen's flat were the same as in MacLennan's bedroom. Aileen pointed out that was not surprising as they were both government flats. So Chartong promptly unscrewed the lock and laid the bits out on the dining room table. After a few minutes there was a loud "Whoopee! You can lock it from outside," followed almost immediately by a bawl from Kevin down the corridor, "What the hell's happened to the spare room door. I can't get to my books!"

Next Chartong borrowed a set of the police photographs. He sat there a whole day going through them with a magnifying glass and a strong light. By supper time he had only one word to say:

"Sloppy."

"What is?" asked Aileen.

"Police procedures here. I used to be a scene-of-crime photographer when I was in the Met. The golden rule is that the photographer goes in first before anything is touched. The whole idea is to get a permanent record of everything, from every angle, just as it is found.

"Not so here. The photographs were taken at four different times over a period of days. Even the first set were taken while people were moving things around. Look at this. You see in this picture there's a coat on the back of the chair. In this next picture it's gone. What use is that? This can't be the scene as it was found. It's posed. Look at the way this photo of the notes is posed, with the pen neatly down one side with the watch at the top. I'm sure I read in the inquest notes that the envelope was picked up before it was photographed. So what use is that? Then look at this. A photograph supposed to be how the flat was found—with a crowbar on the floor. Now we know the crowbar was produced by the police after the flat was broken into. What's it doing in a scene-of-crime photograph? But the one that worries me most is this one."

He showed Aileen a picture taken from the bedroom door, of the bed and the windows with the feet of the corpse sticking out beyond the bed.

"Look at the middle of the bed. There is something sticking up about three inches above the bed. I can't see what it is. But whatever it is, it is leaning against the bed, so it is a couple of feet long, right beside the body. Now look at the full photo of the body. There is nothing leaning against the bed. Where has it gone? Someone was there apparently removing vital evidence while the photographer was going about his work. So to say the least it is sloppy police procedure. At worst it is criminal suppression of evidence.'

A day or two later Chartong had a ring up from one of Aileen's listeners, an ex-policeman called Khan. He had a perennial chip on his shoulder and had been trying for years to establish that he was wrongfully dismissed because he had uncovered loan-sharking condoned by the police. He wanted to tell Chartong all about it. So they arranged to meet at 3.30 that afternoon at the reception desk of the YMCA in Salisbury Road, to assist recognition.

Chartong took a minnibus to the Star Ferry giving himself plenty of time. The magazines and soft drinks stalls were busy as he passed the recently built GPO building and made for the lower ferry deck, the cheap class along with the ropes and the anchors. Even as a hardened ex cop, being among the bustling boats amid the vast panoramic vista gave him quite a thrill. The YMCA was just a few minutes walk from the pier and he turned up at 3.25. This Pakistani was already there. He came up to him.

"Mr Conway?"

"Yes. Mr Khan?"

"Yes."

They decided to go to the restaurant on the roof. The Pakistani led the way and kept on taking wrong turnings. Chartong thought he remembered him saying he knew that place well. Then he began to notice a lack of authority in the voice, a lack of accuracy in the English, wishy-washy logic. This was not an ex-policeman.

Chartong went to the phone to ring Aileen and as he turned round the man got up and fled. Chartong chased him but lost him. Downstairs he found another Pakistani.

"Mr Conway?"

"Can I see your identity card?"

Khan looked a bit surprised, but produced it. Chartong told him what had happened. Jumping to the obvious conclusion, he asked:

"Do you know your phone is tapped?"

"Yes, but I rang you from a call box. Your's must be tapped too."

They were so shaken by the incident they both sat down and wrote statements about what had happened—typical police fashion, before getting down to the subject on the agenda.

It was a rather white and shaken Chartong who returned at tea time to say to Aileen:

"Did you know your phone was tapped?"

"I suspected it, but I wasn't sure."

"Well, it is."

She had a nasty feeling, having the certainty that someone was listening to all her private conversations. She had suspected it before, but that was different. Certainty was a very different thing. But why?

Chartong suggested it was too blatant. "They must want you to know it is tapped."

"Ah, like Quicksilver and his overt surveillance."

"Yes. It's a warning, I should think."

It took about three days for her to get used to the idea. She worried about Boff. There had been a few grumbles from that direction about noisy lines but since they were hardly speaking the matter was not discussed. She realised that apart from the distaste, she really had nothing to hide, or if she did have something she was careful not to disclose it over the phone. In fact after a while she had a lot of amusement slandering all the main characters in the affair over the phone, especially Quinn, knowing there was nothing they could do about it.

Chapter 42

Meanwhile Chartong went about his business with renewed vigour. He went to the Transport Registry to ask about John MacLennan's car and discovered that it wasn't his car at all. It was registered in the name of a lady called Shroff. "They are a very rich family in Hong Kong. Why hasn't she come forward to claim the car? Has she got something to hide? And what about the $250 cheque he cashed the day before he died. Why did he need $250 to kill himself?" Then he wanted to know why the alleged suicide note was on an envelope. Where were the other envelopes? If it was the last of the packet where was the band? Why not on notepaper anyway?

"For heaven's sake," Aileen said, "stop asking questions and give us some answers."

But he just asked another question. "What are envelopes for anyway?"

"For putting letters in."

"Exactly. Where is it?"

"You mean Johnny might have written a letter and put it in the envelope?"

"And wrote the note afterwards as an afterthought. Why else take his typewriter home? Didn't one of the witnesses say he would have expected his friend to write something longer?"

It was about this time that Aileen received feedback on the examination of the exhibits. The sweater, so she was told, showed no evidence of powder on the sleeves. She mentioned this to Chartong who was skeptical. "It depends on how it has been treated since. Powder burns are a kind of dust which fall off in time and get contaminated as well. An FDR test is supposed to be carried out within 36 hours to be reliable. If the sweater had been bagged immediately then there could have been residue in the bag a long time after. But if it had been exposed, which would have been consistent with Hong Kong police practice all through this case, then tests after all this time would be meaningless. So you can only conclude that either the police were completely incompetent in not bagging it and then even more incompetent in sending it off for tests in that state or Johnny didn't shoot himself."

She was also told about the report from the handwriting expert, Derek Davies. Apparently it was pretty lengthy, but the gist was that John MacLennan had written the note. However, he had written the time and date at a different time, probably standing up. Derek Davies added that, from a graphologist's point of view, there was no indication in the writing that the writer was about to commit suicide.

She didn't tell Chartong this. She wanted to hear what he found out first. But she did ask him about Derek Davies.

"Yes, I know him. He came to me some years ago to find out where he could go to study handwriting. I told him there was no formal training. You have to learn it the hard way like I did. I believe he is very good now, but he's a graphologist, not a questioned document examiner."

"What's the difference?"

"They both examine handwriting, but in different ways. Both can tell you whether handwriting originated from a certain person. But the graphologist will go a lot further one way and tell you about the character of the writer and the state of mind he was in at the time of writing. A questioned document examiner will go in a different direction and tell you a lot of other things, such as what sort of pen was used or whether a specific pen was used, what sort of surface a note was written on, whether an envelope has been sealed and opened, what words have been erased or crossed out and so on. And he covers all sorts of other documents, typed and so on. In short your graphologist is more psychological, a questioned document examiner is more scientific. They both have their place. To a large extent they are complementary."

Aileen became increasingly eager that Chartong should get hold of the note and see it for himself. He had already spent hours, days, weeks staring at the photographs with his magnifying glass, but he was very cagey and kept saying he must have the original. He was getting nowhere with the Commission. They seemed to have clammed up and wouldn't let him have access to the note or the gun. So in the end Aileen took a hand herself. She rang up the Commission's lawyers and Chartong got access to the note the next day. He had to get to the Commission Secretary:s, Norman Chan's, office and do his examination under supervision, but he didn't mind that. It seemed he had actually done most of his work from the photograph and it was only a question of clearing up a lot of hunches. He still spent the whole day.

"Well?" Aileen said.

"Johnny wrote them all right."

"Is that all?"

"The armoury register was interesting. The alteration everybody noticed was actually that he had first written 1800 and changed it to 0600. In other words he appeared to be confused whether it was morning or evening."

"And what aboust the note?"

"He wrote it at two different times. He wrote the time and the date at a different time from the rest."

"Are you sure he wrote the time and the date himself?"

"Oh, yes. And with the same pen. But they can't find the pen. They gave me three pens, but none of them wrote the note and none was the Parker ballpoint in the photograph."

"Does it matter?"

"Not for me to say. If the note had been written with the Parker then he could have written it alone in the room. But supposing it wasn't. Then, since it wasn't written with any other of the pens in the room, he might have borrowed a pen off somebody else—a second party. Who? The Parker was an exhibit. I would have said an important exhibit—and they say they have lost it. Certainly my asking for it seems to have made them very embarrassed. I don't know whether that's because they know something or because to lose an exhibit is such gross incompetence—which of course it is. I think I asked for it once too often, because they started to turn nasty."

"And had the envelope been sealed?"

"No. At no time. There was no scuffing. But there was no grain in the writing."

"Grain?"

"Yes, the note was found on a hardwood desk. If it had been written as it was, with a hard ballpoint, there would have been traces of the irregularities of the grain of the wood in the writing. There weren't. There would also have been traces of indentations on the back of the envelope. There weren't."

"So?"

"So I have no doubt whatsoever that when the note was written there was something in the envelope that masked the grain of the wood and took up the indentations. I must say also, though it's a bit outside my line, I found the writing very smooth and controlled for a man just about to commit suicide—on the note, that is. The writing in the armoury register was entirely consistent with somebody in a highly emotional state, I should imagine."

Aileen then told him what Derek Davies had said.

"Yes, he's a good chap."

There was a pause. Then he said "there was something else."

"What else?"

He started slowly at first. "What I have said so far has been from your point of view—how you should see what I have found. But there is another slant and that is how I see it, which is a little different. You see I was there all day. Nobody can go all day without a call of nature, and sure enough Norman Chan had to go out and he sat his secretary in his office ostensibly to look after my every need. Well, the silly girl thought that included a cup of tea, so unknown to Norman Chan I was left alone in his office just for a few minutes, just long enough for me to have a quick look round. His desk drawers were stuffed with everything except the kitchen sink, mostly papers and the like, but in the left hand top drawer I spotted several plastic bags containing exhibits and one contained a pen. I had to close the drawer quickly and nip back to my desk as I heard the sound of tea cups, but not before I spotted the exhibit number, 5C. I will have to see from the lists what that should be. But, as I say, when I suggested to Norman Chan later that there might be another pen he got quite shirty, so I couldn't press the point and you mustn't either. It could get us both in deep trouble."

"I didn't hear all that," she assured him, making a mental note of what he had said. "But between you and me, what is the significance?" she asked.

"Simple. Johnny always wrote with a black ink pen. The suicide note was written in Victorian blue. It is almost certain that the pen labelled exhibit C was Johnny's Parker ballpoint—black ink. Why was it declared 'Lost'. Obviously someone has spotted that if no pen was found which was blue then the note could not have been written in the flat, and the whole suicide theory is shattered. They wouldn't want that, would they? They know perfectly well the pen was never lost. Only too dangerous to be released."

Next Chartong wanted to examine the gun. But he had a lot of preparation to do. First he wanted a rig made up to test the trigger pressure. Apparently to do this with a spring balance, which is what the Hong Kong police did, is very inaccurate and amateurish. Keith makes a particular point of this in his book. So Aileen arranged for Chartong to meet an army sergeant who fixed him up with the appropriate instruments. Then he wanted some one-inch pine board. She got that for him from a friend who was an architect. The army sergeant cut it up for him and fixed the pieces in a box. The theory was apparently that a normal .38 bullet should go through four or five (possibly six) one-inch pine boards. But Chartong suspected that this particular gun had a sloppy cylinder with a bad gas leak, which would reduce the muzzle velocity—particularly, so he thought, when in close contact. This apparently was the standard internationally accepted test.

By arrangement he turned up at the police armoury and he was allowed to test the trigger pull of some thirty similar weapons chosen at random. The trigger pull of the exhibit was about average. No problem there. Then he fired shots from the exhibit gun into the pine boards. The penetration was 2½ boards, not four or five. Apparently the Hong Kong police revolvers were so underpowered as to be scarcely lethal. Then he put one of Kevin' old socks over the boards and fired again. The penetration was 2½ boards. Not much difference. Then he put the lights out and did it again.

"All the time I had this policeman breathing down my neck," he said, "making notes, so I had difficulty in doing the crucial test."

"What was that?"

"I wanted to know the amount of powder coming out sideways past the leaky chamber. So when I put the lights out I observed the flash sideways. It was much more than you would observe with a new weapon, but then this was 25 to 30 years old. But when I put the gun in contact with the sock, as it would have been pressed against Johnny's sweater, the back pressure was considerably greater and the sideways flash was very considerable. I put my left hand about six inches to the side, and when I looked at the palm after the lights were on there was black line. That's the bit I didn't want the policeman to see."

"Why not?"

"Well, everything else supported the suicide theory. The low muzzle velocity supports the possibility of firing five shots into yourself. So long as I apparently supported the suicide theory they co-operated. Have you got a toy gun?"

"No, but next door may have. They have kids."

She was in luck and came back a few minutes later with a suitable specimen—giggling.

"What's the joke?"

"Mrs Fong gave me such a funny look when I asked for a toy gun because a detective friend of mine needed it."

"Wonder what she thought? Anyway, do you see how the cylinder is fitted? If there is a gas leak it cannot go upwards because of the way the gun is made. It goes sideways and downwards. Now, take this and aim to shoot yourself in the waist. Try and hold the gun upright."

She did.

"Now, observe that your wrist is above the gun. There is a good chance the flash will go under your wrist, leaving no visible mark or stain on the sleeve. Now try and shoot yourself in the chest."

She did. It was very awkward.

He continued, "Look how your wrist is now curled round the side. The flash now will go straight onto the sleeve you are wearing."

"But there was no powder on the sweater."

"No, there wasn't, was there, though that could be just police incompetence as I said. But there is an alternative. Try holding the gun with two hands with your thumb on the trigger."

She did. It brought her wrists further towards her chest.

"The discharge of the flash could now go straight on to your wrists and not on the sweater. But the wrists are close to the gun—within six inches. The mark would be visible. Especially with four shots."

"But Dr Wong said he examined the hands and there were no visible marks."

"That's right. What do you think now? Was it suicide or murder?"

"I'm confused."

Chapter 43

Aileen was disturbed. Something was wrong. She knew many things had been wrong right from the start, but up till now it had been fairly open, even if it had taken the form of a cover-up. But now it took on a kind of malevolent unreality. Here was Chartong finding out things that ought to have been done by the authorities long since, and his activities were accompanied by a kind of deathly hush. Something was going on, silently, way under the surface. She couldn't get a clue what it was. Aileen remembered Chartong's first introduction at the inquiry when Conrad Seagroat had referred to his considerable experience in ballistics and handwriting and Justice Yang had readily given him permission to do all the tests he wanted. Now all that openness had gone. They weren't offering help any more. He was having to battle for everything. True, the struggle had got him access to the note and the gun, he was even able to check that exhibit 5C was indeed the pen found on the desk and photographed beside the suicide note, but he was still not allowed to get his hands on any of John's belongings—and that was really why he was here. Why were they ignoring the chosen and authorised representative of the parents? What was the problem?

She took him into the studio for a radio interview.

She brought out his longstanding association with the MacLennan family, how John's uncle and aunt had been guests at his wedding thirty years before, and his close association with the Black Isle. Chartong told a bit about the farm, about what simple folk the parents, Joe and Katie were, about Joe's blindness, and the impracticability of either of them travelling to Hong Kong.

He told how they had first heard of John's death being described as a 'shooting incident' on the BBC and the frustrations of the whole family when they could find out nothing more. The local press had followed the inquest but there seemed to be something wrong. After the inquest there was a great deal of consternation and comment throughout the whole community and when they heard the Attorney General had taken a hand in the matter it added further to the confusion.

Chartong, therefore, approached the family and said he was prepared to go to Hong Kong at his own expense and find out what he could. Then the inquiry was announced, so they asked him to go as their representative. Aileen asked him about his past experience.

"I was a serving police officer for fifteen years. Then I was an experimental officer in a forensic science laboratory in Belfast. Most of my duties were concerned with the examination of firearms and questioned documents. After that I was self-employed in my own business in handwriting and document examining for ten or twelve years. In my latter years I was employed as a civilian with the Northern Constabulary and much of my work there was concerned with the licensing of firearms. I advised sportsmen on the type of weapon, in particular the appropriate calibre, for shooting at various forms of game."

Then Aileen led on to the question of financing his stay in Hong Kong.

There was an immediate reaction. Listeners rang up offering to contribute to a fund to support him. Although there was no real money problem, she wanted the Commission to approve his stay and the only real way to ensure that was for them to pay him—anything.

After the broadcast the phones were ringing.

One or two of the reactions were rather strange. Both the Police and the Secretariat Public Relations Departments rang to say they didn't realise he had that sort of expertise. Odd! Why hadn't they been told? Where were they when it came out in court? Perhaps they had been concentrating too hard on other areas of his background. But in the end Aileen got the call she wanted. First one of the lawyers, then the secretary of the Commission, rang to say there was never any question of their not supporting Conway. It was only a question of finalising the administration. There followed a request that she not broadcast any more on the subject as it would be settled in a couple of days.

It was. They gave him the same allowance as a local witness. Nothing like enough to live on in Hong Kong but the important fact was that with that act they had conceded that he represented the parents.

Actually the official figure for the whole inquiry was a cost of $100,000 every day it sat. The pittance allotted to Chartong seemed to indicate the relative importance they attached to the representation of the parents, or was it just one more indication of some undercurrent building up against him? Had he asked just too many awkward questions?

Meanwhile Vincent Carratu was preparing a list of people he wanted to interrogate. A newspaper stated that Aileen and Elsie were on it. Aileen's lawyer was on the phone as she walked into the office. He sounded quite jittery, as if someone had told him something he didn't want to pass on to her. She had just put the phone down from that call when the Commission's lawyer rang to ask if she would go to see him. She called back her lawyer.

"What's all this about? What am I supposed to know?"

"You must be very careful. Obviously you have upset somebody. It might be the police or the Commission, it might even be triads. After all, there was a lot of talk about John MacLennan's triad association at the time of the Yuen Long affair. If his elimination had been triad-instigated there might be quite a lot of nasty characters after you. Don't worry too much about it. Actually, your position in the public eye—or ear—is a good protection to you. For all that, I am very glad you are on radio and not on television

The next morning TVB rang and asked Aileen to appear on <u>Focus</u> TV program.

"No, I couldn't, I couldn't possibly."

"But you must. It is about being a phone-in host. We can't do the program without you."

"I'm afraid you will have to."

The TV station tried hard but she was firm. Besides she had another appointment to keep.

She told Nick she was on her way to be questioned by the Commission's lawyer. Monday was never his best day and this was Black Monday.

Chapter 44

The solicitor for the Commission was a Mr Murray Burton. He was twenty minutes late. Aileen's usual laid back attitude to life disintegrated with unpunctuality. She took the view that she could not belate either. Finally, this somewhat overweight young man came diffidently in, clutching his sandwiches. He tried to apologise but he was not very adept at dealing with Amazons and he did not succeed.

"You'd better get on with it, I can only give you seventeen and a half minutes."

"Well, I only want to know what you have to tell the inquiry." He said.

"Nothing."

"But surely something must have transpired during your association with the MacLennan case which could cast some light on the mystery."

"No."

"But, er . . . er . . ."

He was rather a personable young man with a round boyish face and he was only trying to do his job, possibly that excuse for being late that she hadn't listened to might have been a good one. She dipped into her handbag and produced Slasher George's tape. She tossed it onto his desk with a clank.

"Perhaps you'd like to listen to that."

He seemed relieved not to have to listen to her and put the tape on with alacrity. In no time at all he started to display a hidden ebullience as Slasher George started talking about being gay and going to bed with

John MacLennan. He alternated between rubbing his hands like Fagin and writing notes furiously. It seemed to make him far too happy, so she gave him the tape of Lloyd Conway saying the cremation was against both John's and his parents' wishes. That took the smile off his face. Aileen got the impression he didn't care for Lloyd Conway.

Then he leaned back in his chair and said that the Commission was most upset over her broadcast message to Mr Neligan.

"I wouldn't have sent him that message over the air if I hadn't considered Mr Neligan's action to be most improper in the first place."

He did not reply, and she had the distinct feeling that he was not enjoying this one bit.

It was a strange interview. She had expected a kind of CIA interrogation and instead found herself playing a character part of some over bearing dowager. She thought he was not used to having theatrical overemphasis brought so close to his nostrils. They parted without either of them having the slightest idea what the other was really like.

Aileen's phone rang in the studio. It was Vincent Carratu himself.

"Could I see you tomorrow?." he said after an initial introduction.

"I'm afraid I have to go to Stanley prison."

He sounded surprised. Aileen continued, "I have to see an inmate that is due to be released soon. I am trying it find him a home. If you would like to come to my apartment though in Plantation Road I will be back there by 4.30."

He was already there when she arrived. Ah Sun had prepared him some tea and cakes and he was sitting on the veranda revelling in the magnificent view over the harbour.

Aileen thought he looked as if he had walked straight out of a TV detective series. He was just what you might imagine a private detective to be, a sort of Barnaby Columbo. He was immensely charming, having lost some of the slimness of youth and a fair proportion of his hair as well, but shrewd, searching, with an incredible memory for detail, and, above all, down-to-earth, companionable and easy to talk to.

At first the conversation was quite lighthearted. He joked about the local police force

"This isn't Fred Carnot, it's Meccano—full of holes. All the top echelon are suspect, with one possible exception—Li Kwan-ha. He's as straight as a laser beam. Got quite a future, I should imagine, if he can survive the pressures of corruption all around him."

He gave the impression he was leaking inside information, though few of his confidences were of any value. Indeed, at one stage he confided he and his assistant had been sworn to absolute secrecy. If anyone was going to wheedle information out of you, this character was going to do it—by the bundle thought Aileen, though she wondered what was so secret this open inquiry needed to guard.

She was quite relieved when Chartong came in and sat down between them, without an invitation, and said "Ah, Tea!"

The rival investigators' antagonism towards each other glowed immediately almost radioactively. This was not the private tete a tete Vince had in mind. After several long silences and snide comments Aileen offered him some head phones and the Slasher George tape. This was the second recording, easier to listen t but the one without the names. He was clearly very interested.

"I shall find him."

"How? You don't know anything about him."

"I know all I need to know. I shall find him," and he went off without even asking her the name of the restaurant where they had met.

He found him.

Chapter 45

It was around this time Aileen had become aware of some very obvious clicking on her home telephone. Many of her callers would break off in mid conversation and ask if her phone was tapped. She consulted a telecommunications engineer who gave her a lot of technical claptrap about high impedance circuits, phantoms and sensitivity which convinced her, even though she understood not word, that, with modern technology, if someone wanted to tap the phone covertly, there was no way you could know, not even by sophisticated electronic tests. She drew the only conclusion—that some person or persons unknown were determined that she be constantly reminded that her phone was tapped. And yes it was unnerving.

It was around this time Kevin brought Alan Yim home to dinner one night. He was a colleague on the electronics division of the Institution of Engineers with whom he wanted to discuss how information technology should be handled, was it electronics or something else? Aileen played hostess very properly through dinner but over coffee she couldn't resist airing her current obsession.

"Alan, what do you know about telephone tapping?" Kevin scowled. Alan raised an eyebrow. "A certain amount, why?"

"If someone taps your phone can you tell?"

"I depends on who is doing it. Let me explain. When you dial 109 to make a complaint about a number, the operator will use a facility provided to tap that number. Though she will hear the conversation, she is disciplined not to listen to it, but only to note that the line is normal. She will then reply to your complaint. Those taking part in that conversation will not know what has happened."

"But I thought you needed some sort of warrant to tap a telephone."

"Yes, it's supposed to be provided by the Governor in Council, though in practice he delegates the authority to certain posts. Having said that, obviously the operators on 109 are exempt. But now you come to a rather sensitive issue. When telephone exchanges are installed, the supplier is required to provide so many lines per ten thousand for 109 use. In practice the number is a lot higher than needed by 109 and the remainder is directed surreptitiously to military intelligence or MI6. Now they don't need, certainly they don't get, authority from the Governor in Council. This is because in practice they are above the law. Any enquiry or complaint against them is met by the usual 'In defence of the realm' or 'In the national interest'. They are simply not accountable."

"So why on earth do they go through this charade of getting the permission of the Governor in Council?"

"Oh, that's very simple. Unless they do that they can't use what they hear in evidence. But if all they are seeking is intelligence they often don't bother."

"But you said the person using the telephone wouldn't know."

"That's right. Technology is so advanced these days that the tap done the way I have described is absolutely inaudible. But access to such methods is very restricted. If a private investigator wanted to tap a phone he would have to do it physically at the terminals somewhere between the exchange and the instrument, or put a bug in the instrument itself. And I guess he would be most unlikely to get permission, so it would be illegal. Any of these methods can be detected, and if not done professionally could well be audible."

"This doesn't make sense. Alan, would you do me a favour. Would you mind picking up that telephone and listening?"

"Sure." He did so. "Sounds alright to me. Just dial tone."

"Perhaps you need to dial a number. Could you dial your home?"

"Sure." He did so. He was connected to his maid to whom he said he would be a bit late home. During this a smile crept across his face. As he closed the call he turned to Aileen. "Yes, I see what you mean. I would say that's what we call an overt tap. They want you to know."

Kevin was visibly upset and returned the conversation quickly to information technology. After Alan had gone he was very abrasive with

Aileen accusing her of misusing his important guest. She put up with that and the clicks for about a week before she rang up the managing director of the Telephone Company. His secretary, a charming girl, asked her business.

"I'll tell him that when I see him."

"I'm afraid he doesn't normally see anyone without knowing the nature of the matter they wish to discuss."

"In this case I am afraid I can't tell you. Would you just ask him if he will see me."

Ten minutes later she rang back.

"I'm sorry, Mr Walker would like to be told what you want to talk about."

Aileen disliked bringing pressure to bear on people to do the right thing but she had no choice. "I'm afraid that is putting me in a difficult position. I have a query and if I mention it on my program it might create the wrong impression about your company. However since I have been unable to get a reaction from Mr Walker we will have to face it."

Three minutes later the phone rang. "Eric Walker here. When would you like to come?"

"Tomorrow."

"Shall we say three o'clock?"

"Certainly."

Halfway through the program the next morning, the news was thrust in front of her with the usual thirty seconds to prepare. The first item described the progress of the show trial in Peking of the "Gang of Four", Mao's wife, Jiang Qing, and three other conspirators who had planned to overthrow the Government. They had been found guilty. It was therefore not until she was actually reading the second item on air that the bells began to ring. An antique dealer, it said, was found dead in his Peak flat. He had been bound and gagged. She looked for the usual 'No foul play is suspected.' It wasn't there. That's when the bells began to ring.

As soon as she had the opportunity she sent up to the news room for the name for the dead man. They didn't know. She asked them to find out—fast. A couple of hours later they came back with the answer. It was *Ian McLean*!. Yee Gods, she had a tape describing a victim of homicide as an evil homosexual with lots of enemies. On top of detectives, phone tapping, interrogations and threats, she was now involved in a murder.

Chapter 46

Aileen now had a new problem. She had played Vince Carratu the other tape, the second one. The one that did not mention Ian McLean. On the other hand, the first tape mentioned so many names it was too hot to handle. And then there was that anonymous short story she had broadcast about the murder of 'Inspector McNaughton'. How did it end?

She got it out and looked at it again.

'But he breathed again when the authorities stepped in and declared it suicide; because as soon as this one blew over there was another one he had to get rid of.'

Coincidence? Or was she an accessory before the fact?

She rang her lawyer.

"It's no use worrying about it," he said. "Because you have only one possible course of action. Give the police the tape."

"But I've already played the other one to Vincent Carratu."

"Then give it to Vincent Carratu and tell him to give it to the police. But get rid of it as quickly as you can."

"What about all the other names on it?"

He thought for a moment. "Can you edit them out?"

"Yes."

"Then do so."

An hour later the dirty deed was done and she was dialling Vince Carratu.

"Vince, I've got a bit of evidence I think you'd better have."

"Jolly good. What?"

"It's a tape—er, have you heard the 12 o'clock news?"

"No."

"Well, you remember the tape I played you of Slasher George?"

"Yes."

"Well there is another. A fuller one with names on it. I didn't play you that because it was in a restaurant and there was a lot of background noise."

He sounded unconvinced. She continued, "Well, one of the names was a man who has just been murdered.'

"Oh, yes. Who?"

"It's an antique dealer called Ian McLean."

The effect was a little unexpected. There proceeded from the telephone a stream of language quite out of character from the middle-aged charmer she had met the day before.

She played the innocent. 'Sorry, I didn't quite hear. There was a crackle on the line. Is something the matter?'

"Only that I had lined up an interview with him tomorrow. He's—or rather was—one of the key witnesses in the MacLennan case. He knew more about the gay scene in Hong Kong than anyone."

"Oh, er, would you like the tape?"

"I'll send a car up for it now."

Eric Walker, the managing director of the Telephone Company, greeted her on the dot of 3pm. He looked as though he'd been looking forward to their meeting all day, which is of course the impression all the best managing directors give.

"Now whatever is this great secret you can't tell me over the telephone?"

"My telephone is tapped.

"Really."

He didn't seem the least bit surprised. "Of course you are a public figure and you are taking not a little interest in this case going on at the moment involving all kinds of questionable people." He went on to tell her he had even had to have his own checked at one time when one of his staff was on a corruption charge.

"The only thing I can assure you, Aileen, is that it is not done with my sanction."

He explained that it could either be done at her block of flats, which was difficult for him to monitor, or by agents planted among his staff. He told her of an actual case where this had happened and a fraud was carried out by using triad members infiltrated among his numerous employees.

She left without much consolation and with an ugly feeling deep down that she was living in a police state and that nobody cared. Not even Boff—any more.

Chapter 47

"Let's go sleuthing."

Chartong seemed to have more than his usual bounce this morning. He was obviously up to something.

"I thought you were always sleuthing," said Aileen.

"Yes, I suppose I am. But this morning I've got the keys to John MacLennan's flat. Do you want to come?"

"Do I! I wouldn't miss it for the world."

As they drove down the winding tree lined road, the flashes of sunlight seemed this morning to add a new expectancy to the air. Something was going to happen today. They continued down steep Garden Road between the pink storks in the botanic gardens and the huge prison-like headquarters of the Public Works Department. Then the vista of the harbour was unveiled and it too glittered with a new excitement. Down on the waterfront to the cross-harbour tunnel seemed busier than ever, the local drivers even keener than usual to cut in and jump a place or two in the queue.

Homantin flats are not far on the other side of the tunnel. Aileen drove her car towards the huge Oi Man housing estate, turned left and right and into Homantin Hill Road, where the government service flats were situated at number 19. The road wound up an incline.

She asked Chartong if he knew the Chinese called it the Home of Evil Spirits.

"No, tell me about it."

"In World war II the Japanese took over the high ground and used it for surveying the area and much worse. After the war the area was leveled for rebuilding, and the excess material was used for reclamation. They unearthed mass graves dating back to the Boxer rebellion, when fighting triads massacred many Christian 'foreign devils' and later the Japanese added many more victims to the cemetery."

"Gruesome!"

It was an odd block, obviously not designed for visitors, mainly because there was no indication whatsoever how to get in. There was a watchman in a glass-fronted box in the centre, but he only waved his arms. They wandered around a dungeon-like car park for a bit until they found the wide windowed office of the Manageress, Mrs Janet Gafoor, who was out at the time so they tried some stairs. They came to a deserted marble vestibule with a couple of potted plants and a notice board advertising next Sunday's film. The flats were built like a compound with the iron railed balconies facing inward and surrounding a yard with washing hanging up, accessed from some doors at the back. Had there been an alternative they would have tried it. There didn't seem to be.

Off the corner of the yard were some stairs going down. Obviously the wrong direction. They wanted to go up. They tried another. Here were some stairs going up and tucked round the corner where you would least expect it was a small lift. They tried that and pressed the button for the fourth floor. It was eerie. It was all so deserted. It was as if the usual customers were dead.

Taking a double turn out of the lift they came through a door into a long balcony, open to the sky on the left, a row of front doors on the right. At the end where they stood was a window looking out onto a kind of partly enclosed sheer drop. The first front door was 401B—John MacLennan's.

It was a spooky feeling putting the key in the lock and opening the new door. The original, of course, had been broken to pieces. Aileen didn't know what she had expected. It may have been the tidily furnished apartment she had seen in the photographs, or a room seething with policemen, or just deathly silence. But it was empty and almost bare. There were a few items of government furniture, but all Johnny's belongings were gone. The flat was tiny. Four strides took you the length of it where you could look from the lounge window over another sheer drop to the railway line through the trees below, and beyond over seething Mongkok.

She hovered there for a while wondering how Johnny might have stood there, looking over the city with one of his girls, or his close friend Matt Handley, talking about life in the police or about Scotland. Perhaps the lights were twinkling and dusk was falling, and he would switch on the standard lamp, draw the blinds, and go to the little kitchen by the front door for his Scotch and water. Then Johnny was there, offering one to Aileen, and she was sitting in the wooden-armed easy chair, while his broad figure stood smiling like the picture the press had all used, telling her how he loved life and wanted to be a good policeman.

"You're not much of a sleuth, are you!"

She came to, suddenly, to the bare empty day lit flat, with Chartong waving a magnifying glass like some unbelievable cliché. All that was missing was the deerstalker.

"There's not a sign of any ricochet marks on the floor."

"Should there be?"

"I need to know there aren't. It means the bullets went direct."

"Direct where?"

"Come on, I'll show you."

They went into the bedroom, even tinier than the lounge. Just inside the door on the right was a built-in walk-in wardrobe. There was a single bed with the head against the wall on the right. On the centre of the wall opposite the door was a built-in dressing table with small windows on either side. The wall on the left was blank.

Chartong went over to the window on the far right. Beside it was an air conditioning switch. He pointed below it.

"That's where one bullet hit. The other went downwards into a chest of drawers here about a foot off the floor." He pointed to the bare wall on the left.

"But they are in different directions."

"Completely."

"How did that happen?"

"That's what I propose the find out. Here, take this pen and pretend it's a gun. Stand by the bed on the same side as the window and see how you have to stand for the bullet to hit the air conditioning switch."

Aileen tried it. She was back to the windows, facing across the end of the bed towards the right of the door.

"Now fire another shot so it goes in a chest of drawers here."

It was impossible. It was more then a right angle.

"Perhaps the first shot swivelled him round, 'she said.

"Perhaps. But there's one snag."

"What's that?"

"The bullets through the body were only slightly downwards and the bullet in the chest of drawers was also only slightly downwards a foot off the floor."

"You mean he couldn't have been standing up?"

"That's a possible explanation. Now, you know about Johnny's religious upbringing. What do you think he would have done if he was about to shoot himself?"

"Say his prayers?"

"Where?"

"Beside the bed, just like he had all his life."

"All right. You do it, and see what happens."

She tried. She knelt as if she was going to say her prayers. Then she pointed the gun.

"Which was the first shot?" she asked.

"I think the suicide note tells you that."

"How do you mean? It only said 'Tell my parents it was an accident.'"

"And how do you think he would make it look like an accident?"

"Not by shooting himself through the heart like Professor Gibson said, that's for sure."

"But accidents can happen, indeed have happened, when you stick a gun in your belt. He was wearing a belt and no holster."

"You mean, if the shot through the waist was the first shot, he might have thought it could have looked like an accident?"

"It's a possible explanation."

"But it didn't kill him. So he had to fire some more."

"All right, try it."

She did. The first shot was easy. Going as if to put a gun in her belt and imagining it going off, provided she was facing a little towards the foot of the bed there was no difficulty in imagining the first bullet hitting the wall by the air conditioning switch.

"Now fire the next shot," said Chartong.

There was absolutely no way she could make the next bullet go into the chest of drawers. It needed a pirouette on her knees.

"Supposing the shots were the other way round," said Chartong. "Try that."

That seemed possible. By facing the head of the bed she could make the first bullet go in the chest of drawers, but there was no way she could get the second on the other wall.

"It's impossible," she said.

"All right. Let's just try something else. Fire the first shot into the chest of drawers, but this time imagine the result. You have just fired a red-hot .38 bullet through your waist. Imagine the shock, the pain, the tremendous noise and the flash. What do you do?"

"Collapse, I should think."

"All right. Do that. Not on the floor, because we know he wasn't lying down when any of the shots were fired. So collapse forward on the bed."

She did. And suddenly it all became reality. John MacLennan was there. He was all around her. She <u>was</u> John MacLennan and she experienced the terrible physical and mental agony of having shot herself. Her whole abdomen burned with pain. Her head overflowed with the enormity of what she had done. The shock made everything blurred and unsteady. She could see for the first time, the overwhelming desire to finish it and the utter impossibility of doing so.

Then Chartong did an unexpected thing. He grabbed her by the right shoulder, which caused her to twist in a way she could not do naturally herself, and he took the gun off the bed and fired the next four shots himself. It was incredible. Suddenly everything fitted. The bullets went in the right direction. But more. Those four crippling shocks, the unbelievable pain, the inexorability of them, one after the other, came with her arms limp by her sides, her weight balanced on her knees held stable by Chartong's firm grip and it all became possible. When he released her and she fell on the floor, she fell in exactly the position John MacLennan was found, with her ankles crossed. Even her shoes came off. It was uncanny.

"But, how could that be?" She said. "There was no-one else in the bedroom."

"Who told you that, the Attorney General?'

"But the door was locked and he said there was absolutely no way it could be locked from outside."

"All right. Let's put that to the test. Come here."

They went out of the bedroom door and shut it.

"Now, you see that round plate at the back of the handle?"

"Yes," she said.

"Try and unscrew it."

She couldn't, but Chartong gripped it in his large hands and after a bit of strain he unscrewed it. The handle came off. Inside was a square bar. He gripped it and twisted it to the right. Then he replaced the handle.

"There you are." he said. "The door is locked."

"But who else would know you could do that?"

"Every policeman would know that. Quinn would have known, Trotman would have known, so would most of the others there. They had an odd-job man too, if you remember. He would have known too."

"Then why break the door down?"

"Why indeed! It was absolutely unnecessary. Because they could have unlocked it simply by reversing the process."

"But that would have made a mess of the suicide theory."

"True. Mind you, it might have been sheer panic. They had just broken down the front door, they might have broken down the bedroom door, out of habit, so to speak. But it might interest you to know that they not only forced the door with the crowbar, they battered the lock clean out of the door. It was photographed separately. And now it's missing, which is a pity because if I had it I could have discovered whether it had been undone in the way I have just shown you."

"You mean it has disappeared?"

"Completely."

"But, wait a minute. You've just proved someone could have got out of the bedroom, but he would have still had to get out of the locked flat."

"I thought that had already been done by a reporter. Still, let's look at that. It couldn't have been easy otherwise it would have been obvious. Where shall we look first?"

"How about the window?"

It was a strange window. Two of the frames opened with the hinges at the top and one with the hinges at the side. There was no ledge outside. About ten feet away and below was a tree.

"I suppose someone could have jumped into that." She was thinking aloud. "But he would have needed to be a bit of an acrobat."

"How could he have shut the window? There is nowhere to grip. But didn't you broadcast a story about someone climbing out on a rope to the flat above?"

"Yes. But that was from the bedroom window. And we know that was impossible because the black paper prevented those windows from being opened. Besides, it would be very awkward with windows hinged at the top."

"There was no black paper on this window." He pointed to the one hinged at the side. "And once on a rope you could push it shut before you climbed up. It's a possibility. But there may be others. Let's look."

They looked at the kitchen windows which opened on to the corridor. No sheer drop there. But they were barred. No-one would climb through there.

The bathroom window opened close to the end corridor window and someone could conceivably have climbed from one to the other. But the windows did interfere with each other as they opened, so it would have been extremely difficult. There was the sheer drop there, also a deterrent.

"But the fifth floor window doesn't get in the way," said Chartong. "You could climb out of the bathroom window and up to the fifth floor corridor."

"Jolly dangerous. I wouldn't want to."

"But you haven't just committed a murder."

"True."

"Supposing he never left the flat."

"How do you mean?"

"How many people were there in the arresting party?"

"Oo, a hell of a lot. There were two parties, weren't there? Quinn's and Trotman's."

"Yes, that could be quite an important point. Two lots of people who might not have known each other. I think, counting the manageress, the solicitor, the odd-job man and the two parties there would have been about twelve people."

"What, all in that tiny room?"

"Exactly. Who would have noticed the addition of one more?"

"You mean someone might have been in the flat all the time?"

"It's a possibility. Let's look at it. We now know he needn't have been in the bedroom. Where could he hide in the lounge or kitchen?"

"There's nowhere."

"Not really. So where else?"

"The bathroom? But Trotman looked in the bathroom when he first entered the flat."

"Looked in. Exactly. Not searched. Do you think he would have seen someone behind the door?"

Aileen tried it. It was more difficult than one would imagine. The door opened inwards and almost touched the bath which ran the full length of the room. So that to see if anyone was behind the door you would either have to go in and close the door, or lean over the bath and peer back at a most awkward angle. It was quite clear from Trotman's evidence he had not done that.

Chartong smiled. "So you see, when a few minutes later there was a crowd round the bedroom door only a few feet away, all facing away from the bathroom, a man could have stepped out and joined them and absolutely no-one would have noticed."

"Do you think that's what happened?"

"It's a possibility. But let's try something else. Suppose the mysterious X never left the bedroom at all. Come on. You stand by the bed and face the wardrobes. I will go inside, there's plenty of room. I have two strides from the wardrobe, which opens the right way, to the bedroom door and safety. When you are ready turn once round and see what happens."

Aileen watched him enter the wardrobe and close the door all but a chink. She then turned round once. Not too fast. Not too slow. As she looked again at the wardrobe it looked exactly the same. Nothing seemed to have changed—till Chartong's grinning face appeared from outside the bedroom doorway. He had done it without sound or trace in a matter of seconds.

Actually, he didn't surprise her nearly as much as he had expected and he looked a bit disappointed. She had worked for a time with a magician, the Great Masoni. She was sawn in half twice nightly. But one thing she had learned at that time was the incredible things you could do in full view of an audience while you distracted them. Chartong's little trick was child's play.

"Now suppose you are not just turning round. You are a photographer. Quinn has cleared everyone else out of the room. You are photographing the body. You are getting in the right position, focussing—then flash—you are temporarily blinded. Just what are your chances of spotting someone do what I have just done?"

"Zero, I should think."

"Well, at least it's a possibility."

"But there's still something you haven't explained."

"You mean who was it?"

"Exactly."

"Well, I don't know, do I? But here's a scenario. Try it out. Think about it. Try and pick holes in it. It might be a useful exercise.

"We know John MacLennan was under surveillance. They tried to tell us it had stopped before his death. But Quinn said in evidence that when he heard that John had been told he was to be interviewed by the SIU he was afraid he might, amongst other things, have fled the country. Do you really believe he would not be under surveillance under those circumstances? I really don't believe even the Hong Kong police would be that careless.

"Now, there are usually two on a surveillance team. What did they do when Johnny went to the armoury for the gun?"

"Followed him?"

"Exactly. And what would they do when they knew he had collected a gun?"

"Well, they certainly wouldn't keep information like that to themselves."

"No. They would have rung up a superior. Let's call him Omega. But they would have continued to keep tabs on John MacLennan. So the question arises, where were they when he fired the first shot?"

"As I see it they could easily be just outside in that twist in the corridor where the lift is. No-one would be seen there."

"So Johnny comes back with the gun. He has determined to shoot himself and try and make it look like an accident. He goes in. Does he take his mind off what he is doing, turn and put all four locks in place on the front door?"

"I've always thought that took some explaining. I would have thought once he had made up his mind to shoot himself he would go on and do it, and to hell with whether the front door was locked or not."

"And the same with the bedroom door?"

Why not?"

"So our watcher outside waits. Perhaps while Johnny goes in, takes his jacket off and hangs it on a chair, changes his shoes, goes and says his prayers, perhaps enough time has elapsed for the watcher to be joined by Omega. There is a bang and they rush in."

"Yes, Sandra Hill's evidence was she heard one bang then a gap, then some more."

"Omega sees the suicide note, takes out the letter inside and scans through it. He is horrified. Perhaps he is named. He goes into the bedroom where John is collapsed over the bed, groaning. A quick glance at the bleeding shows the wound is not fatal. If they call an ambulance, and he recovers, everything in the letter would come out in the inquiry. Whereas here there is a perfect suicide set-up. 'We'll have to finish him off.' And I've just shown you how it could have been done."

"Then all they had to do was to make sure it looked like suicide. They locked every lock they could find . . ."

"Thus overdoing it. That made me suspicious from the start."

"And with three pairs of hands they could easily have done the rope trick at the lounge window or helped the smallest of them out of the bathroom window and up to the fifth floor corridor . . ."

"Or simply left him here to mingle with the crowd when they arrived. No, Aileen, if this Attorney General of yours wants to prove it was wholly suicide, I am afraid he has got to be a lot more convincing that he has been up to date."

As they drove home Aileen said, "But I still don't understand why they needed four shots to finish him off. Why not just the one through the heart? I know Elsie mentioned it was a triad signature, but you are saying it was the police themselves."

"Who says they were not triads?"

"Who says they were?"

"Elsie does and I think its possible. I have been doing some digging. What's the Cantonese for 4?"

"Say."

"And what's the word for death?"

"Say."

"It seems the Chinese have an obsession with numbers. The number 4 is associated with death because it sounds the same. It has also been adopted by the triads and all members have a code number beginning with 4. Ordinary members have the number 49. Officials have particular code numbers. 426 is the martial arts expert or 'red pole' and 432 is the official messenger or 'straw sandal'. The most important is the 489 or

Shan Chu, who is the society's head. So you see, the fact that Johnny was issued with a gun to shoot himself, number 4894, might have been coincidence, probably was, but it might have been a warning to all triad police that that's how the Shan Chu deals with people who mess with the triads. That would explain the 4 shots. Remember they couldn't give him a short barreled CID gun, which would have been correct. They said they hadn't got one, but maybe they hadn't got one with the right number on it. Did anyone check with the register to see if any CID guns were in fact available? If not, why not?"

Chapter 48

On 3rd October the inquiry was adjourned for the sixth time, this time for three weeks. Only a few days before, a group from the British forces had got themselves into the <u>Guinness Book of Records</u> for their ten-pin bowling score over 24 hours, the proceeds going to the Phone-in's Christmas 'toys for orphans' appeal, SANTA. Aileen opened the show with the announcement that the Commission had taken up the challenge and were trying to get into the same book for the most adjournments.

"Meanwhile," she said, "their opportunities and credibility are going down like skittles. They are taking so long their key witnesses are being murdered. If they go on like this they won't have any left. McLean—MacLennan, there is more than just a spelling link here."

The reaction from the authorities was dramatic and could, Aileen thought, only be interpreted as an over-anxiety to cover up any link there may be between MacLennan and McLean. After the program there were calls from three Government Departments. The Police Public Relations Bureau were first on the line waiting to speak to her while her *sign off* signature tune was still playing.

"We would like to request that you did *not* link the death of Ian Mclean to the suicide of MacLennan' said Terry Combs in his formal 'I've been told to say this voice', "unless you have actual evidence that there is a link. In which case we would like you to pass to us what ever information you have". He was still on the line when Frena pointed to the grey phone at the back of the turntable. It was the Assistant Director of Government Information Services who pressed the point that as far as they were aware there was *no* link whatever between the two deaths. Aileen was surprised by that call, not so much because the call had been made, there was a close relationship between the production side of the Talk-Show and that Department, but rather the high rank of the person who gave the message.

"My, they are uptight," she thought.

The third call came half and hour later when Frena and Aileen were in the office discussing how they would arrange collection boxes for the public to donate their gifts of toys for the Charity event at Christmas. It was the Secretary for the Commission, he had no evidence of any link, he declared, and sternly advised Aileen not to insinuate one. "McLean was not a key witness," he added and went on to say, "just someone who might have been able to add a little local information about homosexual activities."

Aileen couldn't suppress a giggle, "Oh, you wanted to know how they do it!" There was a thud as the receiver was slammed down. Next day the press took up the possibility of a link and denials and counter-denials flew about everywhere. *'There is no link'* continually stressed the authorities.

In the end the phone rang and a voice mysteriously told Frena "I need Claire."

Aileen went to the canteen and made the call that gave the link. It was, Raven said, the procurer Sunny Chan—a happy little Chinese gay who had advertised in the English press for four years with complete immunity. Immediately the inquiry started he was slapped smartly in jail. Now he had been remanded four times without a charge.

"You see," said Raven, "he was used by the SIU to procure informers, hence the immunity. He procured the informers on MacLennan. Let's face it, nobody's charged them, have they? But he was also the procurer for top policemen, high-ups in government, some at the very top, and also Ian McLean. You can tell Vincent Carratu that the shutters are down. He won't get anything out of the gays now. His only hope is to employ a gay policeman. If he can't find one I will help him. And incidentally, MacLennan was investigating forged $500 notes. If one had come from one of the informers MacLennan might have been investigating him legitimately."

Aileen rang Vince after the program and suggested they meet in the Mandarin Coffee shop. They sat across a quiet table.

"Did you tell anyone else you were going to interview McLean on the day he was murdered?" Aileen asked.

"Not a soul. But it was written in my office diary for all to see."

"Vince, I'm not trying to pry, but how are you getting on with your enquiries among the gays?"

"Not at all. They won't talk to me. Do they talk to you?"

"Never stop."

"Then why won't they talk to me?'

"I suppose because they don't trust you like they trust me. I have been trying to get the outdated law concerning homosexuals changed for years. Elsie has been fighting for it too. We've seen the lives it has wrecked. Long before the MacLennan affair began."

She gave him the suggestion she had from Raven.

"God, that could make a big difference."

His chubby strong hand covered hers, and his piercing steely eyes seemed to penetrate her thoughts.

"I appreciate your confidence. You can trust me, you know".

The next day Nick came into the studio just before Aileen was to go 'on air'. The few minutes before going on-air she liked to collect her thoughts, and visitors were strictly off limits. However it was more than Frena could do to prevent the Station boss from entering the studio. Besides he had discovered something and it wouldn't keep.

"Now look what you've done. You were quite right. There is a connection between MacLennan and McLean. Ian McLean was down in Disco Disco the night before he was murdered, threatening to shoot his mouth off."

"The hell, he was!"

"And it's all because of you and Elsie. If you hadn't lifted that stone none of this would have happened. Now there will be murders all over Hong Kong."

Frena dived in between them, but Nick was tall and simply shouted over her head.

"Interfering busybody, that's what Elsie is. Now she's dragged you into confrontation with the Police, the Attorney General, the Archbishop, the . . . the . . . ."

"It may have escaped your notice, but my Sig Tune is playing . . ."

"She'll drag you into court. She'll get you fired. The big boss upstairs is VERY UNHAPPY . . . . She'll get you murdered. There will be murders all over Hong Kong!"

"In ten seconds I'm ON_AIR!"

"I can only protect you for so long . . . . the boss upstairs will fire you . . . . there will be murders."

Her hand was on the fader "In three seconds you can say all this on air. I wish you would go away."

"All right, I will." And he did.

"He didn't mean it." Said Frena.

"Oh yes he did. And he's quite right. There <u>are</u> going to be more murders in Hong Kong. I'm going to kill him."

Chapter 49

Aileen opened up the program in the usual way. None of the large multi—national listening audience had an inkling of the acrimonious scene that had just taken place. Aileen's first caller talked about the iniquities of the Housing Department who, having accepted one of the families of the teeming millions, did not check thoroughly that they were really long time residents.

"I know one lot, climbed over the fence not more than a few months ago. It just isn't fair"

Another caller joined in on the protest adding that others who were long term residents were in very different circumstances now from when they first moved into public housing.

"You would be staggered by the number of Mercedes Benz parked outside the cheap public housing. True they were in need once, but they've made it now. Some of those blighters could easily afford to keep Government. They rent out the apartments and pocket the change. Totally unethical"

The program went on in this manner until Aileen promised to get on-air the Director of Housing to state the policies of his department and justify them to the listeners.

In the outside studio the phone was ringing. It was Quicksilver. He rang to say he had been offered money for photos and a statement about MacLennan. While a commercial was broadcast Aileen rang Vince.

"Do you offer money for information?"

"Never."

"Then who is?"

He was very perturbed. They concluded it must be some overseas publication trying to dig up some dirt. The MacLennan affair was a serious matter, not some scandal for a cheap overseas rag to make a few quick bucks out of and drop overnight. In the second half of the program Aileen broadcast a warning to people not to accept money. The Commission was alerted and all their photographs were put under lock and key.

At the end of the program Barry, an actor friend of Aileen, rang.

"Hello, Aileen . . ."

"Hang on a minute, Barry, I've just got to give a time check."

Just then Jerry from the news room came in.

"Nick says you have a good story broken on the program about agents paying for information."

"Yes, hold on, I've just got to give a time check."

The red light came on.

"The time is half past twelve, Longines time. You're not dressed your best unless you're wearing Longines."

The technician was recording, Jerry the newscaster was reading the news bulletin and the guest on the second part of the show was standing on one leg. They had been talking about yoga. Aileen knew she had a 105-year-old mother at home and arranged for the Company Transport to take her home. At the end of the news she told Jerry the substance of the call from Quicksilver and her announcement on air. It was not until then she noticed the phone off the hook. She picked it up:

"Hello?"

"That's the longest time check ever. Now who's trying to get into the Guinness Book of Records? All I wanted to know was can I go back to your flat for a sleep? There is a pneumatic drill outside mine and I have a first night tonight."

"Yes, of course, Barry, I'll just ring the amah so you are expected. I don't suppose Boff will be there but if he is don't bother him, he's not in a good mood these days. Anyway, he'll be alright with you."

She rang her home number—no reply. She found out later the amah was at the market and Chartong was out with the dog.

"But how do I follow up on Quicksilver?" Jerry was still standing there.

She gave him all the contact numbers of Vince Carratu and off he went.

She grabbed her bag. She wanted a word with Nick. You couldn't knock on Nick's door, it was always open. So she swept in.

"Nick, what do I do about this phone-tapping business?"

"Drop it. You've no proof."

"I have. Mine is tapped."

"Everybody thinks their phone is tapped."

"But I know mine is. I can prove it." And she told him about Robert being beaten up after a phone call with her, Chartong's incident with Khan and her interview with Eric Walker. In the end he was not only convinced, he changed right round.

"Yes, of course you must follow it up. It's an outrageous invasion of privacy. But see our lawyer first. Keep in close touch with him all the way."

As she went out she realised something much more important at that moment than the phone-tapping. They were friends again.

But when Barry turned up at her flat and said he had come to go to bed, he had a lot of explaining to do to a suspicious amah backed up by an ex-policeman.

But Chartong had other things to think about than sleepless actors. He had just had a ring up from Alan Harrison, Seagroat's solicitor, to say the Commission were getting very embarrassed by his presence in Hong Kong and would he go down and see him.

He lost no time. He grabbed Aileen's miniature tape recorder, stuffed it in his pocket and was there within the hour.

"Why should I be an embarrassment?" he asked. Alan Harrison was a bit cagy.

"Why did you want to do all those tests with the gun?"

"Because all we have so far is the opinion of a couple of so-called experts that John MacLennan could have shot himself five times in the chest, and five million people out there don't believe it. I want to prove it, one way or the other."

Harrison did not seem too consoled. Perhaps it was the implication of ' . . . the other.'

"You see," Chartong continued, "you have had this trouble all along. Whenever I have been called to give expert evidence in court, I have never been asked my opinion—not starkly like that. I have always been asked to provide a supporting explanation. I have to do tests and take enlarged photographs and explain them in court to be satisfaction of laymen. This has not been done in this inquiry nor in the inquest. Witnesses have come along, often not even expert witnesses, and simply given an unsupported opinion—like Trotman and Matt Handley recognising handwriting as that of MacLennan. That's no way to present evidence. It's absolutely puerile. No member of the public is going to believe it. It will simply convince them it is a cover-up and every witness is in the pay of the police—which of course Trotman and Handley are.

"And look at the evidence about the bedroom door. All you have is Quinn's opinion that it was locked from inside, Quinn's opinion that the only way in was to force the door. Only the other day I was in the flat, I undid the back plate with my finger and found I could lock and unlock the bedroom door from outside without any difficulty. Why, they even had an odd-job-man there at the time who could have done it for them. Why did they have to go into all the drama of hacking at the door with a crowbar and breaking the lock away completely?

"And there's another thing. If I could have examined that lock I could have told whether it had been dismantled recently and if anyone had gripped the inner bar. But where is it? It was photographed at the time, completely broken away from the door, but I have asked everywhere. They have the door, but no lock. Nobody has got it. It is vital evidence. Where is it?'

Harrison had none of the answers and was clearly disconcerted. But before he could comment Chartong was off again.

"And then there's the pen. When I examined the note I was given three pens. None of them wrote the note. But none of them was the gold-topped Parker ballpoint photographed with the note. Where is it? It is vital evidence. I had understood it was an exhibit."

Harrison knew the answer to that one. "It was an exhibit. It is lost."

"But that's incredible. Who is responsible for all the vital evidence being lost? First they cremate the body before they had taken vital evidence off the hands of the corpse. Then they lose the doorknob which could have virtually answered the question whether it was suicide or murder. And now they have actually lost a labelled and recorded exhibit. And, you know, that could almost have told us as much as the doorknob. Just think of what it would mean if that pen hadn't written the note either. It would mean John MacLennan had borrowed a pen. Where from? Who from? Was there a second party in the flat when he wrote the note? All this destruction of evidence just isn't good enough. It's almost as if there is a policy only to present to the Judge evidence that will lead to the conclusion the government wants."

By this time Harrison was more than disconcerted. He was unhappy. Chartong reckoned he had joined the other members of the Commission who were embarrassed. He changed the subject.

"I have the death certificate for you."

Chartong took it. "That's not the death certificate."

"I assure you it is."

"I assure you it is not. It is someone different. This is a death certificate on John Richard MacLennan. We are investigating the death of John MacLennan. That's a different man."

There was a lengthy hush. The air conditioner grumbled. The distant traffic rumbled. Finally Harrison rustled through his papers.

"But the inquest was carried out on John Richard MacLennan."

"Then the inquest was carried out on the wrong man."

Chapter 50

If Chartong's objective had been to increase the embarrassment of the Commission over his presence, he had done a good job. They were in turmoil. They discovered he was quite right about the name. The inquest and the death certificate and lots of other documents were on the wrong man. They discovered he was quite right about the door handle. They set Vince Carratu on to it and he confirmed everything Chartong had said but even he, with all his resources, could not find it. They knew he was right about the pen, but it was surely gone.

Aileen knew what she would have done in their place. She would have determined that Chartong had to be discredited and got rid of—at any cost.

They called him down the next day to the solicitors of the Commission. It was set up for the third degree. He was invited to sit before several interrogators and an obvious and menacing microphone and recorder turning all the time. They taped every word he said. And there were a lot of words. He was there for several hours non-stop.

They went right back through his life history. They knew it all anyway. They knew all about the petty theft. They knew all about the perjury charge in Sheffield. They had a fat dossier on him. They had a thorough go at discrediting him.

But he gave as good he got. He told them about the phone-tapping. They laughed.

"Do you think this is because of you or your hostess?

"I have no doubt it is because of her good relations with the gay people in Hong Kong."

"Oh, yes. And what has she done about it?" one of them said with a leer.

"She has been to see the general manager of the Telephone Company who wasn't a bit surprised and said he thought it could be widespread."

All the laughter and smiles and leers were instantly replaced by frowns and furious writing of notes. Oh no, they weren't getting all their own way by any means.

Then they turned to the questions of his description in the press. They asked him if he would be willing to write to the press disclaiming the word 'expert'. He willingly agreed. He had been embarrassed by it anyway. But he pointed out that the use of the word was none of his doing and that not all the papers had used it. He also pointed out that Carratu had been described as a legendary expert which was just as wrong. They didn't want to know about that. However, he made the point that if he was to write such a letter Carratu should do so too. Their only comment was in effect 'No way'.

"I'm going to draft a letter that does what they say in a way they won't like,' he said afterwards to Aileen. It went like this"

'I have been asked by the solicitors to the Commission of Inquiry into the death of Inspector MacLennan to give them the support of my experience in the matter of the use of the word "expert"

'The word "expert" has a precise legal significance and can only properly be used in connection with giving evidence when a court has recognised a specialist as having the best knowledge of the subject available. Hence, although I have given 'expert' evidence many hundreds of times, I have had to be accepted as the expert in each individual case.

'In the present case I am representing the parents of Inspector MacLennan and it may be that I will not be called as an expert witness at all.

'However, two of the English newspapers described me as an expert while the other two correctly quoted Mr Conrad Seagroat as describing me as a former Metropolitan police officer with considerable experience in ballistics and handwriting.

'The Commission and I are as embarrassed by this misuse of the word as I am sure Mr Carratu is by being described is the South China Morning Post as a legendary fraud squad expert.

'In defense of the press I must say the mistake is widely made. Indeed I used to be described as one of the only two handwriting experts in England by no less a document the English Law List.

'I would therefore respectfully request the press not to use the word expert in my connection in this case.'

He passed it to the Commission. They were absolutely furious. They drafted another which he refused to sign. As he said to Aileen:

"How can I sign something in direct contradiction of the English Law Lists?"

Aileen could see that this entry in the English Law List might assume some importance. So she asked a QC friend of hers if he could get her a copy.

Meanwhile Vince Carratu rang her. He started off with his usual apparent confidences mingled with a few choice remarks about the Hong Kong police. She wondered if she should tell him the phone was tapped. She decided to let him find out for himself. She needn't have bothered.

He asked her if she knew anything about how the parents were informed of the death of their son. She said she only knew what John Conway had told her.

"What was that?"

"Why don't you speak to him? He's here."

"Oh no, no need to disturb him."

He wriggled and struggled. He clearly did not want to speak to John Conway, but in the end he had to.

John gave him the full background. How they were told it was a shooting incident by thr BBC. They had no written information for weeks. Got most of it from the press. Actually had a six-foot grave partly dug. They didn't want him cremated, against their religion.

Vince listened, muttering at intervals. Finally he said:

"That's quite different from the story I've been given by the police."

The next day Aileen received photocopies of pages from the 1972 and 1973 UK Law Lists. Sure enough, there he was. John Conway was listed as one of the only two 'Handwriting Experts' approved for free entry.

She really couldn't make Chartong out. He had been described to her as the biggest con man in the business. Lots of people took an instant dislike to him (especially Kevin).

Now they had this great dossier on him and were talking of embarrassment and trying to get rid of him, and yet what had she

220

actually got against him? Nothing. He had come at his own expense. Johnny's parents and the family trusted him and now, on the one occasion when she had the chance to put one of his claims to the test, he was proved right and everyone else was proved wrong.

She didn't know whether she was sitting on a bomb or a gold mine.

Chapter 51

When you really get immersed in something, information starts coming in from the strangest quarters. All this time Aileen had kept up her charity work and had always looked upon that as another part of her life, a way of getting a bit of relief from John MacLennan—till she was talking to the treasurer one evening, who had taken her daughter to a top Mayfair make-up artist to have an ugly birthmark camouflaged on her face. Aileen recognised the man at once from her description, as a former young struggling make-up artist at one of the leading suppliers, who used to do demonstrations for drama students, and was gay. Apparently they talked about Hong Kong and he had told the treasurer about a very dear friend of his, who then lived in Hong Kong, John Slimming. He had last seen him when he visited Hong Kong for a longish holiday in 1978.

Now, John Slimming was Director of Information Services at that time and in 1979 was found gassed in his flat under what some people regarded as suspicious circumstances. Aileen remembered that at the time all the media had been asked by his Deputy—David Ford—to play it in low key out of deference to his wife. So almost nothing was said about it.

But now it took on a different appearance. A top government official is visited by a longstanding homosexual friend just at the time the SIU was established. A year later he died under circumstances some people regarded as suspicious while his wife was away on holiday. The comparison with John MacLennan became quite curious. Aileen thought of Nick's 'murders all over Hong Kong'. She wondered if he included murders by suicide. Just how far-reaching was this scandal they were beginning to unearth?

The next day the Commission put a sudden chop on Vince Carratu's enquiries. Immediately the question went round town: 'What was he on to?'

Aileen was going down to Happy Valley to see a gay journalist called Hugh Gibb, one of Hong Kong's most prestigious writers. He wanted to discuss the case with her. He told her about how the SIU had recently called on the Editor of the Star, Graham Jenkins, in the middle of the night, to search his flat. He rang Hugh up between four and five a.m. He had had hours of interrogation but he told Hugh they were all very polite and were only interested in pimps and procurers. He had asked the police if he could call his lawyer. They said if he did they would arrest him. If he co-operated, they said, they would do nothing to him provided he gave them his address book. Hugh was worried because Graham's name was in it.

"Can you brainwash anyone in a few hours?" he asked Aileen. "Have you read 1984? The SIU seem to work exactly on the 1984 concept. They find your weakness and work on it. They found John MacLennan's weakness. The simplicity of his parents and his love for them."

"On the way home Aileen had to pass the front of Lee Gardens Hotel and who should she bump into but Vince. Not so surprising, he was staying there.

"Hello, have you got time for a quick coffee?" he said.

They went into the coffee shop for a very very long coffee.

Chapter 52

His opening remark was: "My God, the pressure. And just as I'm getting somewhere they cut me off. I've been given a week to leave."

"What were you on to?"

"Well, I can't really say. But all the time I have been limited to just things clearly related to MacLennan. And suddenly they've said "That's enough". Now I am only going to complete the picture of the pressure on John MacLennan, but not why. Nevertheless, I have come to my own conclusions.

"The pressures on the boy were tremendous. The tactics of the SIU and the police in general were diabolical. I'll tell you one thing. Hard as I try, I cannot find out where he was the night before he died. Don't you think that's strange? He wasn't in his flat and nobody seems to have a clue. Still, you'll be pleased to hear Elsie is going to come out with flying colours."

"I'm delighted. I hope you mean it."

"Oh, I do. You know. I've met a lot of people since I've come out here, and I've met a lot of rotten eggs. But, I don't mind telling you, that you and Elsie are two of the nicest people I've met and that's funny."

"What a magnificent way of ruining a compliment."

"No, I'll tell you something. When I arrived, one of the first things I was told was that you were a pair of dangerous women. Well, I believe in going straight for the lion's mouth, which is why I made a point of seeing you both as soon as possible. All I can say is they were wrong."

"As a matter of fact, Vince, I can't tell you what your coming has meant to us all—me in particular. Elsie and I have both been under a lot of pressure."

"I know. You don't have to tell me."

"We felt at times we were taking on the whole government—and people like the A-G can be pretty scary. But it wasn't just that. It was the things we didn't know. The triads, the SIU, the procurers and so on. Somebody's been committing murders. I know for fact Elsie had been afraid for her life several times, and I must say I've had my moments myself.

"Then John Conway came and seemed to be the answer to our prayers. The first person we could rely on not to join in the cover-up. Now things have turned sour with him.

"Then you arrived and I've got to admit Elsie and I treated you with the greatest suspicion."

"Yes, I know all about that."

"But as time went by it was obvious you weren't part of the cover-up. Then I began to ring you up with problems and you always had time for me and usually you got me an answer. I shall be very sorry to see you go. But it's a great comfort to know your report will be there. They'll find that difficult to cover up."

"I think they will. Mind you, there's a lot in it they're not going to like."

"Have you found out whether John MacLennan was gay or not?"

"I'm afraid he was a bit of a mess. He was bisexual, but I'm not sure I can prove it. I have statements from women about some extraordinary sexual antics he got up to."

"What?"

"I can't tell you. It would embarrass me. You know, I met a gay policeman the other day who told me he can remember exactly the time when he looked at himself in the mirror and knew he was gay and knew he either had to do away with himself there and then or learn to live with it. He reckoned John MacLennan looked at himself that night and chose the former. I know you can keep a secret?"

"Of course."

"I've gone and put up a terrible black."

"What?"

225

"I've interviewed the eight male prostitutes for hours. They're all lying. But I could only prove it with one, who broke down and admitted he had never met John MacLennan and had never been to his flat. He admitted he had been put up to the whole thing. He then said he was afraid for his life, so I took him upstairs and put him in an empty bed in the next room to mine with one of my men. In the night he not only did a moonlight flit, he pinched several thousand dollars. If this comes out it will be bad for my reputation."

"Your secret is safe with me."

He smiled. "I know."

It wasn't so safe with the Commission. It took about three days for the press to get hold of the story. But Aileen wanted to know more.

"How do you think it is all going to end?" she asked.

"There are bound to be scapegoats in the police. In my view Li Kwan-ha is the only really clean one in the top echelon. I should think a lot of quite high-up influential people will have to go. That's what I think will happen. But I worry that there could be a massive cover-up with just a few minor scapegoats. I hope that doesn't happen. My big problem is that people have told me things. But will they stand up and say them in the witness box? So many have said to me, 'What's going to happen to me? My future is in Hong Kong. I want to stay in Hong Kong.' I say, 'You have a duty to say it.' But they say. 'It's great for you. You are leaving. We stay here. What happens to us?'

"It's just like Watergate, isn't it?" he continued, "One mistake compounded another. There was a hell of a blunder at the beginning. So they covered it up and things got worse and ended up with an inquiry. In Nixon's case it finished up with him getting the sack. If they had only come clean at the beginning it would be all over. Now they have to pay. But what are the people in the media saying about it all?"

"I've heard a lot of people say that your terms of reference are simply to prove suicide come hell or high water and that you are being very well paid for it. I even know how much."

He grinned. "And what do you think?"

"I once described you as 'someone who was devastatingly charming, absolutely ruthless that I didn't trust an inch'."

At first he smiled, then he frowned, then he smiled again. "Do you think it is murder or suicide?"

"I am inclined away from suicide."

"But last time you said you thought it was suicide."

Aileen thought—what a fabulous memory! But she said, "It is getting into an area where it is none of my business. I can't betray a confidence. But in any case I swing from one to the other like a pendulum. What do you think?"

"I am pretty convinced it was suicide. If anyone else had fired those shots MacLennan would have lunged forward. It would have taken three people to kill him, two to hold him up and one to shoot him."

"What makes you think he was standing up?"

"What makes you think he wasn't? Mind you, I must say the inquest jury were absolutely right to return an open verdict. They couldn't do anything else."

"Then why did the coroner put such pressure on them to return a verdict of suicide?"

His face turned blank. "I don't know."

They talked for a long time. He was obviously feeling the strain because he forced himself off the case and talked about his family at home. He didn't see much of his wife, Sylvia, but he was obviously a great letter-writer and Aileen gathered that in fact they were very close. As soon as he finished in Hong Kong he was off to Brazil on a big assignment there. He was very proud of his son who had gone into the business.

Inevitably the conversation returned to Hong Kong. Aileen told him about the phone-tapping. He took it very seriously. He was clearly not surprised. In fact once or twice Aileen got the impression he had seen some of the transcripts.

"There's one thing," she said, switching the subject for the nth time, "that puzzles me."

"You've come to the right place. What is it?"

"John Richard Duffy. Here's a clever lawyer, gay, right at the middle of all this, and they let him come out of jail last week, claiming he's got a signed statement from a man alleging to have been to bed with one of the top men in government, and they haven't even subpoenaed him."

"No. If we had he couldn't have left Hong Kong. We had a gentleman's agreement so he could have a couple of weeks in the Philippines."

"Philippines be damned," she said. "He's in the UK He rang up a friend of mine yesterday."

"My God!"

"You're quite sure he doesn't know so much they don't want him in the witness box?"

"Oh no, nothing like that. You really are a suspicious lady, aren't you?"

"I've been brought up in a hard school."

He knew exactly whom she meant. He asked her what she thought of the Attorney General as a man. She said, "I liked him. At a different time in a different place I would like to have met him again. He's intellectual, charming and humorous."

"But you crucified him on air."

"Because he made a cock-up of the press conference, and a man in his position can't do that, however nice he is. I played the tape again only a few days ago and that press conference will be his downfall if I ever broadcast it again when all this is over."

"I know. And he must know it. I reckon he was told to do it."

"You're not the first to say that. Because he is far too clever to make such a goof on a subject he really believed in."

They parted, with Vince saying, "And I'm not even going to have time to buy Sylvia a present from Hong Kong."

Chapter 53

The next day a rather surprising article appeared in the press, the author being Kevin Sinclair of the <u>South China Morning Post</u>. It read: ' . . . One of the new witnesses who has not already given evidence at the inquiry and who is expected to be called is Commercial Radio broadcaster Aileen, who had discussed many aspects of the case on her radio talk-back program.' Several other names were mentioned including Elsie Elliott and John Richard Duffy.

Aileen rang Murray Burton, the solicitor for the Commission, and he denied all knowledge of it. He suggested Vince Carratu must have submitted a list.

So she rang Vince and he said he hadn't submitted a list at all. So she rang Murray Burton back and asked if Kevin Sinclair was now running the Commission. He ignored the remark.

"Perhaps it came from the Counsel for the Commission, Mr Beveridge. Would you like to see him?"

"Not much. Would he like to see me?"

"I'll ask him."

He rang back about three minutes later to say could she take tea with Mr Beveridge in his suite in the Mandarin Hotel the next day at 3 p.m. She accepted the invitation and went off to decide how to get her own back on Kevin Sinclair.

She teased him the next day on the program.

"I see," she sent over the air waves, "that Kevin Sinclair has subpoenaed me to appear before the Inquiry. If the Commission backs him up I suppose I will have to go. I have heard he has been conducting the Foreign Correspondents' Club choir in a little number dedicated to me, John Richard Duffy and goodness knows who else." She then replayed the Lord High Executioner singing 'I've got a little list.'

She had a good story break on the program that day. She had it on the best authority that the ICAC had approached a well-known homosexual actor to play the part of the commissioner of police in a short film they were shooting at 2 a.m. So she broadcast that too, just for good measure. It was a good job she wasn't a limited company. The bottom would have dropped out of the stock market that day.

Chapter 54

It was with some diffidence that Aileen reported to reception in the Mandarin Hotel and took the lift up to the gods. As she raised her hand to knock on the imposing door of the Tanqueray Suite, it was opened by a tall aristocratic man, hair swept back, dressed in a long pink dressing-gown. It was in pink floral Thai cotton with a mandarin collar. It was slit up the sides to his thighs. He looked ravishing.

The effect was spoiled ever so slightly by a slight twitch of the head towards one shoulder. She later noticed this became more prominent in moments of stress.

"Do come in."

He turned on every ounce of charm that he had, which actually wasn't a great deal, but he tried hard and she was grateful because she was rather scared.

It was a sumptuous room. She had been there before under more pleasant circumstances to interview Richard Dunhill, the cigarette man. It hadn't changed. There was the fabulous desk from which Richard Dunhill had done the interview. In the corner sat a secretary typing continuously all the time she was there. The huge window gave a millionaire's view of the harbour. On the left was a plush sofa on which she was invited to sit. John Beveridge sat beside her. It was almost cosy.

"Let me say straight away I am not treating you as a journalist."

"Let me say straight away I am not a journalist."

He gave a slight twitch. "A radio broadcaster then. I want you to know I cannot hold any of this inquiry in camera."

"Then you won't get half the witnesses."

"Oh yes I will. But you see there is no alternative. Everything said in camera must be heard by counsels, solicitors, secretaries, typists and something would be bound to leak, to the complete discredit of the Inquiry. So it all has to be open."

He was a very formidable man. He had been educated 'privately' according to <u>Who's Who</u> and was now Recorder of the Western Circuit since 1975. Pretty big stuff. He was on the Westminster City Council, was a Freeman of the City of London and master of the Westmeath foxhounds. His hobbies were hunting, shooting and travelling which was an interesting variation on the usual three. Obviously not a man to trifle with and here was Aileen trifling with him. Which was funny because he reminded her vaguely of God.

She looked up to find him glaring at her. "This man Conway is an embarrassment."

"You know, you really are overreacting to him."

He and his secretary looked as if no-one had ever spoken to him like that before. He began to show sign of stress. She continued, "In any case, it is you that are keeping him here."

"How can that be?"

"Because all he wants to do is to settle the estate under his power of attorney, which you are stopping him doing. You won't let him get at any of John MacLennan's belongings. Why not? You want him to go and he wants to go. What are you keeping him here for?"

"I am going to put him in the witness box."

"What on earth for? That's not what he came for at all."

"I have a whole dossier on him. He really is no expert."

"He never said he was. The press did. And anyway he is." And she produced the Law List photocopies like a conjuror with all the dramatic attack she had learned to command. To say the least he was disconcerted. But he recovered himself sufficiently to say that he wasn't interested in her photocopies and he was going to put her in court too.

"What for? I don't know anything."

"That's exactly what I want you to say. Many members of the public think you know a great deal and I have to lay that one to rest. And I shall demand names."

"I won't give you any."

"Oh yes you will. I won't accept privilege of journalists, priests, doctors or anyone else."

"Llewellyn, MacLennan's solicitor, has already been granted privilege."

"Members of the legal profession are different."

"You can say that again."

"They are the only exception."

She thought—bloody discrimination. She said, "I still won't give you any names."

"Then I will have no hesitation in putting you behind bars for contempt."

"I won't enjoy that. But no matter."

He looked puzzled, twitched slightly, then changed the subject. "Do you think Mrs Elliott will object be being called?"

"She will be mortified if she isn't."

They discussed the possible subjects Aileen might cover as a witness. He didn't want to know about Robert or Quicksilver or anything else come to that. He just wanted her to say she didn't know anything, because everyone in town thought she did.

She left on reasonably friendly terms except that she didn't get a cup of tea.

Chapter 55

Two days later Aileen was served a subpoena instead. She thought Kevin Sinclair must have been relieved, unless of course he delivered it.

She rang up her lawyer.

"What am I supposed to do now?"

"You will have to send them a statement."

"Saying what?"

"Anything you want to bring out in court."

"But there isn't anything. I don't know anything. At least, that's what Mr Beveridge wants me to say."

"The trouble with that is it may be a trap. If you start up saying you know nothing and then they question you and find you do, you will be declared a hostile witness."

"Is that bad?"

"Well, it's not good. You will be discredited in public. That can't be good for your image. Besides, if you make a statement they are supposed to limit their questions to the subject of it."

She found Chartong had also asked to appear in court. He hadn't been subpoenaed. But apparently he had been asked to produce a statement. So they sat down together and wrote them. Neither of them wanted to say anything. They were like a couple of kids kept in after school to write an essay they didn't want to write.

She told him what her lawyer had said.

"But I don't see how I can be declared a hostile witness. I'm not a witness at all. I'm the representative of the parents."

"Perhaps that's all you need say."

So that's what he put:

'Since the Commission has employed Inquiry Agents, it is clear that my place is simply to represent the parents, and no more. However, in view of my past experience in some fields of forensic science, they would think it strange if I returned to Scotland without examining both the ballistics and handwriting aspects of the case to the best of my ability.

'I would stress, however, that I intend to do this purely for the enlightenment of the parents, because the Commission of Inquiry is employing its own experts in these matters. I therefore do not feel that I have any evidence that would be proper for me to offer, or place before, the Commission of Inquiry.'

They thought it was pretty good. They didn't see how the Commission could do anything to him after that. It seemed to let him right out. He just wasn't a witness.

As they were preening themselves Kevin came through the front door.

"Hi, Boff. Come for your Brandy dry?"

"No thanks." He went straight to his room.

Chartong looked rather embarrassed.

Aileen brought him back to business with "Come on, let's get on with it." They turned to Aileen's statement. This was a bit more tricky. She had to ensure that she couldn't be caught for concealing anything and yet say nothing. She got round this by briefly referring to all the information broadcast.

'I am aware that everything I broadcast is transcribed, if in any way related to this inquiry, and is passed to the Attorney General's office. Hence I treat this information as already available and which therefore need not be repeated in this statement.'

She was rather pleased with that. There was no way they could accuse her of concealing anything since she had, in effect, included everything she had ever broadcast. That dealt with the hostile witness bit. Next she felt she had to say something. So, in the end, she decided to ignore Mr Beveridge's instructions to her and put in about Robert and the phone-tapping.

235

Next day they put their statements in and waited. More witnesses came and went. Quinn was recalled and grumbled about how badly he had been treated. He wanted to sue Elsie and they wouldn't let him. Aileen, he said, had a hate for him, had called him a murderer and a sadist said the most distressing things about him which had thoroughly upset his family. This actually was quite true, but the only time she had used those terms had been on the telephone to trusted friends, so Quinn could only have got the information from the phone tap. She rubbed her hands with glee.

Then John Conway was called into court and they crucified him. It was an absolute deliberate character assassination. Why that was necessary against the parents' representative who had come with power of attorney to collect Johnny's effects was not made clear. They brought up the petty theft:

"Were you or were you not convicted of a small theft charge? Answer yes or no."

"Yes."

"Were you or were you not prosecuted for perjury over evidence you had given as a specialist in fingerprint photography? Answer yes or no."

"Yes, but the case was dismissed."

He was asked to confine himself to answering the question, but he managed to blurt out that in the court he was not required to say a word in his defense.

As the examination finished he waited for the counsel for the MacLennan family to come to his defence as defence counsels always had in the past.

But no-one rose to their feet.

"No further questions."

And that was that.

Most of the press saw right through it and didn't even report the incident. But one did and that was more than enough. Most of the media thought it was unjust and improper and felt that far from discrediting John Conway it had in fact shown the Commission to be highly discriminatory in its approach and no respecter of individuals. After that Beveridge started to get the title of reputation-wrecker in the bars and coffee shops.

The repercussions went a little deeper than was expected. It just so happened that the Bank fraud case, that Chartong had been working on in 1978, returned to another court at that time. Handwriting experts were called. The police handwriting specialist, Ronald Edgeley, still said the signatures were forgeries, while a UK expert, Ian Renshaw, held the same view John Conway had, that the plaintiff had forged her own signature.

Ian Renshaw, cross-examined by Mr John Swaine QC, who appeared for the plaintiff, agreed that the bank had also consulted Mr John Conway for an opinion on the signature.

Counsel: "This was Mr John Conway, the self-proclaimed document examiner, who has been thoroughly discredited during the course of the MacLennan inquiry, was it not?"

Mr Renshaw said it was.

Aileen rang up her lawyer and asked him the ethics of this.

"Here is a QC, in a ten million dollar fraud case, trying to sway the judgment by introducing a so-called discreditation in another court, completely irrelevant to the case, when this so-called discreditation was based mainly on a dismissed charge. I thought if a charge was dismissed you were not guilty and it couldn't be raised again."

He replied somewhat guardedly, but his opinion was obvious.

"I am afraid this sort of manoeuvre is sometimes used in court when things are getting a bit desperate. I wouldn't do it myself because in my opinion both events were improper. But I must stress it is only my opinion. This is to say I would not bring up a dismissed charge because I consider to do so is unethical, but other people may not think so. I certainly would not quote such an incident in another court in order to sway the judge however desperate I was, because I would think it improper. But that in itself is a question of personal judgment. Other people might consider it quite proper."

In the end the judge in the bank fraud case, Mr Justice Bewley, had the final say. In giving judgment against the plaintiff he said: "The plaintiffs had also called Mr Ronald Edgeley of the Hong Kong forensic laboratory. He has assisted the court many times and his assistance is always welcomed."

Then came the blow for justice. The judge added that Mr Ronald Edgeley was not an expert witness on the level of the two brought from England (Mr Renshaw and Mr Conway).

So John Conway had been put back where Aileen was sure he belonged, as an established handwriting expert and a cut above the local man.

Soon after that Margaret Thompson, an old friend of the MacLennans, who used to have Johnny round to her house very often, was called to go to court. She rang Aileen up the night before. "Aileen, I don't quite know what to do. The Commission want me to cut out some of my statement."

"Which bit?"

"It's four clauses actually. One where I say the parents were not informed properly about the death; second, I put that they had the wrong name on the casket of ashes; third, that a full-length grave had begun to be dug; and fourth, that cremation was against Johnny's religion."

"But Margaret, if that's what you want to say I'm sure they have no right to stop you."

"That's what I thought. It's what I hoped you'd say."

She went down to the court and the solicitors immediately nobbled her and explained that she hadn't worded the clauses very well and that the points would be better brought out in cross-questioning. They charmed her into signing a new statement without the four clauses and, would you believe, they didn't come out in cross-questioning.

Aileen thought she would have to prepare herself well against all their tricks. And when Mr Barlow, the counsel for the Legal Department, got up in court and said 'There is an abominable lack of respect to the damage done to reputations in these proceedings,' she began to wonder if this Commission's main objectives were to cover up the truth and destroy the reputation of witnesses.

Chapter 56

The problem of reputation did not exist with the male prostitutes, the potential informers on MacLennan. They had no reputation to destroy. Despite that they were brought into court in a long procession and addressed only by a fictitious first name. As Carratu had predicted they were nearly all found to be lying, so the so called charges against MacLennan were in effect dismissed. All but one. This was the evidence given by a prostitute they called "Peter". There was no doubt from the evidence he gave he had been to MacLennan's flat. He described MacLennan as 'John the ICAC Man,' working for the Independent Commission Against Corruption (ICAC). His evidence was over two days, so that evening Chartong suggested he and Aileen nobble him after he was released to see if they could find out why.

"Problem is," he said, "the Commission brings them to court by car and takes them away afterwards. I expect it is to avoid the press. So I don't suppose they take them very far. We had better be ready with a taxi."

So it was that as soon as Peter was dismissed, Chartong nipped out and called for a taxi while Aileen stood guard. As soon as Peter came out and was bundled in a government car, with an AM number plate, Chartong said "follow that car."

"Gosh," said Aileen, "this is like a Hollywood movie."

They left the Government Headquarters in Lower Albert Road, turned left and left again down Garden Road, then along Queensway into the red light district of Wanchai. There Peter was unceremoniously bundled out and left on the pavement. Aileen and Chartong were on to him in a flash and pointed him in the direction of a particularly sleezy Chinese restaurant. Being mid morning it was not crowded nor too noisy. Aileen ordered Tsing Char (clear Chinese tea) and Chartong started.

"This is Aileen, the Commercial Radio Talk Show host."

"Sure, I know."

"Really?"

"Why you think I come with you? I could easily done a bunk."

Chartong tuned to Aileen. "Nice to know talk show hosts have their uses."

Then he got down to business. "Now, why did you really go to John MacLennan's flat?"

"He invited me there."

"Why?"

"Who are you, anyway?"

"I'm the representative of John MacLennan's parents. I want to know the truth."

"So them up there aren't going to know about this?"

Aileen chipped in. If he trusted her, they ought to be maximising that trust. "Honestly, Peter, this isn't to help the Inquiry or the Police in any way. We just want to be able to tell John's parents the truth." There was a long pause.

"Well, it wasn't what they say it was. He wanted information what for some reason he didn't want in the police records."

"What was that, Peter?" she coaxed.

Well, I done a job for Quinn and DC Lau paid me thousand bucks for it. I got the bar over there to change one of the $500 notes and it turned out it was a dud. John MacLennan found out about it and traced me through the bar. But he was quite friendly about it and said he wouldn't charge me."

Chartong was suspicious. "That doesn't make much sense. There is a proper way of investigating things like that. The police don't invite witnesses back to their flat."

"No, that's what I thought. But he was very friendly and I thought it was just an excuse to fuck me. So I went."

"But it wasn't, was it?" said Aileen.

"No, first I thought he was just after Quinn. But then he got on to the triads and how they procured boys, real young boys, for the Gang of Four."

Aileen was astounded. "The what?"

"No not them Chinese lot. No, that's what we used to call them big nibs up on the Peak. They used to have a do off and on in one of them big houses up there. I think one was something to do with a bank, a couple of top policemen and Molo used to say one was a judge, but I never knew about that."

Chartong really had his nose down. "Did you ever wonder why John MacLennan wanted to know all this?"

"Yeah, but I never make much sense of it. I mean, he wouldn't have got very far if he had tried to blackmail one of them, would he? They would have had him chopped so pretty fast he would never know what hit him."

Aileen couldn't resist adding, "perhaps they did have him chopped pretty fast."

There didn't seem much more Peter could add, so they drank up and went their ways.

Next the Commission put Mike Fulton on the stand. They probed deeper and deeper into the most intimate details of his sex life. It went on day after day and the top lawyers couldn't catch him out. Aileen got a University Professor, Peter Harris on the program to ask about the effect of day after day of cross-examination. He said that most people can take only so much. After a while they begin to get a conviction reversal and will start to say things they don't believe. Indeed, after seven days of it Fulton did start to crack up, but he never shifted from his conviction that he was asked to set up MacLennan by Chief Inspector Quinn.

Chapter 57

The weekend came and Aileen decided to go round the corner from their flat to a sale. It was no ordinary sale. It was to dispose of the affects of Ian McLean, a nasty piece of work rumoured to b e the procurers of boys for the top homosexuals. After all, you don't get to where a murder has been committed very often so she went just for the devil of it.

There was a long queue and she nearly went home. But the sun was shining and it didn't seem a bad day to stand in a queue, so she stuck it out. There was a lovely view over the islands and the sea way below them sparkled. Once inside, the passage way was very dark and she blinked to try and get her bearings. But the flat itself was fascinating.

There was a long false wall inside with plants growing behind it with daylight lighting. It looked very realistically like an outdoor garden strip. The narrowing of the room was compensated for cleverly with full-length mirrors so the effect was quite spacious.

Through to the back and down a couple of steps was the lounge with a small Japanese garden, the end of which appeared to be a cliff edge and way below was the harbour, Kowloon City and the distant hills of the nine dragons. Off the right of the lounge was a bedroom furnished as if for some eastern potentate. The bed was a huge mattress cased in below the picture window with everything to hand, TV remote, TV recorder, hifi, telephone, telephone recorder, loudspeakers and automatic dialling system. He must have had a whale of a time on that bed—until he finished up dead on it.

Then she saw a very large box of tapes, most open reel, the sort she used every day. She thought at the rat she got through tapes they would last her six months. A lot of them were unused and she could easily erase the rest.

So she paid $450 for Lot 54 and went home with what looked like a lot of rubbish. Kevin had spread his files from the Institution of Engineers all over the dining table and was sorting masses of documents. As Aileen struggled through the front door Kevin looked up, "Want some help?"

"No thanks." She dumped the box on the coffee table and started to sort the tapes.

Those in the first batch were middle of the road and disco. Then there was a voice, by its quality a telephone recording. She was shocked to realise it was the voice of the murdered man, a voice from the grave. She was transfixed as he spoke to another. It was intimate. It was mysterious. It was intriguing. Kevin took no notice so she turned up the volume so he could no longer ignore it. At first he looked irritated by the noise. However, as McLean was clearly doing dirty deals, in Paris, London, New York, making detailed arrangements over long distance for the shipment of jewelry—so he said—Kevin could suppress his interest no longer.

"Jewelry? Or was it heroin?" said Aileen. "McLean, who was murdered, was a known dealer."

On another tape McLean called the man at the Hong Kong end 'dear', and then a woman's voice came on and accused him of stealing her husband, but that was alright as long as he didn't let it affect the business. In another he referred to the next shipment of "rare lacquer boxes which you will find of particular interest." You could almost see the steam coming out of the equipment as it played.

Kevin returned to his work shaking his head and muttering "Oh no. Oh my God. What next!"

Aileen made a copy of them all and rang up Anthony Polsky, reportedly an American spy who set up the FBI office in Hong Kong. "Tony, have you any idea of a possible connection between The antique dealer, Ian McLean, and Paris, London and New York?" And she told him the whole story.

"Well, of course it could be legitimate, antiques and jewelry are shipped to and from all those places. But it could be a leftover from the antique business set up by the triads in Paris under their leader Curio Chang. It was said to have been crushed, but it might not have been. Perhaps it was still going on. Maybe MacLennan was on to it."

Aileen then rang up PPRB.

"Police public relations wing. Can I help you?"

"Yes Terry. What's your homicide bureau like?"

"Best in the world, Aileen, why?"

"I was just wondering if they did a thorough job of searching Ian McLean's flat when he died."

"Naturally."

"Because I went to the sale yesterday and bought all these tapes and they're full of intimate telephone conversations between him and all sorts of peculiar characters."

"My God! It would have to be you, wouldn't it?"

"Well, what shall I do with them?"

"Leave it to me."

Within half an hour a guy from homicide came to collect them.

Towards the end of the week she broadcast some of them because she wanted to make a point. She took the opportunity to say that two months after a man is murdered they sell his private telephone conversations to the public, whereas ten months after John MacLennan died they hadn't released his gold-topped pen, his cufflinks, his kilt or his watch to the parents' representative. She chose those particular items because she knew those were the items they had lost. She checked that it was duly transcribed and sent to the Commission.

She then sat back and waited for the reaction. It wasn't quite what she expected.

She received a solicitor's letter threatening to bring a charge against her of criminal libel, not because of the McLean tapes but because of the short story about 'Inspector McNaughton! The short story she read on air that stated emphatically that it was murder, a murder carried out by the police.

She rang her lawyer.

"What's the penalty for criminal libel?"

"Life imprisonment."

Her heart stopped. She visualized in a flash the claustaphobic cell, the bars, the bullying warders and worst of the loss of professional integrity. She felt quite dizzy and nauseous,. She couldn't bear the thought of loading this on Nick Demuth. She rang the station owner, George Ho. He knew more about what was going on than she imagined and assured her the station would support her, which was some comfort. But what about Kevin? Why were the implications of her actions so catastrophic?

Chapter 58

Aileen's day in court arrived. She was cross-examined by John Beveridge, then by each of the counsels in turn. The Commission paid for her to have her own counsel and, on advice, she chose Corinne Remedios, who was very supportive and leapt to her feet every time Aileen was in any way threatened. One such was when the counsel for Senior Superintendent Jack Trotman questioned her credentials as a broadcaster, which the judge agreed was outside the terms of reference of the Inquiry. Beveridge also was as good as his word. So long as she stuck to the story that she knew nothing other than what she had broadcast he raised no ugly evidence. Not so the counsel for the Police, Andrew Hodge. He had before him transcripts of numerous broadcasts and seemed determined to catch her out in some way. Criminal libel might well have been on his mind. Fortunately he kept losing his place and couldn't find the references he needed. He came at last to the short story by Simon Blake, describing its broadcast as irresponsible. Corinne Remedios was on her feet objecting that such a piece of fiction added nothing to the Inquiry and the Judge agreed. Hodge tried several more tacks, each time with the same result. Finally John Beveridge addressed the bench to the effect that Aileen knew nothing useful to the Inquiry and the cross-examination should be brought to an end. The Judge addressed Andrew Hodge with the words "this lady is not on trial." And he terminated her appearance. Andrew Hodge turned to Aileen saying in a loud voice "you have been very lucky, madam", but not in as loud a voice as John Beveridge who called out "No! No! No! No!", from which one might assume that there had been some prior agreement among the counsels which he was breaching.

Once Aileen was safely on record as knowing nothing, she felt she was then free to go ahead and find out.

In the studio the next day, however, she was somewhat distracted reading the news. The Queen's Chief Inspector of Constabulary, Sir James Cane, had completed a visit to Hong Kong, with two of his chief superintendents, Alfred Wallen and Sidney Pleece, who had been there for a month. They had been investigating the organisation of the Royal Hong Kong Police. She wondered if they had unearthed its triad organisation.

As soon as she could get away she rang Raven. "This is Claire."

"How can I help you?"

"John MacLennan was under surveillance. Why weren't the tails called as witnesses."

"Why don't you ask them?"

"Who, the tails?"

"Of course."

"But I don't know who they are."

"Ring me back tomorrow."

Raven, as usual, came up with the goods. "You'll find one, P.C. Ma Sun-yuen, in Yuen Long. The other seems to be P.C. Cheng Tung-sing, but I haven't tracked him down yet."

"Never mind, thanks. One will do."

"Now just be careful, Sweetie. You'll be in very hostile country."

It turned out to be extremely hostile. Mike Fulton tracked P.C. Ma down and arranged for a very burley friend of his to go with her one afternoon. But that morning the news that came on her desk reported P.C. Ma Sun-yuen, a triad, had been found murdered in a building entry in Yuen Long at 4 pm the previous day. She asked Mike if he could find Cheng Tung-sing. He said, "what makes you think you can get there first?"

So she turned her mind to the credibility of Chartong.

The trouble with dealing with any professional is that you feel afterwards you have been subjected to both his expertise, which you more or less have to accept, and the limitations within which he works. Aileen felt this very strongly about Chartong. Firstly he had taken her through a piece of detective work with such skill that she wasn't sure how many alternatives might have been glossed over. Secondly, his experience in ballistics and general detective work had not taken them into fields she would have liked to see investigated. So she decided to do a bit of sleuthing on her own.

To begin with, that business beside the bed in John MacLennan's flat. It was all very slick, and she wasn't sure how repeatable. So one afternoon when Chartong was out she invited Barry, her actor friend, up to the flat. She wanted to try out a few stage falls.

They arranged the coffee table in the lounge so that there was a good expanse of soft carpet beside it. She still had the neighbour's toy gun, which was quite realistic, and the stage was set. First Barry stood at the foot of the coffee table, 'shot' himself, dropped the gun and fell. The gun fell at his feet every time, just where it was in the photograph of John MacLennan, but on no occasion did he end up with his legs crossed or his shoes off.

"Try Kevin's sloppy bedroom slippers," she said. "After all, John MacLennan's shoes looked like pretty soft loose slippers."

So they tried it again. The shoes still wouldn't come off.

Then they tried the 'saying the prayers' theory, and immediately she could see the clue that Chartong must have seen. When you kneel with loose shoes the heels come off before you start shooting. So they tried it again. But Barry met the same trouble she had. When you try and get the bullets to go in the observed directions you can't swivel on your knees enough to make it plausible. However, they tried it a few times, but mostly Barry fell on one side with his knees bent and pointing towards the left, and with the gun beside them. The amah kept giving some very strange looks, but they ignored her.

Finally they tried Chartong's theory. To Aileen's surprise she found that when she grabbed Barry's right shoulder with her left hand she could balance him without undue effort in the twisted position. They tried it over and over again and every time he finished on his back with his legs crossed and nearly every time his shoes came off.

But Aileen was left with the gun. And then she realised something Chartong had not shown her. That when Barry shot himself from the kneeling position the gun always dropped at his knees. When she was left with it she could drop it where she liked and the most obvious place was at his feet. But it was the wrong place for a kneeling suicide.

When she pointed it out to Chartong that evening, he said he knew about that all the time, which was very annoying. But she still felt that her own knowledge of the relaxed stage fall had enabled her to support what was up till then only conjecture.

Chapter 59

It so happened that Aileen's producer, Frena, was also an author having published several books. She was now writing a book about the occult and had arranged to interview an eastern hypnotherapist, Lim Ming. He had agreed to take her back to a past life and, since she was not sure how much of it she would remember, she invited Aileen to come with her with her tape recorder. Aileen suggested Graeme came too, as the presence of a Western doctor might be a useful source of subsequent comment. She mentioned this to Barry and he said he would love to come as he had never witnessed anyone under hypnosis and he never knew when he might be asked to play the part of someone being hypnotised. Just as he was leaving her flat he added, "Since you are digging up evidence about MacLennan, why don't you see if you can get someone under hypnosis to write a suicide note. It would be in their handwriting."

"What a marvellous idea. I don't know whether I could, though, it is Frena's occasion and it's all about going back into a past life. But I'll bear it in mind."

Aileen could see this might upset one of Chartong's theories, so she typed out MacLennan's suicide note on an envelope, just as it was in the Attorney General's photograph, and slipped it in with her tape recorder. She warned Frena she was bringing another guest, but did not tell her about the note.

Lim Ming's clinic was in an old office block in Mongkok. The entrance was narrow and dingy with a few steps up to a bored looking guard on a tatty chair and two lifts with sliding iron linked gates and brass handles. Adventurers who took one of these to the fourth floor went in a series of jerks and on arrival were faced with a semi-glass door, embossed with "Lim Ming, Acupuncturist and Hypnotherapist", leading to a small waiting room with walls smothered with press cuttings and photographs of his achievements. The articles were mainly from Kuala Lumpur and Ipoh in Malaysia, where he was born and studied hypnosis. In order to perfect his powers, he stood on the beach and gazed through half closed eyes at the sunrise. As he gazed, he chanted prayers for the powers of healing and for purity. He repeated this exercise again before noon and once more at night when the moon was high in the sky. On a moonless night he would gaze at the stars and say his prayers. He kept it up for 108 days and then he was content that his power of healing was strong and he was pure. He was confident that if a beautiful woman was completely under his influence he could resist all temptation, even if she was the temptress. He also learned the hypnotizing shout. Western hypnotists use a quiet persuasive voice. Lim included a shout, which, he claimed, stimulated and controlled the nervous system. In one of the pictures he was presiding over a subject stiff as a board with head on one chair and heels on another with no other support. In another a group of people were sitting in a semicircle, all fast asleep. In a third he was with two policemen, this time wide awake.

Lim was treating his last patient of the day and by the time he had finished it was seven o'clock and all those taking part had arrived. When he came out Aileen asked him about the two policemen. "They came to me as students of hypnosis," he replied. "As far as I remember they were Mike Farnham and Brian Webster. They wanted to learn how to get victims of rape or violence to remember the detail of their trauma and their attackers"

His consulting room was bright and spotless. He turned down the lights and they got to work immediately. Frena was to be the guinea pig and Aileen turned on her tape recorder and sat back. The idea was that Lim would hypnotise her and take her back to her childhood and then back into a previous existence. This he did and before long she was an Icelandic fisherman in a previous century describing the scene and the boat and tackle in great detail. By this time Lim was really in the spirit of the thing and offered to pass his power to Aileen to see if she could exercise it. This was unexpected, and at first she wondered what to do because she had intended to take Lim into her confidence, once Frena was in a trance, but now the onus was on her. She withdrew from her bag the long brown manilla envelope with the words:

'Please, Please tell my parents that this was an accident and that I was a good Police Officer.'

She had another blank envelope ready. She said to Lim, "If I tell Frena the first is a name and address and I want her to copy it, will she copy it in her own normal handwriting?"

"I should think so."

"And will she believe she had written a name and address?"

"Almost certainly, I should think."

So he passed his hypnotic power over and told Frena to do what Aileen said. Just for good measure Aileen put a new tape in her recorder and set it going with a fresh start. Then she said to her, "Frena, you see this envelope."

Frena replied softly and drawn out "Y-e-s" in an almost unrecognisable voice.

Aileen continued "You see, it says 'Mr Smith, Star House, Tsim Sha Tsui, Kowloon.'"

"Y-e-s."

"I want you to copy it."

Aileen put the pen in Frena's hand with the blank envelope on the table. After a while Frena slowly started to write. Sure enough, despite what Aileen had told her the words were, they appeared as 'Please, Please tell my parents . . .' and Aileen was breathless with excitement. They were about to produce a suicide note in Frena's own handwriting and she would think she had written a name and address. Let the Attorney General explain that one away, she was thinking as she turned to Frena and was appalled to find she had dropped the pen, was gasping in agony and holding her side. "He's dead, he's dead, he's dead. They killed him," she was saying.

At that moment they all felt an extra presence in the room. None of them had any doubt.

Lim Ming tried hard to bring Frena out of the suffering and get her relaxed. He succeeded to some extent, but she rambled on, obsessed by her sudden integration with John MacLennan's death. She spoke in a half whisper. It was eerie.

"He killed himself. They destroyed him."

"Who did?' Aileen asked.

"They were going to do something. Not what they said they were going to do. Something else. They told him they would arrest him, but they were going to do something else."

"What else, Frena?"

"It's very complicated. He wanted to tell about something. Something he knew about people. Something about government. Something organised."

"Was it to do with money?"

"No. It wasn't homosexual either, it was something else—something he knew, something—they were organising something they were doing."

"Did anyone else know?"

"Yes. He had a friend called Andrew or An-something. He knew the secret. It was something organised, something they were doing. It was to do with secrets. It is why he resigned.'

"Was it criminal?"

"No. Not criminal, not directly criminal. But it was wrong. Something like conspiracy. Conspiracy to use the government. Yes, something like that. It doesn't go right to the top."

"Is the Attorney General involved?"

"No, he's too late. It started before he came to Hong Kong. It's people who were here before that. Several years ago. Just after the cultural revolution in China."

"Are you sure it's not to do with money?"

"No, it's not money. It's doing something, organising something. It's not sex either. They just said that. It was what he knew. He killed himself. They made him do it."

"So what is involved. Frena?"

"It's a number of top people. Not just police. Though they are involved. After the riots the police became a para-military force. Hong Kong is still run as a police state with that justification. It's maybe something to do with that and the people who control it. It's a number of top ones."

"Is the Head of the ICAC involved?"

"No Jack Cater's not. And the Governor doesn't even know about it. There are some top Chinese involved. Some in private enterprise. It's power. It's something to do with power—also with China." And she tentatively listed half a dozen names that left them all reeling.

Then Aileen thought of the recent scandal where serious breaches of security were disclosed concerning the secret MI6 communications centre at Little Saiwan. She asked if it had anything to do with that. Frena puzzled for a moment. "Yes, I think so. I think there is a connection."

But she kept coming back to the physical agony she had first experienced. She kept remembering the pain. "He's dead. He killed himself."

"Why did he shoot himself, Frena?'

"Because of what they were going to do to expose him—as a homosexual."

"But why expose him?"

"Because he wouldn't shut up. He had to tell. He felt he had to tell. He told Anders, and somebody who's not here now. Anders is very unhappy. He is very afraid. They will destroy Anders. There are a small number of people who know. And he wrote it down."

"Wrote it down. Where?"

"I don't know. He wrote it down. But the wrong people have it. It's to do with civil order. They're all afraid."

"Are the triads involved?"

"The triads are being used. Most other things are being used. It's people with power, but not just in government. He killed himself. He wanted to tell the story. It was all there. It could have changed the future of Hong Kong. If it came out it could change things. It's to do with trust. It's been betrayed by people here. It's stopped now. If people knew. He knew. He's dead. Because he wasn't brave enough to survive."

Lim was getting more and more agitated. He kept muttering, "I had no idea you had this in mind" and Aileen kept saying "I didn't. I had no idea either," but the fact was they were all sweating and shaking and Lim stepped in at this point and put a stop to it. He told Frena to forget everything that had happened. He warned everyone present never to disclose to Frena what had happened "it could damage her mind." Then he brought her round. She was bright and relaxed and wanted to know what had happened but everyone else was spent and shattered and they were not about to tell her. They just told her she went back to Iceland. They broke up the session as soon as they could and went their ways, but not before Aileen had drawn Lim on one side and persuaded him to have an inquest later. He insisted he would not allow Frena to be present. Aileen respected his expertise in this and agreed. This time it was to be in Graeme's flat three days later.

Chapter 60

Aileen couldn't wait for the appointed time. Had they just heard the meanderings of a comatose mind, or had they had some supernatural experience which had opened chinks in the whole MacLennan cover-up? As she drove over to Barker Road to the seclusion of Graeme's flat the words of Brutus kept running through her mind:

'O conspiracy;
Sham'st thou to show thy dangerous brow by night,
When evils are most free? Oh, then, by day
Where will thou find a cavern dark enough
To mask thy monstrous visage?'

The fact was that if the ideas that had come from Frena's lips had any substance in them, who would have the courage to do anything with the information?

Graeme and Barry were full of eagerness and expectancy. Aileen did not share their ebullience. She was overawed by what they might discover. Lim Ming was serious too. Very, very serious. However, as he opened the discussion he was coldly scientific.

"What we experienced the other night could have two explanations. Keeping it within the limitations of hypnotic science, I would say that Frena is a journalist with wide knowledge of current affairs and local gossip. Under hypnosis her mind was freed from all her personal prejudices and was able to make a much better job of piecing together information objectively than she could have done consciously."

"Yes," Aileen said. "That explains something I found very surprising. She would never accept John MacLennan committed suicide. Yet under hypnosis she insisted he killed himself."

"That may simply mean that consciously, as a journalist, the sensationalism of a murder appealed to her, whereas her subconscious accepted that the facts pointed to suicide."

"But do they?"

"That's not the point. All I'm saying is that the facts stored in Frena's mind may lead to a logical conclusion of suicide, but those facts could still be incomplete or incorrect."

Graeme looked most disappointed. "So what is the value of what we heard?"

"Well, if my thesis is correct, we have heard the correlation of a lot of facts and gossip, probably high quality facts and gossip, that we could not have obtained in any other way. Because Frena is intelligent and well informed, probably better informed than even Aileen, because she's plugged into the network. I would say that a lot of what we heard has substance."

Barry was puzzled. "But there wasn't much substance in what she said. She kept making reference to organising things and conspiracy. But even when she mentioned names I got the impression she was only guessing."

"Isn't that just what you would expect?" said Lim. "If Frena had all the answers she would have either made history or been locked up months ago. What we observed was probably the best distillation of the incomplete information she has picked up so far. Probably it is no better than a series of leads."

"But Lim," said Aileen, "how can we possibly allow ourselves to be led in those directions? It's political dynamite."

It was Graeme who reminded them, "Didn't John MacLennan once say just that? That what he knew would blow the lid off Hong Kong?"

"Okay," Aileen replied. "But where do you think it can possibly lead?"

"I think you've only got to look at the newspapers to answer that. What were the headlines in the papers today?"

"I don't know. Something about the Peking trials, wasn't it? Something about the Gang of Four."

"Right. I've got it here. It says, 'Hong Kong is too important to change'. It was a statement by a senior Chinese government official that the riots that had rocked Hong Kong and Macau in 1967 were the result of 'ultra-leftist influence'. However, whether or not Lin Biao and the Gang of Four, the primary figures of the Cultural revolution, had planned the takeover of Hong Kong, Chairman Mao Zedong and Prime Minister Zhou Enlai would never have agreed to it because both recognised the importance of Hong Kong to China.

"Now, the point is, Aileen, that we can be pretty certain from a statement like that there was a plan to take over Hong Kong. Such a plan would be so much more practical to carry out if the perpetrators had got the co-operation of influential people in Hong Kong, that we can be pretty certain that there was a gang of three or four or five in Hong Kong at the time, in direct communication with the gang in China. Now when the Gang of Four were clobbered in China, what do you think happened to our lot here?"

"Went into hiding, escaped perhaps?"

"What on earth for? If nobody knew what they had been up to what was to stop them continuing their legitimate activities? If nobody knew. But if John MacLennan knew, he would have to be got rid of, wouldn't he?"

Barry looked as if he had seen a vision. "That's the first plausible motive for this whole affair anyone has ever produced yet. I never did believe he committed suicide, or was murdered, because he saw a name or two on some list of rumoured homosexuals that everybody knew about anyway. But this is different. This is a real motive."

But Aileen's mind had been racing through all this. "Do we want all this to come out?"

"Why on earth not?" asked Graeme.

Aileen was very thoughtful. "I was talking to the Commissioner of the ICAC the other day and he was explaining some of the difficult judgments he has to make. 'What do you do,' he asked me, 'if you find someone in a top position, steeped in corruption, but such a key figure in the export program that to remove him would inflict the most severe damage to the economy of Hong Kong?' He gave me the impression that he left such people well alone. Shouldn't we do the same? After all, our gang of five or whatever have stopped this particular conspiratorial activity now. They must have. To disclose their previous activities now could harm Hong Kong much more by their removal than to cover it up.

My God! That's exactly what the Attorney General told me over dinner, and I didn't know what he was talking about."

But the professional in Lim could not accept such an unethical approach. "If it's true, you can't let them get away with it."

"I'm afraid it's the way Hong Kong works," said Aileen. You do the thing which causes least damage to the economy. You've got to admit it's a highly successful policy. The trouble is it results in the discriminatory practices so many homosexuals have been complaining about, namely that the purges are against the middle people, to show something is being done, while the top people are allowed to get away with it."

Barry broke a long silence. "Lim."

"Yes."

"You said there were two explanations. What was the other?"

Lim smiled. "It's not very scientific I'm afraid."

"Never mind. What is it?"

"Some people might say, those who believe in the supernatural, that what we experienced the other night was not just hypnosis but a séance. They would say this would be possible if somebody present, or possibly somebody who lived in the house, had appropriate powers, ESP or whatever you like to call it."

Aileen said, "I must say I felt John MacLennan was there. At least at first."

Barry and Graeme readily agreed. Then Barry added, "You mean it could have been John MacLennan himself trying to tell us something?"

They talked around the subject for a while till they noticed Graeme had gone very quiet.

What's the matter, Graeme," asked Aileen.

"I've just had a flash of enlightenment I wish I hadn't had."

"What? Tell us."

"Frena kept referring to a friend of MacLennan called An-something. She called him Andrew and Anders."

"So?"

"Well I know one. One of my patients. His name is Anson Che. And I know for a fact he did know MacLennan. But how could Frena possibly know that?"

Chapter 61

Graeme wasted no time in contacting Anson Che to see if he would be willing to speak to Aileen. He was, so it was arranged they would meet in the Captain's Bar of the Mandarin Hotel, which was about as dimly lit and secluded as they could get. It turned out he was an officer in the Community Relations Branch of the Independent Commission Against Corruption (ICAC).

"I first met John when I was stationed in the Sham Shui Po Branch of the ICAC. It was there principally as a report centre for members of the public to tell their stories and give us leads. John was working an easy tram ride in Yuen Long at the time. He had had brown manila envelopes regularly left in his office drawer with money in and he didn't know what to do about it. I took them over and had them officially recorded. Then he got caught up in all that triad nonsense, when he was dismissed on fragile evidence and reinstated. I caught up with him again when he was moved to Homantin. He was investigating forged $500 notes. His difficulty was the same. He had traced one back to the police and wanted to know what he should do about it."

"Yes," said Aileen, "I heard about that. He got it from one of the male prostitutes."

"Yes. I couldn't help him very much with that either except to feed it into the system."

"Why did Peter in the Inquiry describe him as John the ICAC man?"

"As far as I know I was his only contact. They must have found out something about our relationship. He actually contacted me quite often from Homantin, basically when he came up against triads in the Police.

"Its actually a very interesting story. Did you know that Dr Sun Yat Sen was a high up triad officer. So was Chiang Kai Shek, who was originally a broker in the Shanghai stock exchange. They used to say he was called a broker because he broke the arms and fingers of those who crossed him. So the overthrow of the Qing Dynasty was triad instigated. The follow up is even more curious. At the end of World War II President Roosevelt had a secret agreement with Chiang Kai Shek, by then a triad office bearer, to keep the British out and hand Hong Kong back to him at the end of the war. Had that happened, Hong Kong would have been overrun by the communists and finished up like Shanghai. Am I boring you?"

"No, its fascinating. You mean America was in league with the triads?"

"Exactly."

"What went wrong, or should I say right?"

"There was a very courageous Englishman, Arthur May, a civil servant in the electrical section of the PWD and a distant relative of a past Hong Kong Governor. He was interned by the Japanese. I have reason to believe he was an MI6 agent. He operated clandestine radio receivers and had sewn up a Union Jack in one of his mother's cushions. When the news reached Hong Kong that the war with the Japanese was over, he and a friend broke out of the camp by night, proceeded on a very hazardous journey across the harbour in a leaky boat, woke up his mother who had not been interned but was living in Kennedy Road, and took the British Flag up to the Peak and raised it. He then set out alone in a small sailing boat towards Macau to try and get a wireless message through to Britain that the flag had been raised, since there was no radio contact from Hong Kong. He was captured by pirates, but such was his persuasive power, he had an old pistol which didn't work, that he got them to take him to Macau, where he radioed the message. He then thumbed a lift on a junk bringing rice to the starving people of Hong Kong with a young boy you will know very well, he is now the Senior Member of the Legislative Council, Roger Lobo. They arrived simultaneously with Admiral Harcourt and the British fleet led by three

British destroyers. So Hong Kong was kept from the triads and returned to the British."

"I know Arthur May. He rings up my program sometimes."

Though Anson did not tell Aileen very much about John MacLennan, she had the feeling there was a strong undercurrent to their meeting. Perhaps he was sizing her up. Certainly she was convinced he had a lot more to tell her at an appropriate time.

There was an interesting corollary to that story only a few days later. It was the day of the wedding of Prince Charles and Diana. One of the ex PoWs rang the program to say he could see a very special Union Jack hanging from a balcony across Happy Valley.

"Not THE Union Jack, the one that kept Hong Kong British?"

"Oh, you know the story. Yes that's the one. Arthur only gets it out for very special occasions."

Chapter 62

The Inquiry was nearing its end. The Commissioner of Police, Roy Henry, was called as a witness, but counsels were strictly limited to questions about John MacLennan. They were not allowed to mention Roy Henry's private life. John Conway could see his part in the affair was also drawing to a close. He made one last effort to retrieve John MacLennan's effects that had been requested by the parents, but was refused. So he flew back to Britain, just missing the trial of a bar captain accused of murdering Ian McLean which ended with the judge, no less a person than the Chief Justice, Sir Denys Roberts, sentencing him to three years imprisonment, which was generally regarded asa a bit fishy. Back in the Inquiry there was a fascinating exchange between John Beveridge and the final witness, the Attorney General—two top lawyers on top form and clearly antagonists.

The following day, scheduled to be a free day, the inquiry was unexpectedly opened at the request of the Governor, Sir Murray MacLehose. The Counsel for the Crown, Andrew Leggatt, generally regarded as the Governor's mouthpiece, said Sir Murray wanted Justice Yang to draw the inquiry to an expeditious conclusion. He should resolve allegations against the police and others. If found innocent they should be clearly exonerated. Sir Murray did not expect gratuitous criticism which did not relate to the main events. One of these was the part played by the Attorney General. Sir Murray had been satisfied after the inquest that MacLennan's death had been suicide and that there was evidence he had been involved in homosexual activities. Others saw it differently

Mr Leggatt said that Sir Murray regarded two of the Inquiry terms of reference as of paramount importance: was the death other than suicide and were the charges properly brought and evidence properly obtained? Justice Yang's report must be concise and intelligible to the man in the street.

After the weekend summing up by the various counsels began. The first day was entirely occupied by Conrad Seagroat, Counsel for the MacLennan family. Though he spoke all day it should be remembered the court normally only sat for 4½ hours each day, which may have contributed to its lasting 10 months. Society had good reason to be grateful to those prepared to question authority. Public servants have a duty to earn the confidence of the public. On personalities he said Quinn was less responsible than his superiors, Superintendent Brooks and his colleague Inspector Angus Graham, who was stamped by bigotry and maliciousness. The inordinate interest in the case was demonstrated by small snippets of information being passed up to a very high level. Some suggestions from top police officers, Ross, Clancy and Moor were 'arrogant, blinkered nonsense' He dismissed the male prostitutes as unreliable and noted that none of them had been prosecuted. They appeared to be a deliberate smokescreen. He particularly singled out the Attorney General for his inaction on warnings from Lindsey and Elliott. Furthermore he had omitted reference to the set-up in his press conference for no conceivable reason.

He thought John MacLennan probably committed suicide though there was difficulty in establishing a credible motive. He was also probably bisexual since to argue against this would indicate that there had been a conspiracy of mammoth proportions to concoct evidence against him. Nevertheless, he had been a victim of the police. There had been gratuitous attempts to attack the credibility of witnesses, such as Fulton, while Director of Personnel and Training, Eric Blackburn's attitude to MacLennan during the reinstatement after the Yuen Long incident had been disloyal and disgraceful. Indeed, Roy Henry had made a faulty judgment at that time in his dismissal of MacLennan, who had been shabbily treated and then considered disloyal for reasonably seeking help outside.

Elsie attended the inquiry that day. She thought Seagroat's summing up to be the most important because he, being the Counsel for the family, was the only one likely to make the case for John MacLennan's defense. She was therefore devastated at his concession that the death was 'probably suicide' and as soon as she was home telephoned Aileen to express her displeasure. "If the Counsel for the MacLennans supports the suicide theory what hope have we got!"

Aileen was taken aback too, and asked Elsie to confirm the words were 'probably suicide'.

"Yes, Aileen, I was shocked."

Aileen thought a moment. "You know, Elsie, that's not the same as definitely suicide, or suicide beyond reasonable doubt. He might have chosen his words very carefully. 'Probably suicide' allows an element of doubt. After all, none of the evidence presented to the inquiry led to any conclusion other than suicide. What else could he say? By conceding an element of doubt, possibly reasonable doubt, Conrad Seagroat has in fact supported the Jury's open verdict, which is as far as he could go under the circumstances. Indeed, he was probably made aware by his solicitor of the tests Conway had done, so he may have had good reason to doubt the suicide, but could not say so for lack of evidence presented to the inquiry."

"In that case why didn't he object when they crucified John Conway in Court?"

"I don't know, Elsie. Perhaps he had no grounds for objecting to the accusations against Conway. I have wondered about that myself and have been unable to come up with an answer."

Chapter 63

The counsel for Senior Inspector Michael Fulton, Mr A.M. Niamatullah, surprised many in the court by launching into an attack on the Governor. The submission on His Excellency's behalf, he said, showed disrespect to the Inquiry Commissioner, Mr Justice Yang, and was possibly contempt of the High Court, of which the Inquiry was a judicial proceeding. Some of the comments were objectionable and unfortunate and caused him great concern. He urged Justice Yang to make it clear in his final report that the commission was truly independent. Contained in Mr Leggatt's submission, he said, was innuendo that the report might not be all Mr Justice Yang's own work.

Mr Niamatullah also attacked the Attorney General as misleading the public, unfair, and heavy handed. His later action in telephoning Senior Inspector Fulton's lawyers to try and stop a statement being issued by them was "evidence of a guilty mind". There was no doubt, he continued, that the SIU had a hold over his client. He had been asked by the SIU to set-up MacLennan by introducing him to one of his friends so that a homsexual act could take place in order to provide evidence of homosexuality. The SIU were clearly under pressure to produce evidence against MacLennan. This pressure built up after Senior Inspector Fulton refused to help them and complained to the Commissioner of Police—though the complaint was intercepted by the Director of Criminal Investigation, Mr Patrick Clancy, who had not been truthful in his evidence to the Inquiry. After the lunch break counsel for the SIU, Mr Kemel Bokhary, said the temptation for Senior Inspector

Fulton not to be frank about his informing activities was very strong. He was unreliable, in danger of being influenced by others and his account was embellished. Kemel Bokhary was particularly concerned about the allegations against Chief Inspector Quinn, who had had his day in court and had been, in his opinion, completely vindicated. All the evidence of the male prostitutes had been tested thoroughly and there was no basis for thinking the case against Inspector MacLennan had been manufactured . . . It was clear that MacLennan took his own life after being told by Senior Superintendent Jack Trotman that he was to be interviewed by the SIU. Superintendent Bob Brooks and Chief Inspector Michael Quinn of the SIU were both unhappy about that action. If people thought John MacLennan was hounded to death why was there no mention of this in his suicide note? The allegation was entirely unfounded. It had been his dying wish that his parents should not learn of his homosexuality.

The final submission that day was by the counsel for Senior Superintendent Jack Trotman, Mr Charles Ingham. He gave detailed reasons why Justice Yang should conclude the death was suicide for which there was overwhelming evidence. Paul Stevens must have been mistaken in his recollection of the suicide note. There had been absurd suggestions like "the man in the wardrobe". This was pure fantasy. Broadcasts by Aileen and Mrs Elliott had caused distress to innocent people.

Having established the certainty of suicide Mr Ingham turned to motive. MacLennan had admitted knowledge of "Peter" to Llewellyn and had some connection with the Star Ferry where male prostitutes frequented. It did not make sense for MacLennan to commit suicide if he were not homosexual. The motive was therefore that he was leading two separate lives and feared disclosure.

Mr Ingham urged Justice Yang to vindicate Senior Superintendent Trotman for his decision to inform Inspector MacLennan that he was to be interviewed by the SIU. Trotman, he said, should be judged on the police procedures at the time and the overwhelming evidence of suicide. He asked for no less than a public exoneration of Trotman and others regarding the allegations of murder. If such had been true they could have led to the most serious charges. "My client and his family have had to live with this for over a year."

Chapter 64

The next day the inquiry was diverted from summing up by a submission from another counsel who put forward the opinion that Mr Leggatt's submission had been misconstrued. "No warning, direction or other interference whatsoever, with the exercise of the powers as commissioner vested in your lordship alone, was or is intended by His Excellency or by Mr Leggatt."

The summing up then proceeded with submissions from counsels for the Legal Department, Mr Max Lucas and Mr Barrie Barlow. Mr Lucas pointed out that no one had contested that the charges against Inspector MacLennan were properly brought. Furthermore, it was pure sophistry to suggest that if the Attorney General had acted promptly on complaints that MacLennan was being set-up he would not have died because that set-up complaint had nothing to do with the charges which led to the suicide. Besides, the complainants were unreliable and manipulators. One, Howard Lindsay, was embittered with a grudge against Chief Inspector Quinn. The other, Mrs Elliott, was clumsy and careless about the facts. He went on to read one page of his statement twice and, having noticed this himself and apologized, admitted that it bothered him that no one else seemed to have noticed. Extravagant headlines demonstrated the charged atmosphere in Hong Kong about the death.

Mr Barlow added that the Attorney General had taken the allegation of a set-up plan seriously. Counsel for Elsie Elliott, Mr Albert Sanguinetti, rose to his feet to say his client felt that a great wrong had been done to John MacLennan. He had clearly been selected from among the many police officers who were under investigation and were concerned, he thought, with being homosexual. As many as 17 of these had been confirmed. She maintained that the late inspector was hounded to death. "Whether it was suicide, murder or otherwise, whether he had been practicing homosexuality or not and whether or not the charges were properly brought against him, the fact remains that he was selected. This might have been because it was considered he was disloyal to the police by invoking the aid of several people including that of my client."

Mr Sanguinetti blamed those higher and in charge of the SIU rather than its own staff, in particular the SIU Charter drawn up in secret, It was left to Mr Moor, in conjunction with the Attorney General, to decide who to target. By identifying the investigation and types of people to be targeted it produced selectivity. It was a discriminatory charter. It was unfair and unjust in every sense of the word. It had a sinister and dangerous smell about it.

Mr Sanguinetti criticised the Attorney General for suggesting to Mrs Elliott she take the matter up with CAPO as he knew full well that her informer was a police officer whom, she feared, might lose his job if exposed. She regarded it as absurd for a man of his intelligence. He should have taken it up with the Deputy Commissioner Peter Moor so that at least something would have been done to alter the course of events.

Finally he added that his client was sad, very disturbed and concerned by Sir Murray's address to the inquiry apparently instructing Justice Yang on his findings.

The next day's hearing was opened by Mr Andrew Hodge, counsel for the police. He suggested that instead of the late inspector being the victim of a police vendetta he was the victim of his own sexual tastes. Mrs Elliott, on the other hand, had abused the responsibility of a public figure and willfully misused the issue to further her own vendetta against the police. This, he claimed, indicated a mentality warped beyond reason by blind adherence to her own messianic vision. She completely distorted the information given to her by MacLennan and Judge Daniel about the Yuen Long incident to fit in with her own unhealthy suspicions about the force. Having distorted and mis-stated the Fulton allegations, she was able, taking two matters together, to publish the scandalous allegations and innuendoes. He then turned to the media. Activities by parts of the media, he said, should be deprecated by all those who profess concern for the standards of responsible journalism. Other members of the "publicists", according to Mr Hodge, were former Crown Counsel Howard Lindsay, former Senior Inspector Michael Fulton and former solicitor Richard Duffy. The evidence against Inspector McLennan was properly obtained and there had never been any attempt to cover up the death or surrounding circumstances among the 60 police witnesses represented by Mr Hodge the motivation of several were specifically defended Deputy Commissioners Eric Blackburn and Peter Moor he said had always acted properly, fairly and in good faith. Special operations group chief Bill Ross would not have permitted any improper pursuit and targeting of Inspector McLennan. And police Commissioner Roy Henry's decision to dismiss Inspector McLennan in 1978 had been taken honestly and in the interests of the public, the police and Inspector McLennan. If the allegations of homosexual conduct against Inspector McLennan were to have been made public by his arrest he had the courage and strength of character to put five bullets in himself. They were the last desperate acts of a desperate man.

Mr Hodge concluded that the fairest view of John McLennan's death was that the various skeins he had woven in life had been knotted. The only disillusion he saw was final. He sought to save his family, friends, colleagues and supporters, or those who had trusted him from betrayal and shame. And there the matter should have rested in decency. But there were those who would feed the fire of their public vendettas with his death, his body. His last and best intentions were thwarted and in the charred remains the truth of John McLennan became unrecognisable. Its recreation had been a pain-filled protest. Many have suffered. Let us hope they hold in their breasts more charity than did the misguided pyromaniacs.

After Mr Hodge had finished his submission, Mrs Elliott's Counsel, Mr Albert Sanguinetti, said mistakes and errors could be made, as Mrs Elliott in her evidence had candidly admitted. But he said it was beyond all propriety to say she was guilty of fraud, asking the Commissioner, Mr Justice Yang, to disregard the accusation. Mr Sanguinetti said it should be treated with all other vituperous allegations made to the commission.

Chapter 65

The final submission in the McLennan inquiry was made by counsel for the commission John Beveridge, who said that the inquiry had already performed a valuable service to Hong Kong by relieving grave doubts in the community about the administration of justice. It had arisen, he said, out of a personal tragedy, which resulted in a number of persons—both public-spirited and responsible—expressing suspicion that the death might be murder. This arose through a widespread distrust in certain elements of the police. The worst aspect, he said, was an apparent conviction that influential persons in the colony could always protect themselves and the inquiry would not be effective beyond a certain level. It showed a fundamental lack of trust in the integrity of life in Hong Kong and aspects of administration, including the rule of law.

He urged the Commissioner, Mr Justice Yang, to make it clear that the commission's findings were free from external influence and whether the submission made two weeks before on behalf of the Governor Sir Murray MacLehose amounted to an infringement of the judiciary's independence. Furthermore, the suggestion made by Mr Andrew Leggatt on behalf of Sir Murray, that it was not in the public interest to make findings critical of the Attorney General, could not assist Mr Justice Yang. He argued that the role of the Attorney General in the McLennan affair was relevant. If so the status of his office might make it more necessary to the public interest that they be included in the report. Furthermore, he felt the Attorney General had been in error in setting his own views against those of the Inquest Jury. It was essential that the inquiry should attract public confidence, for one of its primary functions was to satisfy the public that truth had been uncovered. Nobody—including Sir Murray—had the right to influence the way in which the commission carried out its functions. The greatest safeguard of the individual within the British constitutional system was the rule of law, before whom all are, and must always be seen to be, equally answerable, from the highest to the lowest.

Mr Beveridge gave his own views on certain aspects of the evidence. That Inspector McLennan committed suicide, he said, had been established with an absolute and compelling authority rarely to be found. But the late inspector's homosexuality or bisexuality had not so clearly been established. Regarding the special investigations unit, while it might be concluded there had been reprehensible and improper behaviour, together with breaches of police standing orders, there was no evidence that the case against McLennan had been improperly brought with the purpose of driving him to suicide. The Commissioner might decide there was evidence of a readiness because of resentment about McLennan's behaviour—in accepting outside help to fight his dismissal—to take up information against him while similar information on other officers was not followed up. This might deserve strong criticism, he suggested. The evidence from Senior Inspector Michael Fulton of a proposed set-up of McLennan possibly fell short of an allegation to make a crime, and in any case no offence had been committed. Nevertheless it might be considered improper and undesirable.

There were several matters of particular difficulty that Mr Justice Yang had to resolve. These included: Police Commissioner Roy Henry's decision to dismiss Inspector McLennan in 1978; the extent of and reason for continued police interest in the late inspector; the process and decision of targeting him; and decision to prosecute.

To close the proceedings, Mr Justice Yang made a short firm statement. "In order to clear the air", he said, "I would reaffirm, if affirmation is necessary at all, the sanctity of judicial independence which brooks no interference from any quarter." He thanked all counsel for their submissions but stressed that in the end he would use his own independent judgement, and his alone. He added, "I would like to publicly pay tribute to the press who have covered this long and complicated case conscientiously and faithfully and with a degree of independence which orderly society demands and receives."

The 10 month inquiry was reported to be the longest judicial inquiry in English legal history. The evidence came from 110 witnesses and 57 statements read out by lawyers. The transcript ran to 13,000 pages. It was estimated to have cost around US$2½ million, most of which were legal fees—at least 17 parties were represented by counsel at some time.

PART III
THE AFTERMATH

Chapter 66

Everyone then had a lengthy recess while Justice Yang wrote his report.

Aileen and Kevin were due for leave and they decided they would go to Britain. Then Aileen received a most extraordinary phone call from the Director of Community Relations of the ICAC, asking her if she would be prepared to take John MacLennan's effects back to his parents. How he knew she was going to Britain, why he had the belongings and not the Police or the lawyers, why he should choose a broadcaster and not the family representative with legal authority, were questions she found completely puzzling and to which she never found answers. Anyway, she collected the box and found to her disgust that it did not contain several items the parents had requested, such as the gold topped pen and the kilt, but it did contain the bullet ridden sweater and shirt John MacLennan had died in, which would have caused untold distress to the parents, along with his typewriter, watch and other more reasonable items. She removed the offending items. It was then decided, after quite a lot of persuasion towards a reluctant Kevin, to take a self financed side trip to Scotland.

On arrival at Heathrow Airport they just had time to deposit their two large suitcases in left luggage before catching an internal flight to Scotland. It was a very special internal flight. As a promotion British Airways were operating some internal flights by Concord, though not supersonic. It was such a thrill that Aileen and Kevin actually spoke to one another on the flight and, being away from the stresses of Hong

Kong, there were the first signs of their relationship thawing out. On arrival they hired a car and drove into Inverness for lunch, after which Aileen drove on to the Black Isle to see John MacLennan's parents, Joe and Katie, and give them Johnny's effects, while Kevin set off into the town to visit his uncle Hamish, whom he said he hadn't seen for years. They arranged to meet after the visits at the railway station so they could drive on towards Ullapool on the West coast for a short break.

Aileen found Togorm Farm with some difficulty, as it was not signposted and the locals seemed to be speaking a foreign language. She was irritated that Kevin would not come with her, he would have been such a useful navigator. However, as he had become quietly more aloof as the MacLennan case had continued she felt she had to agree to his seeing this mysterious uncle, even though he had never even mentioned him all their married life. However she finally made it and a little way past the farm house was a small stone cottage with a steep ridge roof alone in acres of pastures and corn fields. She made her way through the side wicket gate round to a small front door in the right hand side, concealed from the road. She knocked. She had corresponded with Katie, so was expected and warmly welcomed. Katie, tall and lean with curly grey hair and a weary smile, led her into a sparsely furnished living room, with only a small window to let in some pale sunlight while keeping out the cold in winter. Joe, in a huge navy sweater was sitting in his favourite upright armchair by the fireplace and smiled warmly when Aileen spoke, though he could not see her.

There was still a lot of sadness, though after 18 months much of the pain had gone and they could speak of Johnny freely. Yes, he was all the things Aileen had heard from his friends, jolly, full of fun and practical jokes, yet deeply religious and clearly of high integrity. Katie proudly threw open a wardrobe door to reveal stacks of letters he had written home. She had kept them all. Katie confirmed the appalling way the news of his death had been broken, over the BBC news, how they had wanted his body returned, but the Hong Kong London Office would not sanction it. How the casket with the ashes had been sent to an office in Aberdeen, over a hundred miles away, and they had received a curt note to come and collect them. Fortunately Mr Macdonald had stepped in, fetched the casket himself and, having noticed it was incorrectly labelled "John Richard MacLennan", he had been able to get a new plaque made in a hurry with the correct name "John MacLennan" before the parents saw it. They only found out much later when a solicitor called requiring them to sign an affidavit swearing that their son's name was John, not John Richard, as if the blunder had been their fault. They were both distressed at the insinuations surrounding the death and simply did not believe it was suicide.

Kevin arrived at the station forecourt on time, he had lived long enough with a broadcaster to know the importance of radio pips calling for action stations. They drove north to Dingwall then set out to cross the highlands to Ullapool. Aileen did all the talking and told him what she had found at Togorm Farm and how pleased the folk had been with her visit.

"Get any good interviews?" was about all he said.

"No, I couldn't. I hadn't the heart, though I sure would have liked the bit about having the wrong name on the casket."

It was evening, though still bright daylight, and the sun cast a vivid red glow on the mountains. However, hunger pangs told them supper was overdue. A large placard by the road announced a hunting lodge a mile beyond, so that seemed the obvious place to eat. They turned up a winding tree-lined driveway to what the French would call a chateau, a magnificent dwelling turned over to a hotel. It was too tempting. There was a vacant room so they grabbed it. Up a broad, deeply carpeted curved grand staircase they were taken to room 2 and the porter opened it to disclose almost a ballroom with a four-poster bed, a deep pile carpet, huge casement windows and heavy velvet drapes.

Kevin remarked, "We could get our whole flat in this!"

But hunger prevailed and after a quick wash and brush up they were seated in the magnificent stately dining room with Highland beef broth followed by pheasant in red wine sauce accompanied by their favourite Chateauneuf du Pape.

"What shall we drink to?" he asked,

"What about us?"

"Why not." The thaw had taken root.

They took coffee on the verandah, watching the sun go down over the mountains, talking of trivialities as the long twilight faded into night. The first star appeared, then another, then the whole panoply of heaven, a sight seldom seen in the light polluted atmosphere of Hong Kong. The night noises steered them towards the great staircase, the panelled bedroom door, the chandeliers the velvet drapes and the four-poster bed.

They chose their sides, placing them miles apart from each other, and Aileen went first into the bathroom. There came the sound of gushing water and a cheery song through the open door and then a lot of splashing. At other times Kevin would have been in that big bath with her, but he sat in a deep chair and maybe thought a bit. After a while she came out dressed in a towel.

"You won't believe it. I've left my nightdress in the other bag in the car. Be a love and get it."

Instead he dug in the bag they had.

"Have my pyjama top. It comes down to your knees," and he flung it over.

A little later she appeared wearing it. It fitted where it touched, but she seemed happy with it, and not long after he returned, washed and dressed in just his pyjama trousers, to find her on top of the bed combing her hair like a mermaid.

He turned out the light, leaving only the moonlight flooding through the casements to see his way and tentatively joined her, though the bed allowed them plenty of separation. They might have gone quietly to sleep, as on so many nights over the past weeks, had it not been for the tender loving care of the craftsman who carved the bed, or the energy left by the multitude of couples who had shared the bed before them or perhaps just the magic of the moonlight. For somehow their toes met and softly caressed, then two little fingers touched and joined, then slowly the hands met and gripped and squeezed. Their heads turned for first a butterfly kiss then lips pressed together. Kevin's pajamas were quickly reunited—on the floor—while their owners body-rambled, rediscovering all the erogenous paths to ecstasy as of yore until all the pent up passion of months of denial and misunderstanding flooded out in a steaming panting heaving romp leading to a gasping gargantuan climax. They lay in a trance—the same shared trance—nothing said, nothing uttered, filled with love and forgiveness. At last she opened her eyes to see him staring at her, the moonlight glinting in his eyes.

"Why are you staring?"

"Pillow-looking."

"Why?"

"Because I'm so sorry—so terribly sorry."

"How can you be sorry about that? It was the most wonderful thing that ever happened."

"Sorry how I've treated you."

"Nonsense. I threatened your job."

"What job? I'm too specialised ever to be promoted. No one has ever been fired from the civil service. And anyway I've only got a few years to go. No, the truth is I was jealous."

"Rubbish. Jealous of me?"

"No, jealous of all the strangers who claimed your time and your energy and your whole being. I just couldn't compete."

There was a long pause. She kissed him. "I love you. Only you. Darling, don't be jealous."

There was a moment of silence when love passed to and fro between them then engulfed them far into the moon-blessed night.

Chapter 67

They were not early for breakfast. In fact they nearly missed it. But Aileen had been thinking about what had been said. Perhaps he was right, she had been too involved and had ignored him and what he had been doing. She would make up for it. After all, she had not even asked after Uncle Hamish. "I forgot to ask. How was Uncle Hamish?"

Kevin looked very sheepish. He swallowed a mouthful of cereal. "I haven't got an Uncle Hamish. Never had."

"Then what on earth were you doing yesterday?"

"I saw an address in your papers of John MacLennan's Aunt Trixie who lives in Inverness. I knew I hadn't been helping you and thought I would only be in the way where you were going. So I went to see Trixie, who was charming. She gave me the phone numbers of two of Johnny's girlfriends."

Aileen was speechless. She just stared. Then to the consternation of the restaurant staff she leapt up and planted a passionate kiss on his mouth causing milk to dribble down his neck.

The drive to Ullapool was much more lively than that of the evening before. The conversation soon came round to the MacLennan case, in which Kevin had played so little part and taken so little interest. There was a lot of catching up to do which continued during lunch in one of the old stone buildings in Ullapool, surrounded surprisingly with palm trees and tropical plants which reminded them of the lovelier side of Hong Kong. After lunch they went on a boat trip down the bay to see the cliff faces curtained with myriads of seabirds and the seals basking on the rocks. Aileen couldn't help breaking off to tape an interview with the master of the vessel, taking care to repeat the more indecipherable Scottish words for the benefit of her audience, which was statistically predominantly Chinese, male, aged 28. The master pointed out the Polish fishing fleet which had slipped the Iron Curtain to visit their traditional fisher friends of centuries past. He even explained the palm trees—the Gulf Stream.

Kevin smiled to himself; Aileen never missed an opportunity to get an unusual item on tape for her listeners. Why then, he pondered, did her journalistic instincts allow her to leave Katie without an interview. She did not even ask to see the letters.

"There are so many unknowns in this case,' he said. "You don't know how many might be answered or at least referred to in those letters."

"I know, but they were grieving. Joe is blind, so I felt I had to keep talking and, I don't know, it just didn't seem right."

"Suppose I had been there and had kept Joe occupied?"

"It might have made a difference."

"We'll go tomorrow."

"Wow, you're a sweetheart and I love you to bits."

Aileen still couldn't find the way, as she had made so many wrong turnings the first time, but with Kevin to navigate they did a little better. They received a warm welcome. Johnny's sister Anne was home, as it was Saturday, which made the conversation easier. As soon as was tactful Aileen brought up the subject of the letters. Kevin took up the cue and suggested he lead Joe in a stroll round the garden. The three women were left to talk.

Katie opened up her precious collection of Johnny's letters and let Aileen read a few. There were comparisons of the weather in Hong Kong and Scotland and a description of a recent visit to Hong Kong by Lord George Brown who, Johnny noted, was previously Foreign Secretary and Murray MacLehose, now Governor of Hong Kong, was his private secretary from 1965-1967. These two were obviously very close and this showed during the present visit. He also remarked on Anne's engagement ring that she was surely flashing around the neighborhood. Aileen was touched by the tear that rolled down Anne's cheek and the reverence with which Katie folded the letter and eased it into its envelope for storage. How could she disturb this fragile moment by producing her tape recorder? It stayed in its bag and they sat down to tea.

The two men strolling in the garden were silent at first. The physical contact of leading a blind man and a few warnings like "there's a step here," seemed enough, especially when Joe replied "I ken right enough where the steps are." After a while, inevitably, they talked about Johnny and Joe's distress about the circumstances of the death.

Kevin asked, "supposing he had been killed in a shootout with criminals and been given a medal, would that have made a difference."

"Aye, it would, though I'm no sure it wasn't so."

"What do you mean?"

"Well, he was up against criminals right enough, but they were officials."

"You mean, far from giving him a medal, they had to make up scurrilous stories about him."

"Aye."

"How do you know they were officials?"

"He told me."

"Told you what?"

"I canna tell you. He made me swear not to tell anyone. He said it was top secret."

"Joe, it may have been secret then. But don't you think his death has made a difference. Are you going to let the criminals get away with it just because they were officials?"

Joe thought a moment. "You mean if somebody knew what he was really doing it might help bring them to justice?"

"It might. I can't promise anything except to try and let the right people know."

Joe pondered again. "You may be right. But you must promise me you'll only use it for justice and not just for getting yourself in the papers."

"Joe, I'm a civil servant myself. In the first place I know some of the right people. In the second place I'm not allowed to write to the papers. The only reason I am here is in the interests of justice."

Joe sat on the stone wall and took a few breaths of wonderful Scottish air. "Verra well."

Then it all came out, how Johnny had only been in his first posting for a few months when a brown envelope appeared in his desk drawer with $1,000 in it. He took it to his boss saying it must be a mistake. He was told it would be too much trouble to try and trace it as everybody would claim it so he might as well keep it. Next month there was another. After that it happened again several times, but not regularly. He was still quite naive and in a boyish way decided just to regard it as a bonus. After a while, however, he began to see the connection between some big police corruption scandals and the beginnings of crackdowns by another department formed to fight corruption (Joe would have been referring to the Independent Commission against Corruption or ICAC formed around the same time Johnny went to Hong Kong) and Johnny became embarrassed. He would have liked to have come out in the open and help the ICAC, but he had been accepting the money for too long to make that easy. So he decided to do two things. First he would ask to be posted to Special Branch, which held all the confidential information on police officers and might be investigating the source of the brown envelopes. Secondly, on his first leave back home he would try and get into the British Police instead. This was when he came home and confided in Joe.

"He was really very concerned about the brown envelopes. He saw them as a kind of bad omen. Especially since he had foolishly let himself get involved."

"So what did you say to him?"

"I told him he owed it to himself and the kirk to make retribution for the money he had accepted. So he went back determined to do everything in his power to get to the root of it."

"But he did leave Hong Kong and joined the London Police."

"Aye, that's when I next saw him. He would come up quite often when he was off duty. He was nay too happy about being an ordinary constable, while he had been an inspector in Hong Kong, but the worst thing I reckon was his conscience. He told me he didn't really find out anything verra useful in Special Branch, though he had nay been there long when the London Police offered him a job and he took it. After he came back, he could na settle, he felt mad with himself he had given up on it."

"He felt like a deserter?"

"That's just aboot right. But then things changed. Something verra strange happened. At first he wouldn't tell me aboot it. Very secret he said. Then he said I could know a bit aboot it but I musna tell anyone, not even Katie."

"And did you tell Katie?"

"No I never did. But I feel now perhaps someone ought to know. Someone who will know what to do. Someone in the London Police heard what had happened to him in Hong Kong and must have told someone high up. Because he was asked to go to a special place in Scotland Yard—that's in London ye ken—"

"Yes I know."

"—and at the first meeting he was just asked general questions about his work in Hong Kong, but then got on to the brown envelopes and how he had felt about them. They didn't say anything, just thanked him very much, then asked him not to say a word aboot it to anyone as it wouldn't do for such ideas to get around in the London Police. They didn't want him to mention they had talked to him either."

"Is that all he told you?"

"It was not. They called him up again, more than once, and in the end asked him if he felt so strongly aboot it he would consider going back to the Hong Kong Police as an informer for them. At first they just asked him to think aboot it. So that's when he really came oot with it all to me. Said he had to talk to someone aboot it."

"Are you saying they wanted him to be a spy?"

"That's just what I said to him. Funny that, how we both asked the same question. He was a wee bit shocked I think. But after a moment or two he said 'yes, I suppose that's what it would be.' I told him it sounded verra dangerous, but apparently they had already told him that. He said it was more dangerous that I might imagine. He said there were criminals called triodes . . . no triads—like the Mafia, who had infiltrated the Police. They were very tough and ruthless—like thugs, they would stop at nothing. The London Police had promised him absolute secrecy, in fact promised not to get in touch with him at all. If he found anything out he was just to post it to an address of a private house in a village somewhere outside London and there would never be any reply. They added he would be on his own and if he got into any trouble over it they could not help him."

"But I don't understand. Why were the London Police interested in what was going on internally in the Hong Kong Police?"

"Now, isn't that funny too. That's just what I asked him. We must think just alike you and me. He said that the triads were building up in London and because they had infiltrated the Hong Kong Police they were finding it very difficult to get good information back. His work, they said, would be very important in checking the information they got. Besides, he said, there was a section in the London Police that did have er . . . responsibility I think was the word he used, for police forces in the colonies. I suppose that was the lot that were dealing with him."

"Did you encourage your son to become a spy? Knowing how dangerous it was."

"I know. Of course I wish now I had forbidden him. Not that that would have stopped him if he was determined. In the end he was, and we talked aboot it. I don't think I encouraged him exactly, I just helped him get his mind sorted out by asking him the sort of questions you've just asked me. Anyway, he applied to go back and he was accepted and that's the last we saw of him, Katie and me. He wrote of course, he were a very gud letter writer, but for reasons he gave me he never mentioned any of this, so we didn't have any idea what was happening till we heard it on the news."

Aileen came out with Katie offering tea, which galvanised Joe into action. He loved his tea, over which the discussion was on family matters, the tricks Johnny got up to as a child and the very special relationship he had with his sister Anne.

Chapter 68

Aileen and Kevin left with a deep respect and love for the bereaved family, who had suffered the discourtesies and contempt of the bureaucrats with such stoicism, and they made their way back to the Hotel in Inverness subdued and thoughtful. Kevin in particular was wondering how the tables had turned from his disinterest to suddenly being the recipient of information he hardly dare pass on.

Aileen was a little more circumspect. "What you have told me about your conversation with Joe sounds like a colossal breakthrough. But just supposing you have heard the fantasies of a blind old man trying desperately to come to terms with the loss of his son. It could be some sort of defense mechanism."

"That's a problem."

"We'd better check it out."

"How"

"That's what I am going to find out."

The next day they set about tracing the two girl friends, Karen in Stirling and Gillian in Aberdeen.

Aileen said "It's a long way to both. I can't see how we can visit them."

"Get them on the phone."

"But then I won't get an interview."

"You have a go tracing them and I will pop out to the shops and see if I can get bits to tap the telephone."

Aileen tried phoning the numbers Kevin had given her. Karen was at work and could not be contacted. Gillian had moved, but she was given another number. This one was correct but she was told Gillian was a nurse and would be home off duty in about an hour. Kevin meanwhile had found an electronics shop and had bought a microphone in a rubber sucker. He brought it back in triumph and experimented sticking it different places on the body of the phone so he could get the loudest dial tone through Aileen's tape recorder amplifier.

"OK, I'm ready," he called out.

"Is this a covert or an overt tap?

"Don't worry. Completely covert. She won't know a thing."

"Is this legal?"

"I doubt it."

Aileen rang the number and, yes, Gillian was home. Kevin pressed "record".

Gillian and Johnny had been friends for many years. When he resigned and joined the Metropolitan Police he came up on long weekends and saw her quite often. She said what fun he was and how shattered she was when she heard the news. She had actually booked her ticket to go to Hong Kong to visit him 3 weeks after he died. "He certainly wasn't thinking of suicide when we fixed that up."

"Were you engaged?"

There was a pause. "Unofficially, yes. We were going to clinch it when I went there."

"But in Hong Kong they are saying he was gay."

"Oh, no. Nothing like that. No, for sure, nothing like that."

Aileen thought, she should know.

Chapter 69

Back in Hong Kong Justice Yang's report was finally published. The main conclusion was that John MacLennan had committed suicide. There were certain relatively minor shortcomings or shortcomings of a technical nature in the official investigation, although the Attorney General was wrong to give the impression he was overriding a jury. His denial of a frame-up was grossly misleading and he made an error of judgment. The charges were properly brought, though some of the evidence was improperly obtained. The Yuen Long incident had no bearing on the death, but it contained imperfections. There was prejudice and Mr Henry's decision to terminate MacLennan's contract was an error of judgment. In general most investigations were properly motivated except those by Brooks and Quinn which were improper.

Aileen and Kevin, now enthusiastic about getting at the truth, sat up half the night going through the report and had a competition to see who could find the most shortcomings.

"Look at this sentence, its written in Chinglish." she said. "I thought T.L. Yang went to Oxford. Do you think he was the only author?"

"And he's not very accurate. He includes two photographs of a Colt revolver and calls them a .38 S&W (Smith & Wesson) and in the text he argues that the bullet from a .38 S & W would transfer insufficient energy to throw the body. What about a Colt?"

"What does that say about the accuracy of the rest of the report?"

"And anyway, surely the effect of a gunshot is not just the bullet's momentum. What about the reflex action of the body, which might have

286

been violent? The "experts" compared it with a bullet going through gelatine with no reflex action. What was the value of that?"

"I agree. They seem to have limited the evidence to external physical phenomena. No evidence like reflex action or psychological effects of the first shot was presented to the Judge. He had to guess all that."

"He's based the suicide theory almost entirely on the locked bedroom door and the acceptability of the suicide note. I wonder what he would have done if Conway had been allowed to give evidence."

"Yes, I've just read that bit," she replied. "It all revolves around there being only two alternatives, the victim firing all five shots or someone else firing all five shots. But, as Conway pointed out, a much more plausible explanation is that the victim fired the first shot and someone else the next four. That gets over many of the difficulties and contradictions in the evidence. But that variation was not presented to the judge."

"He's had a go at Quinn and his merry men. They got their evidence by threats, assaults and inducements. Fat lot of good that evidence was."

"There are a lot of other photographs in the middle, notable apparently for two omissions, the one that showed the jacket had been moved between the photos and the other that showed a 3 foot long object leaning against the bed that was never seen again."

"But look at this. He says the Attorney General is guilty of grossly misleading the public when Elsie claimed Fulton was told to set up MacLennan and the AG said that Fulton had denied being told to frame him. They are two different activities, Yang says."

"That's interesting, "Aileen replied. "I read something way back, yes here it is. Peter called MacLennan 'John the ICAC man working for the ICAC', and Yang says that couldn't be true because MacLennan had never been in the ICAC. Isn't that just as grossly misleading? Isn't there a difference between being an informer for the ICAC and working in it."

"More inaccuracies."

"And what about this." Aileen was in top gear. "He says the inquest jury returned an Open Verdict by a majority of two to one. That is absolutely untrue and he knows it. They took three votes on different aspects of the verdict. Two were unanimous and one was two to one."

"Just look at this paragraph about Conway. It says the Star newspaper described Conway as an expert in ballistics and handwriting. In the course of his evidence, he admitted that although he had a letter from the parents of the late Inspector MacLennan requesting him to represent the family, he had in fact offered himself to the family and had drafted the letter for them."

"So? Does that make him a criminal?" asked Aileen.

"Yang goes on to say that Conway also admitted that he had no expertise in ballistics and handwriting, and completely denied that he had ever described himself to the Star or others that he was an expert in these fields."

"That is misrepresentation if you like. He said he was not an expert, but not that he had no expertise."

"In addition, he admitted that he was once prosecuted for perjury for having given expert evidence and handwriting, but was acquitted."

"That must be the most damning evidence against Yang yet. Does he, as a Judge, actually presume to use an acquittal as evidence against the character of a witness. Well really!"

"He goes on. He does not accept that Conway had not passed himself off as an expert in ballistics and handwriting or as someone who had considerable experience in these fields, which he clearly was not."

"No wonder Beveridge was so keen not to read the Law List I gave him, which described Conway as a handwriting expert. He would have lost his grounds for discrediting him."

"And get this. In his opening address, Mr Seagroat, Counsel for the MacLennan family, said that Conway was a person with a not inconsiderable experience in ballistics and handwriting. He could only assume that Mr Seagroat was misled, as the public and he were."

"My God. If it hadn't been in a court of law Seagroat could have had the judge for slander. Misled indeed, by the British Law list! What a slur on his reputation as a barrister! They must have been really desperate to suppress Conway's evidence."

"Besides, Yang himself described the two ballistics guys from Britain, Prescott and Mant, as experts, yet they both admitted they had no experience of suicide by multiple gunshots. He calls that 'expert'?"

"Yes that seems pretty inconsistent too."

"And what about these male prostitutes? Yang had complete faith in this one called Ah Tung, who said he had served MacLennan. How did that chap compare with Conway as deserving credit as a witness?"

"And what about the motive for suicide, Kevin continued. "He dismisses this with two quotes from other police officers. One, Inspector

Burns, said he believed John's parents would not have understood had it been proved that he had taken part in homosexual activities."

"But we've just come from the parents. Either they didn't believe it or they did in fact understand it. How could Yang base the motive on an opinion of Burns who had never met the parents and didn't know how they would react?"

Aileen took a few moments to calm down. "So what are we going to do about it?" she asked.

Kevin thought for a while. He scratched his ear. "I suppose— nothing. You can't challenge a judicial inquiry unless you've got something really solid to base your objection on. What have you got?"

"How to lock the bedroom door from outside."

"That doesn't prove he was murdered, only that he could have been."

"None of the pens in the flat wrote the note."

"You don't know that. The one they lost might have done."

"I know the names of the tails."

"One's dead and you never found the other. No I really don't think you have enough to go on."

"Then what do you suggest."

"I suggest you make a statement on air tomorrow to the effect that we've had our Inquiry and now we had better get back to our lives. That doesn't prevent you from revealing something solid later if it did come up."

"Well, alright. But I'm jolly well putting in a bit out of that interview I did in Scotland with Gillian, Johnny's unofficial fiance."

Kevin laughed. "You mean the bit where she says there was nothing gay about Johnny."

"Yes."

"That would be regarded as entirely consistent with your character. Nobody would do anything but giggle."

"But I'm not giving up. Supposing I could find the pen they lost and it didn't write the note then what?"

"What would it prove? Some pen wrote the note."

"But not in the locked flat. I think that would rock the foundations of the Yang Report."

"In any case, if they can't find the pen how could you?"

"Well. I just might be able to. John Conway told me where it was."

"Where?"

"In the desk of the Secretary of the Commission, Norman Chan. He even told me which drawer it was in."

"But that was ages ago. What are the chances it is still there?"

"When did you last clean out your desk drawer?"

"Point taken. But how could you possibly get to it?"

"I just might. Supposing I ask Norman Chan for an interview, you know—now its all over so to speak."

Naturally she couldn't do that before the next day's program so she prepared it exactly as she and Kevin had agreed. The listeners had found many more discrepancies, but gradually the subject died down. She rang Norman Chan and he said he would be delighted to see her on the following Saturday morning.

Aileen was fairly hyped up as she parked her car outside the Government Secretariat where the Commission had its office. She knocked on the door of the Secretary. Norman Chan himself opened it.

"Come in, Aileen, have a seat. What is it exactly you want me to say."

"That's entirely up to you. I just thought now that the Inquiry is all over, and your job is in effect over, your reminiscences over the course of the Inquiry could be most interesting to the public."

She set the tape going and after a few preliminary questions asked "How can an exhibit get lost"

"Such as?"

"I was thinking of John MacLennan's Parker pen. It was found on his desk but later declared lost"

He seemed a bit disconcerted. "I don't see the significance."

"I just thought it odd that the police could have lost it. Do you think one of them stole it?"

"Oh. No. Exhibits are far too carefully listed."

"Doesn't that make it all the more extraordinary it was lost?

"Yes, I see. Would you like some coffee? I'm sorry, I invited you on a Saturday as the staff are off and it is quiet for your recording. But that means I will have to make the coffee."

"That's quite alright. I'll fit up my recorder while you are doing it."

As soon as he was through the open door she dived for the right hand desk drawer. It was a shambles—full of junk. Conway had said it was in a plastic exhibit bag. There seemed to be dozens. Still a pen was a pen. I shouldn't be too difficult.

"Do you take sugar?" he called out. She nearly jumped into the drawer. "Er yes, I mean no—no thanks."

She rummaged through. No sign of a pen. In a panic she closed the drawer and started to set up her recorder just as he came back.

Her hand was shaking so much she could hardly hold the coffee steady on the saucer. But she got herself under control and started the interview. Halfway through she had a flash of inspiration. As interviewer she was sitting opposite the interviewee, so the right hand drawer to her was on his left. Maybe she had been looking in the wrong one. She fluffed the next question so badly she had to rewind a bit and ask it again.

As she wound up the interview, she thanked him very much and started to pack up her things, wondering all the time how she could get him out of the room again. In the end she packed it all except a small microphone and went out with him. At the door she said, "Oh, dear I think I left a microphone on your desk. I won't be a minute."

He followed her in. "Yes, there it is."

She popped it in the case and they went back to the door.

"I'm going myself now. I'll walk you down."

"Don't you lock your door?"

"No. The cleaners do that."

In the lobby she hesitated and he turned to the front entrance.

"My car's out the back, "she said, and turned towards the back entrance. He also turned and came with her. When they arrived outside, her car wasn't there, of course, because she had parked it out in front. "Oh, silly me! I forgot. That's where I park in the week. Of course today's Saturday. There was plenty of room in front. She couldn't get rid of him and she had no choice but to get in the car and drive off. But she knew her way around. She turned left and left again down Garden Road, then first right into the car park of Murray Building, the home of the Public Works Department. She was able to park there and walk through the pedestrian tunnel under the road and come up in the East end of the Secretariat. From there she was able to approach Norman Chan's office from the opposite direction. The remaining hazards were the possibility that Norman Chan might come back for something and the cleaners. As she walked down his corridor the cleaners were already in the offices a few doors down. If they caught her, however, she could just say she left a notebook behind.

She dived for the other drawer. It was as untidy as the first, but very quickly she found, towards the back and under some other bags, one containing a pen like the one in the photograph. The label said "MacLennan Inquiry Exhibit 5C" She stuffed it in her handbag just as an old amah with a vacuum cleaner walked in. Aileen waved a cheery "Choi geen" and returned to the car with as much civil service dignity as she could muster. The amah never turned a hair.

She drove like the wind to Star Ferry car park and ran to Swire House hoping to catch a lawyer friend. He was actually locking his door as she arrived (lawyers were apparently more security minded than secretaries). "Larry, wait," she puffed. We must go back in the office."

"But I'm late."

"Doesn't matter. Go back in."

Reluctantly he opened the door. She produced the plastic bag. "I want you to open this bag, take out the pen, and write your name on a piece of paper."

"What on earth for?"

"Never mind. Just do it."

He did what she said with a puzzled frown. "It doesn't write."

"My God. Of course. It's been in that bag for a year. Perhaps its dried up. No it can't have. Shake it."

He shook it and tried again. "No good."

"Oh, give it to me." She shook it and scribbled vigorously all over his pad. Not a sign of any mark. But no, there was a faint mark. She scribbled again, and shook it, and scribbled and finally it started to write—faintly at first then darker, then normally.

"Thank God for Parker pens."

"So what was all that in aid of?"

"Can't you see. Look at it. It's the key to the MacLennan case."

"Just looks like a lot of scribble to me."

"Not the scribble, you dunk head (yes he was a friend), the colour. It's black. John MacLennan always wrote with a black pen. This didn't write his suicide note. That was in Victorian blue."

Chapter 70

A few months later Aileen was watching Ah Sun scurrying around packing up all her things for her annual exodus to China and be the rich auntie again. The postman came and delivered a letter from Anson Che. It said he would be in the Captain's Bar next Saturday at noon and if she would care to meet him there she would be most welcome.

It was a different Anson she met this time. Previously he had been a typical officer of a disciplined force, in command and revealing only what he thought was proper. This time he looked worried, his bearing was less upright.

"There is something I didn't tell you last time we met. I shouldn't tell you now, only things are getting very uncomfortable and I feel I must tell someone."

"In what way uncomfortable?"

"Someone, somewhere, suspects or possibly knows I have information about MacLennan. Now in my job, I live with secrecy. So if I have information it is only passed on to people who need to know. But in this case I suppose they think I don't need to know."

"Go on."

"John and I became quite friendly. So when he was targeted I suppose I was in a way included. We were very discreet, but it is not always possible to hide everything. John actually told me what he was up to because he thought I could help—and I think I did. He had some contact in Britain he used to report to. He was always cagey about it, but I know he used to write to a private address in London. On the night he died he sent his last report, but in this case he sent a carbon copy to me. It was too hot for me to handle. It showed John had details of triad infiltration in the police that he had obtained through the male prostitute triad network. He identified top triad police officers and listed several others who were in their pay, including Ian McLean who was part of the drug syndicate."

"What did you do with it?"

"Well it implicated the Carrian Group as a source of funds so, as I knew Justice Barker was interested in the activities of the Carrian Group, I sent it to him—anonymously. But I just have the sneaking feeling that someone, somewhere has put two and two together and decided I'm involved."

"Did you keep a copy?"

"Certainly not. I didn't want to have anything to do with it."

"So why tell me about it?"

"For two reasons. One is I'm leaving tonight to go on a course in Scotland and I think someone ought to keep an eye open to see if anything comes up about it. The other is that, apart from Graeme, I think you are about the only person I can trust. I don't want to burden Graeme with it, he's gay and he's a government doctor."

"Well, thanks. But what do you expect me to do?"

"Nothing. Nothing at all. Just keep your eyes and ears open, which I'm sure you always do, and when I come back we might follow it up together."

Chapter 71

Two weeks later Aileen received a surprising phone call. "Aileen? How did you like the Yang Report?"

"Chartong? Whatever are you doing in Hong Kong?"

"I'm writing a book, as I think I told you, and I have a few loose ends to tie up. Now that the report is released it seemed a good time to come back here, while the fares are cheap, and look up a few old friends."

"Where are you staying?"

"In the China Fleet Club in Wanchai. I get it cheap for my service in the Navy."

"Well, you couldn't have come at a better time. When are you free for dinner?"

"Not tonight, but after that, any day."

She took his number and immediately rang Elsie and Graeme. She managed to get them together two days later. It was a balmy evening in mid February. The big sliding windows to the balcony were open revealing what seemed more like a reflection of a starlit sky than a city stretching miles away to the horizon.

The doorbell rang. Ah Sun let in Graeme.

"I think you likee whiskey."

"Thanks, Ah Sun, a wee dram is just what I need."

Aileen came down the corridor and gave him a welcoming kiss. "Graeme, you're early."

"I'm sorry. Am I interrupting something? I know I'm early."

"Not at all, and I can see from your frown you have a reason."

They sat on the balcony.

"Yes. This is all going out of control. Did you see the papers today."

"Yes. What in particular?"

"Anson's dead."

Aileen was stunned. "What! He can't be. Where? When? I didn't see that."

"No, it was a bit obscure. On page 6. It just said: ICAC Officer found dead. His name didn't appear till the third paragraph. Then today it was repeated in the Standard."

"My God. I was only talking to him two weeks ago. I can't believe it. How did he die?"

"A gas accident, apparently."

"Oh, no. Not another. No foul play I suppose. When is all this going to end?"

"Well it may be an accident, but I agree, there have been so many. I get involved in a whole lot that never make the press."

"But why should that make you so worried?"

"Because I am doing the same thing. I am revealing secret matters to people I trust. I am most careful what I say on the telephone, but you never know what's bugged, do you."

"Graeme, I suppose it's alright to tell you this now, but he sent MacLennan's last report on triad infiltration of the police to the Judiciary. Maybe he shouldn't have trusted them. But what have you done?"

"Nothing much yet. The fact is I know too much and I need somebody to share it."

"That's just what Anson said. You had better be very careful."

"I try to be. I've been giving a lot of thought to our previous talk about the Zoo. The fact is I caught a glimpse of a man, who spoke with a Scottish accent, in the Zoo that night. At first he seemed in control of himself, but left about three hours later sounding dazed and incoherent. I got a better look at him then and he certainly looked like the photos I have seen of John MacLennan, though contorted. I remember wondering if he would get home alright and was surprised they didn't ask me to have a look at him. Now, I have seen people like this often enough. Under the disorientation of bright lights, sleep-depravation, white noise generators and the constant verbal hammering most victims come out dazed and incoherent. But they don't all get in the papers for shooting themselves five times in the chest. Another thing that worries me is that you say Elsie is coming in a minute and I don't know if I can trust her."

"You can—absolutely. She has more dark secrets of other people than anyone else I know. But how dazed was this Scotsman you saw?"

"Pretty far gone."

"Could he have been hypnotized?"

Graeme paused. "It's possible. They do practice it in the Zoo. They use it for getting evidence out of witnesses with amnesia, Chinese infiltrators and so on."

"Why Chinese infiltrators?"

"That's most of their work. Putting two and two together I gather Peking are trying to set up a network here. The ones that get caught go to the Zoo. They find out all they can and send them back to China. I only get involved when they really ill-treat them. Although often I am only required to say they are fit enough to be deported."

The doorbell interrupted the flow. Elsie and Conway came in together, she looking her usual 20 years younger than her age, dressed in a grey jumper and long black pleated skirt and he as scruffy as usual but bursting with vigour. She asked for a glass of water. Ah Sun didn't even ask Chartong, she just brought him a cup of tea.

Chapter 72

Aileen quickly brought them up to date. Elsie loved a bit of scandal and apparently didn't know very much about the Zoo. Aileen told them both about Frena's hypnosis and that now she had most of the suicide note written in Frena's handwriting. Frena, however, had no recollection of it. "Lim told me he had taught elementary hypnosis to two policemen, Farnham and Webster. I asked Mike Fulton about that and he said he knew of a Chief Superintendent Farnham whose office was on the same corridor as the SIU"

"Good God, I never thought of that." A surprising admission for Chartong.

Elsie asked, "What does all this mean?"

Aileen summarised. "As I see it, Justice Yang was fed with filtered evidence. He placed great weight on the fact that the bedroom door could not be locked from the outside, whereas Chartong had demonstrated that it could. He placed great weight on the pathologist's evidence that a man could continue purposeful activity for minutes after shooting himself in the heart, but he was not told the effect of a shot through the aorta lodging in a vertebra, either of which could put him instantly out of action. He assumed that the missing pen wrote the note, because if it hadn't it would have meant the note was not written in John MacLennan's flat, so upsetting the whole locked door theory. Now in fact I have found the missing pen and it did not write the note. It's the wrong colour. So the note was not written in the flat.

"How on earth did you do that?" asked Chartong.

"You told me where it was, except you don't know your right from your left, otherwise you were absolutely correct." She told the whole story just as if she were on-air and had them all in fits. Then she became serious.

"So you see, Yang's reconstruction is entirely circumstantial. He had not one scrap of evidence that the death was actually suicide, only that with the evidence he was given he hadn't got an alternative. He dismissed the firm and honest evidence of Paul Stevens who said the note was not the one he saw, simply because it conflicted with the other evidence he was given. Yang had to accept a pretty thin motive, because he was not supplied with an alternative. Just how thin it was, namely that Johnny had seen Roy Henry's name on a list of homosexuals, was well illustrated in the Inquiry when it was virtually confirmed that Henry was a homosexual. Far from blowing the lid off Hong Kong, apart from a few giggles nobody turned a hair. Besides, the whole Inquiry was slanted towards homosexuality. For example, there was only one brief reference to a link with the ICAC, which Justice Yang dismissed just as briefly, but they grilled a gay senior inspector, Mike Fulton, for seven whole days spending much of that time finding out what he did in bed, and even put his partner in the witness box to corroborate what he said. What relevance was all that? It was sheer smokescreen."

Elsie jumped in, "Yes and they didn't call much more important witnesses. We know he was under surveillance. Why weren't the watchers called as witnesses to solve a lot of unknowns."

"I can tell you that. One has been murdered and the other can't be found."

"Where did you get that from," asked Chartong.

Aileen told him about the tip-off from Raven and her unsuccessful attempts to make contact.

"I think you might be wrong there," said Chartong. "You might have been given those names as a diversion. You see, when someone is under surveillance, the tails are often rotated so they are less likely to be recognised. Your pair might well have been on that job for some of the time, but my conclusion is that two of the men that Johnny had been talking to in the station, Station Sergeant Li Chi-lun and Constable Lee Hok-man, took over the job. They followed him, probably because a senior officer told them about Johnny's pending arrest and they quite properly went to recover the revolver. When they heard the shot they walked straight in, as he had not locked the door, and seeing what had happened rang a senior officer. On instruction they lifted Johnny, who was slumped on the bed, stood him up and one shot him four times in the chest, a triad signature, and let him drop to the floor. They then wiped the gun and dropped it at his feet. Sandra Hills heard the shots with a gap after the first and so, incidentally did an Indonesian lady that lived nearby, but she was too scared to come forward. I had to winkle it out of her. But to answer your question, the reason why the tails were not called is that those two men I mentioned disappeared and the rumour is they were spirited out to Taiwan."

"There's a flaw in that theory," said Aileen.

"Never mind, it's the best yet."

"Not quite. If Johnny had dropped from a standing position his slippers would not have come off. That would only have happened if he had been kneeling."

"He had been kneeling, for the first shot, the one that went in the opposite direction. That's when the slippers left his heels."

"How is it you always have all the answers?"

Chartong grinned.

Ah Sun called them to dinner. They took their places causing a short pause in the discussion.

Chartong broke it. "I don't think I told you, but soon after I went back to England after the Inquiry I went to a medical forensic society seminar where the two UK forensic scientists, I think it was Prescott and Mant, that gave evidence had been invited to present their experiences. Peter Morrish, previously African police officer then barrister then judge, was also invited. The panellists explained why they were convinced John MacLennan committed suicide. At question time Peter asked them both what experience they had of suicide by gunshots. They both admitted none, as we heard in the Inquiry. He then explained that he had been involved in many suicides, with both guns and explosives, and he held that it was unheard of for someone attempting suicide with a gun to aim at any other place on the body but the well known vulnerable places such as in the mouth, under chin and temples. Furthermore, he claimed that the shock and pain of the first shot would deter any more. In his opinion it was a triad execution.

"The transcript of the seminar was later distributed to all who took part and the entire exchange between Peter and the presenters had been expunged."

Elsie was enraged. "Which proves the cover-up extends to Britain as well. But going back to what you were saying about the flat, how did it get locked?"

"My theory is," said Chartong, "that the sergeant told the constable to stay inside, lock the front door and guard the body. He went back and telephoned Senior Superintendent Trotman, who was at home."

"No he wasn't," said Aileen, "he was out walking his dog and the call was forwarded to his friend in the RSPCA."

"Sorry. It doesn't affect my case. He and Sergeant Li returned to Johnny's flat and were let in by the constable. On assessing the situation, Trotman repeated the orders to the constable to securely lock the door and stay inside and to hide if any attempt was made to break in. He then returned to the Station and informed Quinn, who was probably shattered. At around 9 am Senior Inspector Grant, Johnny/s boss, knocked on Trotman's door, presented him with the brown envelope and informed him of the large pile of files in his office. The Commissioner and acting Governor were informed, who in turn consulted the Foreign Office in London. Back came the order to treat it as suicide. The police could now relax and follow normal procedures, which we have heard in graphic detail in both the inquest and the Inquiry."

"Why do you put the finger on Trotman?" asked Aileen. "Surely it could have been any number of officers."

"Possibly, but he was the one who had a phone call which seemed to fit and he was the only one who was allocated a Counsel all to himself. To defend him against what? All the others shared the Counsel for the police."

"But what about the note?" asked Elsie.

"Quinn had two subterfuges to execute. First he had to make sure that as many people as possible poured into Johnny's flat so that an extra man would not be noticed. Secondly he pocketed the note with a view to depositing it in the flat. It was only as he was putting it on the desk that he realised the significance of the enclosure and slipped that in his pocket."

"But Stevens was standing behind him, said Elsie. "So you think Stevens really did see more than just the envelope, as he said twice—under oath."

Graeme had been silent too long. "What about the night before?"

"Nobody knows," said Aileen. "Even the great international detective Vincent Carratu had to admit that.

"I think that's another flaw," continued Aileen. "We now know a lot more than Pelly was allowed to investigate. Johnny had a lot of files to bring up to date. So he took the last of them with two or four sheets of file paper and two brown envelopes and his typewriter back to his apartment. He finished them by say 9 o'clock. He then put two sheets of paper in his typewriter with a carbon and started to write a report on his work. If he was arrested the next day he wasn't sure when he would get another chance. Anson Che told me the gist of it. He was investigating forged $500 notes and traced some of them back to the SIU. Johnny had already told Anson about this and asked his advice. The SIU found out and targeted him. He didn't know who else was straight that he could go to. They paid male prostitutes to bring evidence against him, but you and I, John, caught up with Peter, strangely the only one Yang trusted, and he admitted that sex had never been part of the relationship. MacLennon in fact wanted to know where he got the forged notes."

"But there was more, "interjected Chartong. "It involved Chinese in high places, but since he did not have much to go on it was a somewhat raw and sketchy account. One thing, though, apparently it listed high level police in a triad hierarchy, including John Li at the top and Roy Henry surprisingly below him. In fact I found the chart among Johnny's belongings, which the Hong Kong police had missed. Now that <u>might</u> have blown the lid off Hong Kong, and we only have Pelly's word for it that the so called list was of homosexuals. Incidentally, had it occurred to you that the brown envelope he wrote the note on might have been one left in his drawer with corrupt money in it and with some very interesting fingerprints on it?"

"Which was then deliberately not protected," added Aileen, "so the evidence would all get messed up. So you think triads were involved right to the top. Is that why Sir Yeut-keung Kan resigned from the Executive Council so suddenly? I tried to interview him but he wouldn't. Nobody could find out the reason. I wonder if his position became untenable."

"The implications certainly went up that high," said Chartong.

It might have been even higher, said Elsie. "What about China?"

"Yes we were talking about that with the hypnotist a few weeks ago," said Aerial, "Graeme was there"

"Yes," he said, "we were talking about the show trial of the Gang of Four in Beijing.

We wondered if it could have had something to do with them."

"Who were they?" asked Chartong.

Elsie knew all about that. "They were the ringleaders in the Cultural Revolution, committing all sorts of atrocities. Nobody could stop them because one of them, Jiang Qing, was Mao Zedong's wife."

"She was an actress," added Aileen.

"She was also very powerful, said Elsie. "I just wondered if they had designs on Hong Kong."

"I don't suppose we'll ever know that," said Aileen. "Anyway, we now come to the reconstruction where I think vital evidence has been withheld from Justice Yang. Later on that evening, MacLennan comes over to the Station with the final files and his two reports. One he posts on the way. The other he leaves on top of the files in his boss's office. The watchers see him go in and report back, so by the time he comes out again there is a car waiting for him and an officer he trusts. 'Roy Henry wants to see you. If you can convince him of your innocence the whole thing could be dropped.' But they don't go to Roy Henry, they go to the Zoo.

"Now this is where I get a bit stuck," Aileen continued. "But you might be able to help, Graeme. According to all the people who tried to walk from the Station to the flats it could not be done in ten minutes, I think you can confirm that, John, but in that time Yang had to assume that not only did he complete the procedures in the armoury and walk it he also wrote at least some of the note. The timing just does not add up. I think that his report was already in his boss's office, just a few minutes away, and having decided, or having had it decided for him, to commit suicide he added a note to the report. So he wrote it on the outside of the brown envelope, using one of his boss's pens, which was Victorian blue. None of the pens in his flat were that colour. Just before he left he turned and put his initials and the time. Easily done in ten minutes.

"My problem is this, Graeme. In the armory he was only just coherent, probably shattered after writing up all those files, and made three mistakes in the beat register. By the time he got back to his boss's office he was calm enough to write a very smooth note, no doubt guided by the lines of typing inside, like guidelines. But how could this change come about? Mind you, Yang had the same problem and simply ignored it."

Chartong chipped in, "he ignored quite a lot of things: that MacLennan intended to make it look like an accident; why was the note written on an envelope and not notepaper; that he could not have walked to his flat and done the things he was credited with in ten minutes; the colour of the ink in the pen; indeed the fact that the pen, an exhibit, had been lost . . ."

Graeme thought about it for a bit. "To answer your question, Aileen; the effect of brain washing is not consistent. It is entirely possible that he could be confused one minute and calm and coherent the next. No, I don't think that is a problem. Besides he might, under hypnosis, have been instructed exactly what to put in the note, but not exactly what to put in the Beat Register."

"And there's another thing", Aileen continued "We can assume he would then walk as slowly as he liked to his flat, as there was no timing involved. I mean, leaving before 6.15 he would have plenty of time to die in his apartment between 6.30 and 7.30. But, if he were acting under post hypnotic suggestion, my understanding is that nobody can be made to commit suicide that way."

Graeme knew the answer to that one immediately. "That's true normally. You can't hypnotize a healthy mind and persuade it to kill itself. But John MacLennan could not be described as having a healthy mind. If you remember we had a related question in your Studio. Someone subjected to several days in the witness box could suffer a conviction reversal and start saying things against what he believed. John MacLennan had been harassed for many weeks, by all accounts. Not only in the day, but they had been telephoning him continuously so he was sleep deprived. If on top of that he had suffered three hours treatment in the Zoo I can assure you he could well have been suicidal before being hypnotised. Don't forget they would prey on his weaknesses, his love of his family and his church upbringing. Under those conditions he could undoubtedly be persuaded to shoot himself, especially if he only thought he was making it look like an accident. But I certainly got stuck with the five shots. I would expect the first shot to so to speak bring him round mentally, although physically he would be shocked and in some pain. I would expect him to be so dazed he simply would not have the will to carry on. I certainly support Mr Conway's suggestion. But what happened in the flat when they started to break the door down?"

This was Chartong's area. "I don't know, but it doesn't actually matter. Say Constable Lee was left in the apartment to lock it securely from the inside. He could either have gone into the bedroom, locked the door and hidden in the wardrobe, when he first heard the banging on the outer door, merely appearing when the number of investigators in that small room got up to about seven—no one would have noticed him, particularly if had made some comment like 'Nothing in there, sir.' There were you see, more than two teams who didn't know each other. This could account for the discrepancy in the numbers seen by different witnesses."

"Alternatively," said Aileen, "he could have locked the bedroom door from outside, just like you did, and climbed out of the bathroom window with the help of his friend, just like the Star reporter did. He would have needed to be a bit lighter and thinner than the tubby one the Commission chose to photograph trying to do it."

"Do you know," said Graeme, "I think we've wrapped it up."

"No, said Aileen, "there's more. Twice tonight we have mentioned the Chinese. Justice Yang was given no evidence about them so they did not appear in his report. But I have thought about this before and could never work out the connection. Now I may have got it. You see, at the beginning of the Cultural Revolution the Red Guards surrounded the police post on the border at Sha Tao Kok and a gun battle took place. Security, I have since learned, signaled the Foreign Secretary, George Brown, asking what to do. He signaled back 'throw them out.' So it was that a battalion of Ghurkhas did so."

Chartong looked puzzled. "Are you saying there was actually an attempt to take over Hong Kong?"

"I think that might have been the intention, about 14 years ago, though hardly with a gaggle of Red Guards. But it failed because, so all the pundits reckon, Mao Zedong said Hong Kong should not be touched because it was too valuable to him. "That depends" said Chartong, "on whether they had contingency plans to replace the government. It would be absolute madness to take over any territory without detailed plans for administering it after the event."

Aileen looked thoughtful. "I'm sure that's true for a properly organised military and political takeover. But this was all madness. The Red Guards were only interested in annihilating education."

"This Gang of Four sounds as if they might have been power hungry as well." Chartong pointed out.

"Yes, I see what you're getting at. The Gang of Four could not have failed to see at that time the importance of having people in Hong Kong capable of taking over the administration smoothly if it were overrun. Mao maybe would not then object. Perhaps that brings us to the triads. I have always been down on the triads as beds of organised crime and corruption. But they didn't start like that. Originally they were a group of patriotic monks who defended their motherland."

Chartong added to that. "Round the end of the last century the triads were buying up land in the New Territories to try and get it back that way. A lawyer called Charles Russell was sent out to stop it. He did, but not before he had learned a lot about how secret societies operated. When he came back to Britain he reported to Winston Churchill, then Home Secretary, who thought it was a wonderful idea and formed the British Secret Service, based on triad procedures. That was the beginning of MI6."

Elsie added, "and that is the same Charles Russell who started a law firm of that name?"

"Yes, as I told you last year, he was also instrumental in starting Hampton Winter and Glynn, and between them they have handled all colonial law matters ever since."

Elsie exclaimed, "Yes I remember. I always knew those lawyers in the Inquiry were not independent. No wonder they only brought out the evidence the government wanted them to."

"It's not just that." replied Chartong. "It is a characteristic of all British inquests and inquiries in cases of death. Everyone has a right to be represented by Counsel, including the deceased's family, but not the deceased. He cannot defend himself and no one else does."

"Anyway, to get back to triads" said Aileen. "Don't you think it would be natural for the Gang of Four to plant several moles in government and the private sector and surreptitiously finance them with Chinese money. They would have needed a support network, and what better than a secret society? So if Roy Henry was in the triad hierarchy it might not have been a sign he was corrupt, but rather that he had been warned that one day he might have to lead the police in the event of a takeover. If that had been the list Johnny saw when he was in Special Branch then it <u>could</u> have blown the lid off Hong Kong."

Graeme was puzzled. "But, Aileen, are you saying that Hong Kong is full of moles waiting to take over Hong Kong?

"I'm saying it probably was. I suspect these were the infiltrators you say escaped the Zoo. But when the Gang of Four were arrested six years ago the moles lost their control and have been managing on their own ever since. This is the triad story. They start as patriots, but as soon as they are left without a job they turn to crime. That is probably why the police always tried to play them down, but now they are an embarrassment and something has to be done about them."

Aileen's mind was running ahead. "What a broadcast! I'm going to have so much fun undermining the Yang Report and revealing all this."

Elsie was more cautious. "Just remember, if you do you really will blow the lid off Hong Kong."

Graeme added, "and someone might blow your lid off as well."

"And consider this," added Chartong, "aren't we doing exactly what Johnny was doing, disclosing the triad activities? Aren't we doing exactly what the police were trying to stop him doing?"

"What was that?" asked Aileen.

"Obviously I don't know. But just look at it from their point of view. Supposing they were already tackling the triad infiltration in some way. If they were counter-infiltrating the triads it would have to be top secret. Then along comes a humble inspector and tries to get in on the act. They had to shut him up. They were too late to stop him alerting London, why else do you think Sir James Cane and his team came out at such a critical time?"

Aileen pondered a little. "But with John MacLennan it was different. To him it simply looked like triad infiltration. To us it is a government cover-up as well. I don't see how we can overlook that."

"If we don't we might be just as dangerous to them" stressed Conway. "Anyway, it's up to you what you do about it, but for my part I am going to sit on my work until I see what the police are up to. I'll just get my book ready—just in case."

"I wonder if you're right," said Aileen. "On the other hand, there is another conclusion, you know. This one might not blow the lid off Hong Kong, but it might blow the lid off some future Judicial Inquiry if we can get the message through. What this case has proved is that any Government can so manipulate the evidence in an Inquiry that a perfectly honest and upright judge can legitimately draw the conclusion they want, no matter whether it is wrong or in the best interests of the country."

"Exactly," said Graeme. "I have been quiet for some time because I have been listening with just that thought in mind." He produced a bit of paper he had been jotting notes on. "What would have been the result of the Inquiry if they had been allowed to hear evidence from John Conway here, and people like Anson Che, Sir James Cane, Sir Yeut Keung Kan, Sir Denys Roberts, David Ford, Ian McLean, John Richard Duffy, Molo Choi, Sunny Chan, the hypnotist from the Zoo, the surveillance tails, or even Johnny's father? What would it have been like?

Aileen and Elsie both spoke at once, "different!"

"Graeme, you sound just like a detective," said Chartong.

Graeme smiled. "A doctor is a detective."

Time had crept up on them and Graeme, Elsie and Chartong rose to go.

As the doors on their lift closed those on the other opened. Kevin stepped out.

"God, I'm for bed. I'm bushed."

"No supper?"

"I had something on the ferry."

"I wish you wouldn't get so involved. It's only a job."

"You're a good one to talk. What about you!"

"I'm dropping the MacLennan affair."

"I don't believe it."

"It can stay an open verdict."

"Quite right."

"Till 1997."

"I can live with that."

They become entwined in each other's arms. Their lips touched slowly and thoughtfully. Over the balcony the lights winked at them across Hong Kong's irrepressible harbour. A ship hooted. All was well.

Chapter 73

Epilogue

The events described happened up to February 1982. Anson Che Tak-ying died on 15th February 1982. Within a few months the MacLennan affair died down and one can deduce that the British and Royal Hong Kong Police Forces decided the time was appropriate to start to squeeze the triads. By then Rodney (PC Ma Chi-man) and Sandy (PC Yu Kam-cheung) were making good progress in their infiltration, though their task took about three years, all through the time of the Inquest and Inquiry, demanding the utmost secrecy. In April 1982 there was a major reshuffle in the Royal Hong Kong Police. Jack Trotman left to become a security advisor for a Bank, Michael Quinn was posted to Interpol (he died of an alcohol related illness in 1987), and one can speculate that the recommendations of Sir James Cane were being implemented aimed at either getting rid of triad members or moving them to posts where they could do least harm and phase out. In December 1982 Commissioner Roy Henry disbanded his Triad Bureau to the intense consternation of the media, who regarded the action as an admission of defeat. 'Why disband a useful force and leave the disreputable SIU to continue in its evil ways?' This was probably exactly what the creators of the master plan wanted people to say, since the SIU had been established to counter the triads and was given the task of investigating homosexuals as a smoke screen. The triad leaders appeared to take the moves at their face value for within a few weeks 400 of them held a celebration dinner in a Kowloon restaurant.

Perhaps the most significant move was the removal of Superintendent John Li. He had been named in one of MacLennan's documents as the Shan Chu, or boss of the triad organisation in the Police, in which Commissioner Roy Henry appeared in a subordinate role as Incense Master. Li was arrested in 1976 for loan sharking. Despite the fact that a money lender deals with a large number of clients, no witnesses came forward so he was released. He was arrested again in 1978 for corruption. A triad member agreed to be the chief witness, but he was arrested and found hanging in a police station. Li was once more released. He was arrested again in 1982 for corruption. Again no witnesses came forward so he was released. He was said to be the owner of a building where police beat up reporters in 1982. He was forcibly retired on 9th November 1982 under Colonial Regulation 59, (no reason given).

As a matter of interest, on 17th November 1982, P.C. Cheng Tuen-sing, reputed to be MacLennan's second tail, was reported murdered. At the trial it was confirmed he was a triad and Justice Baber said it was unfortunate there were police of such doubtful character.

Just before his retirement in December 1984 Roy Henry started the crackdown with the announcement that there were more than 30 triad societies with a total of 120,000 members. He was replaced, not by promotion of a subordinate, but by a London Metropolitan Police Officer Ray Anning, who was clearly tasked with breaking up the triad organisation. By then he had superb witnesses in the form of Rodney and Sandy. The first arrests of triad leaders were in January 1985, with the police claiming they had around 80 names. There were arrests all through the year at the end of which Ray Anning admitted that 'triads may have infiltrated the police.' Other triad senior police officers were phased out. The Royal Hong Kong Police went through years of tough purging, one of the more recent action being in August 2003, when 8 police officers successfully infiltrated the 14K triad society resulting in 420 arrests in one day in March 2004. The Hong Kong Police (they dropped the "Royal" in 1997) is now widely regarded as the cleanest and most efficient in the Region. Homosexual acts between consenting adults were decriminalised on 11 July 1991.

Roy Henry retired to Malaysia and lived openly as a gay. Aileen met him by chance in Kuala Lumpur, where she was conducting seminars, and he was then most forthcoming. He later moved to London where he died in May 1998.

The crackdown on the triads focused mainly on the 14K, at the time the dominant triad society and the one which had mainly infiltrated the police. This, coupled with concern about how China might deal with them after 1997, led to a huge exodus of triads overseas to the great benefit of Law and Order in Hong Kong and the detriment of many other major cities. It was clearly absolutely essential for the success of the operation that John MacLennan's work was stifled and covered up. In April 2004 Judge Peter Line threw out a case of burglary where a senior police officer described in court undercover police officers participating in the crime as innocent bystanders. The defence described it as entrapment. Apparently the police are still willing to support set-ups and the like but at least the judiciary will no longer accept the manipulation of evidence.

As to the remainder of the characters in our story, Justice T.L. Yang was promoted to Chief Justice soon after the Inquiry. He retired in 1996 and was appointed to the Executive Council of the post 1997 Hong Kong Special Administrative Region of China. Dr Graeme Ross continued to be hounded by the SIU and was on one occasion arrested and charged with possession of drugs, but was released when a straight police officer discovered the suspected drugs were in his doctors bag and completely legitimate. In 1987 he met an untimely death in his locked flat. No foul play was suspected.

On 14 March 1987 120,000 copies of the South China Morning Post were shredded, apparently to avoid references to links between the Deputy Commissioner of Police, Eric Blackburn, and loan sharking and between John MacLennan and the use of $500 notes in loan sharking. John Conway continued investigative work into cases, including the MacLennan case, which he claimed involved government cover-up, on which he published a book, *To Speak for the Dead*, but not till 1994. After publication he was alone in the house one evening and when his wife returned she found him fallen forward into the gas fire, horribly burned to death. No foul play was suspected. Elsie Elliot married at the age of 70, becoming Elsie Tu, and was elected to the Legislative Council, becoming one of the most highly respected citizens in Hong Kong earning many local and international awards. Quicksilver committed suicide. No foul play was suspected. Slasher George contracted AIDS and became a social worker counseling others with AIDS and later died of the disease. Barry also died of AIDS. Michael Fulton was pressured to retire from the police and found re-employment denied to him for a long time. He now works in education. Aileen retired after 14 years on the talk show and became a member of the USA National Speakers Association and is popular on cruise ships. She and Kevin are still happily married.

Years later one of the Commission lawyers said the MacLennan episode was seminal, leading to development and important lessons. It dragged Sir Murray MacLehose down in status, both in Hong Kong and Britain. It showed up the Hong Kong administration to be a decaying colonial regime unable to maintain control. They had continued in a state of complacency that they could cover up anything that went wrong and this showed they couldn't. It was tremendous loss of face as regards the Chinese and would have greatly influenced the 1982-1984 talks and the inevitability of return to Chinese sovereignty. In particular it would have undermined Margaret Thatcher's suggestion that China take over sovereignty but leave the British to administer Hong Kong for 50 years, because this episode showed more than any other the weakness in that suggestion, namely that, left to themselves, the Chinese would have been able to cover up the affair without difficulty.

Clearly the Hong Kong administration learned from it and it may well have influenced Beijing to be far more sensitive to public opinion. As for Britain, though, one cannot be so sure.

Chapter 74

Summing Up

This case rested on four critical questions:

- Was it suicide or murder?
- What was the motive for either?
- What were the victim's sexual inclinations?
- What was the significance of the suicide note?

The evidence before the judge was that the flat was impenetrable and therefore murder was not an option. For this reason the possible motives for murder were not seriously considered. The motive for suicide was accepted as the victim's disinclination to live with his confused sexuality and to have this disclosed to his family. His bisexuality was accepted on the basis of hearsay and of the evidence of one or two male prostitutes who had visited his flat. Because no pen was found in the flat which wrote the suicide note it was accepted that the pen lost by the Commission must have been the one used. Because murder was ruled out on the evidence one must regard the judge's conclusions as reasonable and proper.

In hindsight it is apparent that the possibility of more than one person being involved in the shooting, however unlikely, was feasible, though this evidence was suppressed during the Inquiry. One can now weigh the unlikelihood of the suicide against the unlikelihood of an intruder and come to a more balanced judgement.

If the victim had been investigating triad infiltration in the police and reporting it to London then, bearing in mind our present knowledge of a simultaneous dangerous undercover operation by the police to infiltrate the triads, then he could have been regarded as a spy and there could have been good reason to silence him (though not necessarily to kill him).

In this event the earlier visit to his flat by triad male prostitutes might not have been relevant to his sexual inclinations. Since this was the only hard evidence of his bisexuality then we must resort to the law and say that if a person is innocent until proved guilty then this one should be regarded as heterosexual until proved otherwise. This was not done, so with this later knowledge one should conclude he was not bisexual, that he did not have this to hide from his family and was not a motive for suicide.

The pen that was "lost" by the Commission was later found and tested to be black, not the Victorian blue of the note. Hence there was no pen in the flat which could have written the suicide note and it must have been written with a pen borrowed from someone else, probably found in Inspector Grant's office. This raises serious doubts about the authenticity of the note and whether, as evidence, it was properly obtained.

As an ultimate juror in the case, what is your verdict?

Authors Note

Several people have asked me what I think the verdict should be. I have, after all, lived with this story a long time. I can only refer to the experiments carried out by John Conway, excluded from the Inquiry by falsely discrediting him.

The trouble with any attempt at a solution is that in either case, suicide or murder, too much is left unexplained. This is true of Justice Yang's report as much as any other. He had no answer to the qualifications of John Conway, who was indeed in the UK Law Lists of 1972 and 1973 as a handwriting expert. The Judge knew it, or at least John Beverage knew it and should have told him. Yet in his report he stated that John Conway had *no* expertise in that area, presumably to explain why Conway was not called as a witness. As to murder, Justice Yang accepted the flat was impenetrable and hence no one else could have been involved. Yet I witnessed the experiments of unlocking the door from outside and of someone kneeling by the bed, simulating shooting themselves in the abdomen and falling forward on the bed, to be later raised and shot 4 more times by somebody else who had been hiding in the wardrobe—again I was a witness. Furthermore, he ignored the evidence that no pen in the flat wrote the note. I am therefore moved towards Conway's explanation that it was neither suicide nor murder—it was both. The intention and the first shot were attempted suicide while the other 4 shots were murder. How else do we explain the suicide note that pleaded "an accident", an explanation not tackled at all by Justice Yang or Leading Counsel.

Accidents when withdrawing a gun from the left side of a belt are well documented and should have been taken into account by the court. It is therefore reasonable to regard it as an Open Verdict.

Chapter 75

Bibliography

Hong Kong Law Journal, Volume 12, Part 1, 1982 Pandora's Box: The Inspector MacLennan Case—Henry Lethbridge. History of the SIU

The Trail of the Triads—Fenton Bresler 1980, ISBN 0 297 77771 8. Describes Royal Hong Kong Police in the 1970s as a group of law enforcement officers unique in the annals of crime. Taiwan was the "Isle of Fugitives" with no extradition with Hong Kong. One of the fugitives, Ma sik chuen founded and ran Hong Kong's largest Chinese language newspaper, *Oriental Daily*. It quotes young expatriate inspectors around 1977 undergoing the same experiences as John MacLennan, brown envelopes with $1,000 notes in their drawers, corrupt station sergeants etc. One of taffy Hunt's predecessors as head of the Triad Bureau, Norman temple, was convicted of corruption and jailed for 3 years. Around 1977 a Superintendent and a Chinese colleague made a "Top Secret" visit to report to the Head of the Metropolitan Police Drugs squad, Fred Luff, who was worried about triad involvement in London's blossoming Trade in South East Asian heroin. Despite their security they were met on arrival in London by the press. 70% of all those sent to jail in 1977 had triad connections. Police chief, Brian Slevin, reported to Interpol Annual General Assembly in 1977 that triads had dispersed from Hong Kong to Europe, USA, Canada, Australia, Amsterdam and other countries. The 14K Triad Society elected a new Shan Chu, 489, one of its highest ranks and lodge leader, in 1978.

The Triads—The Chinese Criminal Fraternity—Martin Booth—Harper Collins 1990, ISBN 0 586 21029 6. The Triads controlled 90% of the world's heroin trade, which makes them potentially the single most dangerous organized crime threat now facing the international community. Their traditions have roots in ancient warrior codes of honour and patriotism, not—as now—the dishonour and cowardice of the street thug. Rodney and Sandy resigned from the police and were recruited into the 14K in 1979, an exercise that was most sensitive, and known only to a very few (names provided) police at the time of the death of John MacLennan. Rodney was key witness in trial after massive police raids in 1985 and later resulting in crippling the 14 K.

To Speak for the Dead—John Conway—British Library Cataloging-in-Publication Data 1994, ISBN 0 9522834 0 9. Six stories of unlawful killing or suspicious deaths. The John MacLennan section describes how murder was feasible and in particular that the pen, supposed to have been used to write the suicide note, contained black ink and therefore could not have been used to write the note. In addition it was not lost, but held in a plastic exhibit bag in the desk drawer of Mr Norman Chan, Secretary to the Commission.

100+ recordings of Aileen's interviews and the Attorney General's Press Conference